30-Minute Asian Meals

P9-DIJ-189

30-Minute Asian Meals

250 QUICK, TASTY & HEALTHY
RECIPES FROM AROUND ASIA

Marie Wilson

TUTTLE PUBLISHING
Tokyo • Rutland, Vermont • Singapore

For my mother

First published in 2007 by
Tuttle Publishing, an imprint of Periplus
Editions (HK) Ltd., with editorial offices at
364 Innovation Drive,
North Clarendon, Vermont 05759 U.S.A.

Copyright © 2007 Marie Wilson

All rights reserved. No part of this publica-
tion may be reproduced or utilized in any
form or by any means, electronic or mechani-
cal, including photocopying, recording, or by
any information storage and retrieval system,
without prior written permission from the
publisher.

LIBRARY OF CONGRESS
CATALOGING-IN-PUBLICATION DATA

Wilson, Marie M.
  30-minute Asian meals : 250 quick, tasty and
  healthy recipes from around Asia / Marie
  Wilson.
          p. cm.
  Includes index.
  ISBN 0-8048-3692-2 (pbk.)
  1. Cookery, Asian. 2. Quick and easy
  cookery. I. Title.
TX724.5.A1W525 2006
641.5'55—dc22   2006017931

ISBN-10: 0-8048-3692-2
ISBN-13: 978-0-8048-3692-0

DISTRIBUTED BY

NORTH AMERICA, LATIN AMERICA & EUROPE
Tuttle Publishing
364 Innovation Drive
North Clarendon, VT 05759-9436 U.S.A.
Tel: 1 (802) 773-8930
Fax: 1 (802) 773-6993
info@tuttlepublishing.com
www.tuttlepublishing.com

JAPAN
Tuttle Publishing
Yaekari Building, 3rd Floor
5-4-12 Osaki
Shinagawa-ku, Tokyo
Japan 141 0032
Tel: (81) 3 5437-0171
Fax: (81) 3 5437-0755
tuttle-sales@gol.com

ASIA PACIFIC
Berkeley Books Pte. Ltd.
130 Joo Seng Road
#06-01/03
Singapore 368357
Tel: (65) 6280-1330
Fax: (65) 6280-6290
inquiries@periplus.com.sg
www.periplus.com

INDONESIA
PT Java Books Indonesia
Kawasan Industri Pulogadung
Jl. Rawa Gelam IV No. 9
Blok A14 No. 17
Jakarta 13930 Indonesia
Tel: (62) 21 4682-1088
Fax: (62) 21 461-0207
cs@javabooks.co.id

First edition
10 09 08 07 06   10 9 8 7 6 5 4 3 2 1

PRINTED IN CANADA

TUTTLE PUBLISHING® is a registered trademark of Tuttle Publishing,
a division of Periplus Editions (HK) Ltd.

Contents

Eating Healthy in 30 Minutes or Less

The evidence is all around us—today's lifestyles and schedules put extra demands on the home cook, requiring that meals be prepared more quickly than ever before. Not only don't we have time to cook, we have even less time to shop. But in spite of our changing habits, our standards are higher than ever. The modern concern with health dictates that these meals should be prepared with fresh, wholesome ingredients and be low in calories and fat. And because we have all become more sophisticated about fine cuisine, they must be unusual meals to be enjoyed and appreciated, not merely a means to meet our nutritional needs.

A common misconception is that you have to choose between gourmet but high-fat, unhealthy foods that are delicious and beautifully presented, or low-fat foods that might help you to live longer but are bland and boring. Another misconception is that so-called healthful gourmet dishes are complex and time-consuming to prepare and require a long list of unusual and expensive ingredients. These trends and misconceptions pose quite an overwhelming challenge for the home cook, who too often takes the easy way out. Otherwise, what would account for the staggering increase in sales of frozen dinners and carryout food?

The prospect of hours in the kitchen after a busy day too often leads to relying on over-processed frozen dinners or fast foods. The temptation to compromise lurks in every corner of the supermarket and in the kitchen, but such compromise comes at a high price. What these foods save in preparation time, they sacrifice in taste, quality and nutritional value. Many essential nutrients may be missing because the more processing raw ingredients undergo, the greater their nutrient loss. They are also high in calories, fat and salt.

Reading the labels on the back of a few common frozen dinners tells the story. A popular brand of chicken dinner has 27 grams of fat, 105 milligrams of cholesterol and 730 milligrams of sodium in one serving. Another has about the same amount of fat but 980 milligrams

of sodium. Canned soups are even worse, with half a can averaging 1000 milligrams of sodium. A fast-food hamburger is not only fatty, but has about 1000 milligrams of sodium, and a serving of fast-food chicken can have upwards of 2000 milligrams. The worst offender is the soup marketed as cup of "oriental noodle soup" that contains 1550 milligrams of sodium.

The need for good tasting, healthy, everyday dishes that can be brought to the table quickly is very real, and the solution is found in Asian cooking. Well-known for its health-promoting benefits and its variety of tempting taste sensations, Asian cuisine is very quick and easy to prepare. The recipes in this book have been chosen for variety—each chapter is organized into major categories such as chicken, beef, pork, lamb, vegetables, salads, eggs, noodles, tofu and so on—and for their simplicity and speed in cooking. They have been simplified without compromising authenticity or flavor. The number of unfamiliar ingredients has been kept to a

minimum, and only those available at most supermarkets are included. Also, substitutions are given wherever possible.

Of course, making an authentic Asian meal—whether Japanese, Chinese, Korean or Indian—is very labor intensive. A typical Asian meal includes a wide array of dishes served with rice, with no one dish dominating, but rather each complementing the others and bringing balance to the whole. To produce such a meal takes a great deal of time and effort. However, many Asian dishes can be made in larger quantities and eaten as a "main course," and if cooked with vegetables, need only rice to make a nutritionally balanced meal. The custom of serving one "main course" is a Western idea that seems to be in keeping with today's fast-paced lifestyles.

Most recipes in this book make two servings, reflecting the Asian tradition of eating family style—that is, of enjoying multiple, smaller dishes with rice rather than one large dish. When serving three or four people, you may wish to make two dishes in this collection or simply double the recipe to make one large dish.

The 30-Minute Strategy

The timeframe for making recipes in this book is 30 minutes—the time it takes to cook rice, plus a 10-minute buffer to rectify mishaps, set the table, make that extra dipping sauce or make two quick dishes instead of one. Experienced cooks may have a meal on the table in 20 minutes flat and, if making dishes with quick-cooking noodles instead of rice, probably even sooner. First, the rice is started and, while it is cooking, the ingredients for the "main dish" are washed, sliced and placed by the stove. If an accompanying salad, vegetable or dipping sauce is desired, that should also be prepared while the rice is cooking. In keeping with the Asian custom of ending a meal with fresh fruit, no dessert recipes are included in this collection.

Most of these dishes are stir-fried, a cooking method that takes a minimum of time. Stir-frying is not really frying, but tossing and stirring foods quickly in a very hot wok or skillet with a small amount of oil. It is a kind of flash-cooking that seals in juices and keeps flavors fresh. Fish is moister and more succulent if cooked until barely opaque at the center and vegetables keep their color, flavor, and natural crispness if cooked just until tender. In these recipes, the number of ingredients has been kept to a minimum, as well as the number of cooking steps. In almost every case, the meat, vegetables, and saucing is done in one pot.

To help you quickly find a recipe that fits your dining pleasure—whether it's curried chicken or vegetarian fried rice—or, more prosaically, to find a recipe that uses ingredients you have on hand, each chapter is organized by main ingredients, components, or cooking methods common to that cuisine—for example, beef, chicken, vegetables, noodles, sauces, Japanese hot pot, satay and so on. A visual key accompanies each recipe section.

Health Benefits of Asian Cuisine

In general, people in Asia eat less than Westeners, and meat and poultry play a much less prominent role in the Asian diet. The major health benefits of Asian cooking are due to an emphasis on plant foods: vegetables, legumes (especially the soybean) and starches. Meats play only a supporting role. Just two or three ounces are used for each portion, but it is appetizingly cooked with little fat and lots of vegetables. Rice is really the heart of the diet and it appears at every meal.

The high-fiber content of vegetables earns another plus for Asian cooking. Science now shows that a diet rich in vegetables can reduce the risk of certain forms of cancer and help lower cholesterol levels, and the omega-3 fatty acids in seafood and seaweed have been shown to keep arteries from clogging. Also, some of the same anticancer agents plentiful in dark green seaweed are found in dark, leafy vegetables such as bok choy and mustard greens.

Consider these statistics: American men live an average of 75 years; American women, 80. In Japan, the range is 78 years for men and 85 for women, though in Okinawa, a prefecture of Japan, the average lifespan is even higher. For women it is more than 86 years, and there are some who live beyond l00. These elderly Okinawans are not only healthy but also productive.

What do they eat? A lot of fish and soybean products—protein sources that have benefits meat cannot provide—rice, seaweed, vegetables, and only a very small amount of meat. They eat more fresh vegetables than Japanese mainlanders, who prefer their vegetables pickled. Thus Okinawans take in more vitamins and less salt than their mainland counterparts. This helps account for historically lower rates of stomach and colon cancer. It is also believed that tofu and other soybean products are particularly rich in isoflavonoids—estrogen-like compounds that may help deter osteoporosis by aiding in calcium absorption. Studies have shown that elderly women who eat more soy have denser bones, which might help to explain why elderly Japanese—and especially Okinawan—women seem to suffer fewer bone fractures than American women, though the Japanese consume far less calcium.

Striving to reduce fat to around 25 to 30 percent of daily calories will match what the modern Japanese and Okinawans eat. In keeping with this goal, oils, sodium, meat, poultry and fish are used sparingly in the recipes included in this book. While not designed for dieters, they are for people who want to eat healthful food,

Science now shows that a diet rich in vegetables can reduce the risk of certain forms of cancer and help lower cholesterol levels.

maintain their weight, and enjoy the pleasures of eating.

■ Oils

Approximately ½ tablespoon of oil per person is sufficient. A light vegetable oil is recommended. Olive oil is the healthiest, because it is high in monounsaturated fats, but it has a decided taste and is not suitable for Asian cooking. Canola oil is also rich in monounsaturated fats, has no taste and is inexpensive. A second choice would be the oils rich in polyunsaturates such as safflower oil, corn oil or peanut oil.

■ Sodium

Salt has a tendency to raise blood pressure. The reliance in some Asian cooking on salty condiments—especially soy sauce—is its only shortcoming. The Japanese still consume about 50 percent more salt than Americans do, which accounts for Japan's high rate of death due to stroke.

For health reasons, no more than approximately ½ tablespoon of any high-salt seasoning (such as soy sauce) is usually suggested per person; this amount may be increased at the discretion of the cook. Also, reduced-sodium soy sauce is a good alternative. Salt is not used in most of the recipes. Instead, most recipes use garlic, ginger, pepper and other spices to enhance flavor. But it is also left up to the cook to include it for taste, or to leave it out, for health concerns.

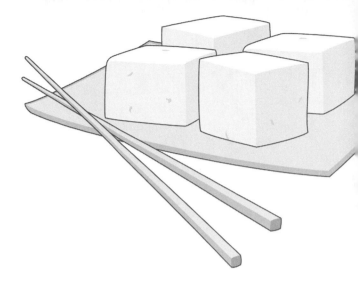

■ Meat, Poultry and Fish

The portions of lean meat and fish in the recipes are generally 4–6 ounces (125–175 g) per person, which is more than is used in the average meal in any Asian country, but considerably less than the 8-or-more-ounce (225-g) portion still prevalent on some tables in the West. Use less or more as you wish.

Helpful Tips for Quick and Easy Cooking

For most Asian home cooks, following a cookbook of specific recipes with detailed instructions is tedious and confining. Most of them learn how to prepare food by first watching others—usually a mother or other family member—and then imitating. Soon they begin to cook the dishes they have observed, but they also cook intuitively and learn to improvise. If you compare recipes from different books that seem to be directions for the same dish, you are likely to find that they are often very different. There are more ways than one to cook even the simplest dish. For example, while sweet and sour foods are always made with sugar, soy sauce and vinegar, from then on

the cook is pretty much on his or her own. Many dishes call for fruit and vegetables, but what fruit, what vegetables? The answer is whatever happens to be in season or available. This also holds true of sauces. Asian cooks do not use measuring spoons, but instead pour or sprinkle seasonings into the food, gauging the amount needed by eye or taste. They know what they like and they make every dish their own.

Try to approach recipes as starting points, with suggested ingredients and seasonings, but subject to variations. Always keep in mind that there is no one way to cook any of these dishes, and no strict measurements for making sauces. It is taken for granted that they will be adapted to individual taste. The following practices will make your adventures go smoothly and help save time.

- Read the recipe through before starting to cook.

- Even though most recipes do not specifically say to rinse fruits and vegetables, fish, meat and poultry, it is a given that they should be rinsed and patted dry.

- Buy fresh vegetables at the supermarket already rinsed, cut, trimmed and chopped. Washed and bagged spinach, for example, saves a lot of work and time. Check packages carefully to determine freshness. It cannot be emphasized enough how important the use of the freshest ingredients is in good cooking.

- Buy boneless chicken for stir-fried dishes. It is so much easier to cut up chicken pieces if they have already been boned. (Of course, if you are a do-everything-yourself cook, you will miss the bones, which you would freeze and use later to make stock.) Beef is often sold already sliced, sometimes called sukiyaki beef.

- Keep a supply of seasonings on hand in a convenient place for the recipes of the countries that interest you. Unusual ingredients have been kept to an absolute minimum, but don't hesitate to substitute or leave something out that you don't have or don't like. Every dish need not be 100 percent authentic, but it should have an integrity that respects the original. A list of ingredients common to each country appears at the beginning of each recipe section.

- Fresh garlic will keep indefinitely in the refrigerator, but fresh ginger will not. However, ginger does very well frozen in whole pieces, and may be taken from the freezer when needed; without defrosting, it may be coarsely grated for whatever dish you are preparing. Fresh herbs may also be frozen and added to dishes directly from the freezer.

- Use well-fitting gloves when handling chiles as they can cause painful skin sensations. If you do not use gloves you must wash your hands several times after handling chiles, and do not touch your eyes. I know from experience how excruciating the pain can be. When cooking with chiles, if you want mild heat, add the pepper whole and discard it before serving. If you want an authentic level of heat, remove seeds and membrane and chop the chile as Asian cooks typically do.

Chile Warning: Handle with Care!

- Do not take the amounts in the recipes too literally. If the recipe calls for 12 ounces (340 g), and you have 14 ounces (400 g), make a larger meal and save what's left for the next day.

- The same can be said for vegetables. I've tried to use units of vegetables rather than weight— for example, one bell pepper or two carrots. But it is not always practical to do this with some ingredients. When cups are used as a measure, do not take it literally. Use your own experience and judgment as a guide. The recipe need not come out exactly as written. If it tastes good and the meal is done in 30 minutes, that is what matters.

- Use the cooking times given in the recipes as guides, not absolutes. The actual cooking time may vary depending upon the kind of pan you use, the intensity of the heat source, and the size and age of ingredients.

- I recommend the use of a spoon when adding condiments, especially salty ones. Pouring out of a bottle as I have seen many cooks do, can be a disaster when you pour too much. A spoon should be used to prevent such a disaster, by allowing only a little of the condiment at a time to go into the dish. Taste it! That is the ultimate test.

- If you prefer brown rice, which takes 50 minutes to cook, to white rice, which takes 20, you can make brown rice in 20 minutes by combining it with twice as much water and soaking it for the day or overnight. Then cook it as you would white rice.

■ Weights and Measures

All weights and measures are given first in American, then in metric equivalents. The American measuring spoon is used in this book. No equivalents are given because measuring spoons differ dramatically elsewhere in the world. Try to think of the proportions as a guide and use rough equivalents. An experi-enced cook does this sort of thing with ease. After a little practice, an inexperienced cook will gain confidence quickly and enjoy the process.

■ Utensils

The most important pan is the wok or skillet (12–14 inch or 30–35 cm) and a spatula to stir the food with. A cover for the wok is necessary for braising or steaming. I can't stress enough how useful it is to have a nonstick pan. The best chefs use them. Less oil is needed, which makes every dish healthier. I have had several woks in my time, and my latest one has been the best. It is made by Circulon, has handles, and is guaranteed to remain nonstick for ten years. If you do not have a wok, a good-quality, large skillet, also nonstick, may be used. It is important that the nonstick surface be in good condition to prevent food from sticking.

Besides a wok or skillet and a spatula for stirring, the usual equipment of any small kitchen will do. A cutting board, a soup pan, a saucepan or two, a couple of mixing bowls, spoons, and a good, sharp knife are all that are necessary. In Southeast Asia mortars and pestles are as important as knives and cleavers are in China and Japan. A small food processor can take their place, and also save a lot of time and work, but it is not absolutely necessary to have one. The recipes are equally successful if the ingredients are finely chopped instead of pounded into a paste.

An Organized Kitchen

I know how difficult it is to be organized in the kitchen, especially when time is limited and one is tired. May I make a few suggestions? These apply especially to Asian cooking and particularly to stir-frying. Because the main dish takes very little time to cook (say 5 to 10 minutes) and should be eaten immediately after it is done, you must prepare as much as possible before you start cooking. The stir-frying method is not difficult to master and is perfect for creating your own recipes. The cardinal rule in stir-frying is to cook each ingredient until it is just done, and not a minute more. A typical stir-fried dish follows the same basic steps, as outlined below.

■ Before You Start Cooking

1. Set the table.

2. Prepare whatever you are going to have with the main dish:

   - Start the rice.

   - If you are having a salad, make it now but leave the dressing off until you sit down to eat.

   - Make the dipping sauce, if any, and put it on the table. If using bread, slice it now and put it on the table. Get serving dishes and/or plates out.

3. Now you are ready to do your prep work.

- Cut ingredients that you will be using in the recipe, and place them in neat piles on the cutting board, in bowls or on paper towels, within easy reach of the stove. Food should be cut into small, uniform pieces or thin slices. Meat, such as flank steak, should be across the grain at a 45-degree angle. It is more easily cut when it is partially frozen. Fibrous vegetables, such as celery, are best cut crosswise on the diagonal into thin, slanting slices. But however you cut them, pieces should all be approximately the same size and thickness so that they will cook evenly.

- If the meat has to be dredged in cornstarch or soy sauce, or if a vegetable needs to be blanched in boiling water, do that now and set it aside.

- Prepare garlic, ginger or any seasonings and sauce mixtures and place them within easy reach of the stove. Once you start to cook, you will have no time to prepare a sauce.

■ Start Cooking

1. Heat the nonstick wok or frying pan on high heat first, then add the oil and rotate the pan to coat it. The oil should be very hot but not smoking.

2. Add the seasoning (garlic or ginger, for example) to flavor the oil, and stir for a few seconds.

14 **30-MINUTE ASIAN MEALS**

3. Add the meat next. Stir and toss until it begins to brown. Remove from pan to a serving plate and keep warm. Never crowd the pan. One pound (16 oz/450 g) or even less is the maximum quantity that should be stir-fried at one time or the food will steam, not fry. If you double the recipe, cook the meat and vegetables in batches, a little at a time.

4. Add a little more oil, and when hot add the vegetable. Stir and toss until it is tender but still very crisp. If you are using more than one vegetable, add the one that requires the longest cooking time first, then add the others in sequence. Some cooks prefer to cook each vegetable separately and remove it to the platter with the meat. For fibrous vegetables, you may need to add a little broth or water, then cover the pan to steam it for a minute or so.

Some recipes call for cooking the vegetables before the meat; others, the meat first. It doesn't matter much, so long as neither is overcooked, and the pan is dry when the oil is put into it.

5. Return the meat to the pan with the vegetables and add the already-mixed sauce. Stir and toss until heated through. Don't be heavy-handed with the seasoning. You can always add more soy sauce but you can't take it away. Proportions for seasonings in the recipes are on the mild side. Taste the food. If it seems bland, add a little pepper or more herbs. If it

still needs something, add a little soy sauce, but be sparing. Place soy sauce, dipping sauce or other seasoning at the table for each diner to add as desired.

■ Hints for Stir-Frying Fresh Vegetables

In general the example of stir-frying a main dish outlined above also applies to stir-frying vegetables by themselves.

- Cut the vegetables into uniform-size slices or small pieces.
- Heat the wok over high heat before adding the oil, add the vegetable all at once and stir and toss uncovered, until it is tender but still crisp.
- Cover and steam longer-cooking vegetables—such as carrots, broccoli, and bok choy—for a minute or two. You may have to add a little water or broth to the wok. The longest cooking vegetable is the green bean, which may take up to 5 minutes depending on size and age.
- Vegetables that naturally contain a lot of water—such as spinach, onions and mushrooms—do not require broth or extra water to cook.
- When cooking several vegetables, add the firmest ones to the wok first, then add the more tender vegetables near the end of the cooking time.

- Or, cook each vegetable separately and then combine them all for reheating and blending of flavors.
- Never crowd the wok. To prepare more servings than you can cook at once, just cook them in two or more batches. Stir-frying is so fast that you can keep the first portions warm in a heated oven while the others cook.

■ Shopping

If possible, it is best to shop twice a week, which means you will have fresh ingredients every day. But busy people have so little time that they can manage to go only once a week, which takes a bit of planning on paper. Your vegetables won't stay fresh that long, so keep some frozen or canned ones on hand to use the last few days of the week.

The recipes have been written for two generous servings. Three moderate eaters will find them to be enough if they add more rice. The quantities may be doubled easily to make four servings, as well as divided in half to make one. If you double a recipe, you will be doubling the main ingredients, but it may not be necessary to double the amount of oil. Remember not to crowd the wok but to stir-fry in batches for best results.

If all this sounds daunting, don't give up until you've tried it a while. Think of food and cooking as an adventure and an art. Keep in mind that Asian cooks do not typically measure ingredients—they cook intuitively and improvise. If you are an inexperienced cook, preparing meals under time pressures can be a challenge at first, but it is a culinary skill that can be mastered with a little practice. Begin with the freshest ingredients, and remember the words of chefs Escoffier and Shizuo Tsuji:

"Cook simply!"

"Let little seem like much, as long as it is fresh and beautiful."

China

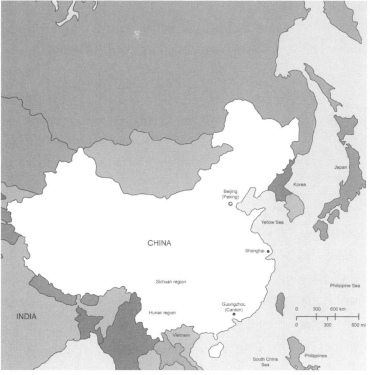

China's cuisine, with a recorded history that spans more than 3,000 years, is the most complex and sophisticated in the world. From earliest times, respect, even reverence, for food has permeated all levels of society, from the peasant working his tiny plot of land for his family's survival, to the scholars, princes, and emperors who placed gastronomy alongside philosophy, literature, and the fine arts. Some even wrote treatises and lyrical poems on the subject. During the Ching Dynasty (1644–1912) when the imperial court indulged in an elaborate style of luxurious living and dining, Chinese cuisine reached a peak that may never be surpassed. The closest western equivalent in technique and philosophy is French haute cuisine and the 1825 book, *The Physiology of Taste*, by Brillat-Savarin.

What characterizes Chinese cuisine is its inventive and adventurous use of so many uncommon ingredients. Every possible taste sensation is relished, from the humble cabbage to the improbable bird's nest. Poetry and whimsy also inform the names of some Chinese dishes. There are squirrelfish, drunken chicken, Peking dust, and monkey head (made of mushrooms).

A humorous legend aptly illustrates this whimsical approach. When a Manchu Dynasty emperor was touring Hangzhou, he stopped at a peasant food stand and asked to be served lunch. The peasant was terrified that he could not produce a dish worthy of the emperor, but he did his best. The emperor was so pleased that he asked the peasant what the dish was called. Not wanting the emperor to know what was really in the dish, he called it "red-beaked green parrot with jade cake." After the emperor had executed several chefs for their inability to reproduce this dish (the emperor's chefs cooked a parrot and served it with a piece of real jade), the peasant was summoned to the palace. He confessed that the dish was actually made of red-rooted green spinach and fried tofu.

and colors. The five tastes—salty, sweet, sour, bitter, and spicy—must all be paid the proper attention so that they are harmoniously combined, with no one accent dominating a meal. The primary purpose of these tastes is the accentuation, rather than the concealment, of natural flavors. Rich foods must be balanced by blandness, bright colors by subtle ones, smoothness with rougher textures, and hot with cold. Contrast, or dynamic balance, echoes one tenet of Taoism, the religion that held a place among the Chinese as important as Confucianism and Buddhism. Taoism (Way of Nature) sees a duality in the universe, a division in its power, with one half working against the other, not in hostility but for the sake of harmonious existence. These two halves are known as Yin and Yang.

Some suggest that the Chinese preoccupation with food is the result of chronic food shortages. With only a small proportion of its total land area suitable for farming, producing an adequate food supply for China's huge population has always been a serious problem. There was not only a scarcity of food but also a scarcity of fuel (which led to the brazier, in which any fuel could be burned), and also to stir-frying—the quick cooking of small pieces of food in a little oil over very high heat.

But economy was not all. Taste was also important. The Chinese philosophy of taste in food has always emphasized the harmonious blending of flavors, textures

The Chinese philosophy of taste in food has always emphasized the harmonious blending of flavors, texture and colors.

Food shortages are no longer a problem in China, and it appears that the majority of the people are reasonably well fed. Food grains are the principal crops, which include wheat, rice, corn and millet. Rice is the leading food grain, and China is the world's leading rice producer. Although traditionally grown in the warmer lands of central and southern China, rice can now be grown in every province as a result of the development of cold-tolerant hybrids. Further, although fishing is less developed than in Japan, China maintains one of the world's largest fishing industries. Its economic development is aided by abundant coal, petroleum and natural gas reserves. But despite the rapid industrialization of recent years—China is now the United States' third largest trading partner—it remains a predominantly agricultural country. In general, throughout China rice or noodles is the foundation of a meal, and vegetables, the main ingredient in any dish, are cooked with only small quantities of meat or fish.

The Styles of Chinese Cuisine

Chinese cuisine may be divided roughly into four general cooking styles: the northern school, encompassing the city of Beijing (Peking) and northern provinces such as Shandong, Henan, and Shanxi; the eastern school, centered on the city of Shanghai and Fujian province; the southwest, or inland, school including Sichuan, Hunan, and Yunan; and the southern school of Guangxi and Guangdong, of which Canton is the capital.

■ The North

In the north where the weather is colder, the conditions are more suitable for growing wheat than for rice paddies. Thus, northerners depend mainly on wheat, from which they make noodles, steamed bread and dumplings. They also grow millet

and barley. Until the seventeenth century, Peking (Beijing), as the home of the Imperial Palace, was the gourmet capital of China. The best chefs were recruited by emperors and encouraged to develop new dishes. The feasts and banquets they produced are legendary. Perhaps the most celebrated northern dish known in the West is Peking Duck. Likewise, Henan is famous for a dish known the world over as sweet-and-sour fish, which is made from carp caught in the Yellow River. Monkey Head is another Henan specialty, made from a large, highly prized mushroom. Northern dishes tend to be light and mildly seasoned with garlic, chives, leeks and green onions (scallions). Other influences in this region's cooking come from Mongolia, which borders China on the north. The Mongols, who were Muslim, conquered China and set up a dynasty that ruled from 1279 to 1368. They introduced the Chinese to lamb, which is the basis for Mongolian fire pot and Mongolian barbecue.

■ The East

The climate in the east is basically subtropical, with warm, wet summers and cool winters, providing a year-round growing season. As a seacoast city in touch with the outside world, Shanghai developed a distinguished cuisine of its own. Having access to wheat and barley, their specialties are baked breads, dumplings and noodles. But if one region could typify China it would be the Yangtze plain, through which the Yangtze River flows. It is the most densely populated area in China. Often called the main street of China, the Yangtze River dominates most of the east. Its delta irrigates vast farming areas in which many varieties of fruit and vegetables grow. Along the Yangtze there are hundreds of shallow lakes around which much of China's rice is grown. While rice and water dominate the lowlands, the hills are a source of fine silk and tea. There are also rich deposits of kaolin, the clay used to make the finest Chinese porcelains. Nanjing and Hangzhou are also important culinary centers because they were the cities to which the emperors and their courts fled when Peking was attacked by the barbarians. With so

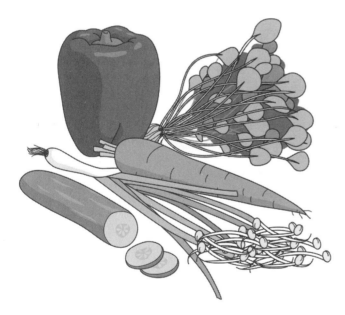

many miles of coastline, the entire region enjoys a remarkable variety of fish and seafood.

Eastern cuisine is characterized by heavily sauced dishes and the liberal use of soy sauce in stewlike dishes known as "red cooking." To coun-

teract the saltiness of the soy, relatively large quantities of sugar are used. Home-style cooking is robust, and slowly simmered casseroles are favored. An example is Lion's Head, a combination of meatballs and leafy green vegetables simmered in stock. Longer cooking, even of stir-fried dishes, is common. Instead of adding liquids only at the very end of the cooking process, a Shanghai cook is more likely to lower the heat after adding liquid and simmer the dish gently another fifteen minutes. The area is reputed to produce the best soy sauce in China.

The Fujian province, which is further south, has a cooking style that is held in high esteem among Chinese gourmets. Its cuisine is simple and emphasizes a respect for the freshest ingredients.

Fujian is noted for its excellent seafood dishes, and though the province produces fine soy sauces, very little is used in any dish. Some of China's finest teas are grown in the foothills of the southern mountains in Fujian.

■ The Southwest

Surrounded by mountains and isolated from the rest of China, the subtropical southwestern inland region of Sichuan (Szechwan) is famous for its liberal use of chiles. These dishes are fiery hot, but also skillfully combine many different flavors—for example, hot, sour and salty—in a single dish. Shredded fresh ginger is also an important ingredient, as are Sichuan peppercorns (a mild, fragrant peppercorn that is first toasted in a dry pan and then crushed). Sichuan peppercorns, unrelated to black pepper, are an essential ingredient in five-spice powder. Star anise, cinnamon and other spices are used liberally as well. These ingredients probably derive from Indian cooking, which was brought to the area by Indian Buddhist missionaries traveling the overland Silk Route. The citrus fruits grown in this region are also used in numerous dishes such as Lemon Chicken.

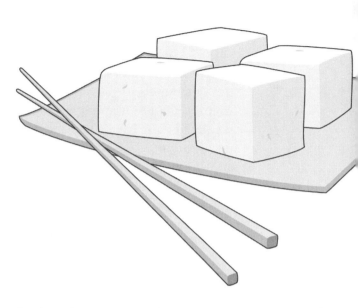

Abundant sauces are rare. Instead, a scant sauce clings to, rather than surrounds, the meat or vegetables. Also, texture plays an important role. For example, a dish called Slippery Chicken is supposed to have the silky texture of satin.

To the south of Sichuan, bordering Burma, Thailand and Laos, lies the province of Yunan, where the Chinese are a minority and live mostly in the cities. The majority of the population here is made up of the hill-dwelling peoples including the Tai, Shan, Miao and Lisu tribes, as well as a substantial number of Muslims (descendants of Muslim officials brought in by the Emperor Kubla Khan to colonize the area). The cuisine of this area is influenced by Sichuan to the north and Burma, Thailand and India to the south and west. Yunan, in particular, makes hot curried dishes and is famous for its hams. Some Yunanese dishes can be found in the northern parts of Burma, Thailand and Laos.

■ The South

The focus for southeastern China is the city of Canton (Guangzhou), in Guangdong, considered to be the culinary mecca of China. Throughout its history it has been a center of foreign trade. When the first Arab merchants arrived in the fourth century to serve as intermediaries between the Chinese and the Greeks, they established a steady commerce between China, India, Africa and Europe. It was via this route that the noodle is said to have found its way from China, through the Middle East, to Europe. Although if you ask an Italian about the noodle, he will say that it traveled in the opposite direction—from Italy, through the Middle East, to China. Canton was the first city to be regularly visited by Europeans, beginning with the Portuguese in 1514, who brought with them plants from the New World. Among these plants was the chile, which would have a dramatic effect on Chinese, as well as Indian and Southeast Asian, cooking.

While Canton has served as the gateway into China, it has also served as the gateway out of it. The people of Canton are viewed by other Chinese as adventurous, restless, receptive to new ideas and able to adjust to new conditions, unlike the stolid, more conservative inhabitants of the north. And so it is from Canton that most of the immigrants have come. Early immigration was mostly to Japan and Southeast Asia. In 1849, news of the discovery of gold in California reached China, and in that year the first group of Chinese arrived to the land of the Golden Mountains, as the United States was called, to join the gold rush and to work in the building of railroads. They also went to Europe, Asia, North and South America, and Australia, and to each of these places they brought with them the cooking style of their native Canton. Until that time, China's culinary art had remained largely unknown to the world.

After just a few decades of Cantonese emigration, Chinese food had become so popular that virtually every fair-sized community had at least one Chinese restarant, and was usually Cantonese.

The southern region is a tropical paradise. A wide variety of tropical fruits grow there, and where agriculture is possible three harvests a year are not uncommon. Rice and sugar are grown in the flatlands, and silk is also an important crop. Because of its tremendous variety,

Cantonese cuisine is considered the finest in China. The art of stir-frying has been perfected here. Only a light seasoning is used to highlight the taste of the main ingredients—ginger, garlic, sugar and a little soy sauce. Oyster sauce is also from Canton. Sweet and sour dishes make use of tropical fruits such as pineapple and lychees, and Canton's long coastline assures a wide variety of fish and seafood. Perhaps the most wonderful food to come from Canton is dim sum, delicious, savory steamed dumplings made with minced meat, shrimp or vegetables and wrapped in dough.

A lesser-known style of cooking is a highly developed vegetarian cuisine, popular among Chinese Buddhists and Taoists who do not eat meat for religious reasons. Some of these vegetable dishes are prepared so that the textures of meat, fowl, and fish are ingeniously simulated using a variety of vegetables, mushrooms and tofu.

To be sure, there are distinct regional differences in Chinese cooking. But it must not be assumed that the cuisines of these regions have remained separate and entirely distinct from one another. Over time, with better transportation and communication, there has been some intermingling not only of ideas, but also of culinary styles.

■   ■   ■

Though not all of these cooking styles be found everywhere outside of China, the remarkable fact is that Chinese food has become the most international cuisine in the world—there is hardly a country, town or city that does not have a Chinese restaurant. In some areas of the world, such as Southeast Asia, where the Chinese have emigrated in large numbers, the impact of Chinese cooking goes further than a few local restaurants. For example, in Thailand, Chinese food is not only firmly entrenched but has influenced Thai cuisine. Some Indonesian dishes are also a mixture of Chinese and Indian or Malay styles, and in Vietnam and Singapore the food is very heavily influenced by Chinese cooking.

Chinese Pantry

To keep shopping to a minimum, and to speed preparation and cooking time, it is helpful to keep these Chinese staples on hand in your kitchen.

Ingredients with a Long Shelf Life

bamboo shoots, canned

black pepper

brown bean sauce

canned black beans, salted
    and fermented

chili sauce or paste

Chinese mushrooms, dried

Chinese rice wine (also known
    as Shaoxing wine) or
    pale dry sherry

five-spice powder

hoisin sauce

oyster sauce

pine nuts

red pepper flakes, dried

red pepper, ground

rice, long-grain white or brown

rice vinegar

sesame oil

sesame seeds

Sichuan peppercorns

soy sauce

wheat noodles

Fresh Ingredients

coriander leaves (cilantro)

garlic

ginger

green onions (scallions)

onions

Rice ■ Mifan

Plain rice is to most of Asian cooking what bread is to other cuisines, the indispensable accompaniment to a meal. Its texture, blandness and whiteness provide an ideal background for colorful, highly seasoned dishes. Cooking rice the Chinese way means cooking it without salt and fat. It also means that it must be washed in several changes of water before cooking. Chinese cooks say that the secret of flaky rice is in the washing, which, they say, rids the rice of excess starch and keeps it from becoming sticky. This appears to be true to some degree. However, washing also removes many of the vitamins and minerals, and because the difference is hardly discernible, I prefer not to wash rice. Another reason for not washing rice is the message on bags of rice found in American grocery stores: "No talc on this rice. Washing is unnecessary."

Both methods are given here. Of course, the simplest way to cook rice is to use an automatic rice cooker. Whichever way you go, keep in mind that precise cooking time for rice may vary depending on the stove and pan you use, and the type and age of the rice. For example, newly harvested rice requires less water than older rice. Not only is there moisture variability in rice, but the type must also be reckoned with. Brown rice, which retains its bran coat and germ, is much slower to tenderize, although more valuable nutritionally, than highly polished white rice. There are also differences in the grain hybrids. Always consult the package instructions, if there are any. For firmer rice, use less water and shorter cooking time. For more tender rice, increase water and simmer longer.

One-half cup of raw rice yields 1½ cups (375 g) cooked rice, a generous serving for one person. However, many Westerners usually eat far less rice at a meal, and more of the dishes that go with it, than Asians typically do. Contrary to popular belief, rice is not high in calories. It contains virtually no fat and only a trace of sodium. The same is true of the potato. It is what you add to rice or potatoes that adds the calories.

Boiled Rice, Chinese Style
Baimifan

1 cup (225 g) long-grain rice
1½ cups (350 ml) water

1. Wash the rice several times by rinsing and rubbing it between your palms until the water runs clear. Drain.
2. In a medium saucepan, combine the rice with the water. Bring to a boil over high heat, uncovered.
3. Cover, reduce the heat to low and simmer for 20 minutes, until the water has evaporated and craters have formed on the rice surface.
4. Remove from the heat and let the rice stand, covered, for about 5 minutes. Fluff with a fork or chopsticks and serve.

Makes 2 servings

Boiled Rice, American Style

1 cup (225 g) long-grain rice
1¾ cups (425 ml) water (2 cups/475 ml)
for softer result)

1. Do not wash the rice. In a medium saucepan, combine the rice and water and bring to a boil. Cover, reduce the heat to low, and simmer until the rice is cooked, 17–20 minutes, or until all the liquid is absorbed.
2. Remove from the heat and let stand, covered, 5 minutes. Fluff with a fork and serve.

Makes 2 servings

Steamed Rice

Steaming produces fluffier rice, but it takes longer. The rice must be boiled for 5 minutes first, then drained and placed in a steamer tray lined with moistened cheesecloth. The steamer tray must be then placed over boiling water and steamed for 30 minutes. Happily, electric rice cookers are often used for steaming. They are simple to use and shut off automatically when the rice is cooked. Follow the directions that come with the rice cooker.

Boiled Brown Rice
Zaomifan

Brown rice retains its bran coat and germ, and contains more protein, minerals and vitamins than polished white rice because these nutrients are lost in the milling process. Brown rice has a chewier texture and takes longer to cook, about 50 minutes. But if it is soaked, it takes only 20 minutes. Both recipes are given here.

1 cup (225 g) brown rice
2 cups (475 ml) water

1. In a medium saucepan, combine the rice and water and bring to a boil. Reduce the heat to low, cover and simmer for 35–45 minutes, or until all the water is absorbed.
2. Remove from the heat and let stand for 5 minutes, covered. Fluff with a fork or chopsticks before serving.

VARIATION: *To cook brown rice in 20 minutes, combine the rice and water in a saucepan and allow it to soak overnight or all day. Then cook it according to the recipe above, but for only 20 minutes.*

Simple Fried Rice
Chaofan

In Chinese cooking, fried rice is a versatile dish that combines cooked rice, onions, soy sauce, eggs and just about any other ingredient—leftover or fresh—that may be on hand. The additions to the rice are stir-fried together first and then combined with the rice. The ingredient that predominates gives the dish its name: chicken fried rice, shrimp fried rice, and so on. When many ingredients are included, the dish is called *subgum* or "many varieties" fried rice. For best results, rice should be cold and dry, preferably a day old. If it is warm or hot, the grains will stick together.

Sauce
2 tablespoons unsalted stock

¼ teaspoon sugar

1 tablespoon Chinese rice wine or pale dry sherry

1 teaspoon to 1 tablespoon reduced-sodium soy sauce, or more to taste

• • •

4 teaspoons vegetable oil

1 egg, lightly beaten

1 small onion, coarsely chopped

1 large clove garlic, crushed

1 small red or green bell pepper (or ½ of each), seeded and diced

1 cup (175 g) diced cooked chicken

3 cups (750 g) cold, cooked long-grain white rice

Freshly ground black pepper

1 green onion (scallion), green part only, sliced, for garnish

1. Combine the sauce ingredients in a small bowl and set aside. Prepare the remaining ingredients and place within easy reach of the stove.
2. Heat a nonstick wok (or skillet) over medium heat. Add 1 teaspoon of the oil. When hot, add the egg and stir lightly until it is firm. Remove to a plate, cut into bite-size pieces and set aside.
3. Turn the heat up to medium-high and add another teaspoon of the oil. Stir-fry the onion until it is soft. Add the garlic and stir-fry 3–4 seconds. Add the bell pepper and chicken and stir-fry about 2 minutes. Stir in the sauce and cook for another 30 seconds. Remove to the plate with the egg.
4. Heat the wok again and add the remaining oil to the wok. Add the cold rice, stirring and turning to break up the clumps and to evenly reheat it. Add the chicken and egg mixture, and continue to stir until heated through, about 2 minutes.
5. Top with the freshly ground pepper and garnish with the sliced green onion (scallion), green part only. Soy sauce or chili sauce may be served at the table.

VARIATIONS: *Cooked ham, beef, pork or shrimp may be substituted for the chicken. Uncooked chicken, beef or pork cut into bite-size pieces may also be used. Add after onion and garlic have been stir-fried.*

Makes 2–3 servings

Savory Fried Rice

Follow the recipe for Simple Fried Rice on page 27, adding, in Step 3, the following combination of ingredients.

¼ cup (30 g) diced cooked chicken
¼ cup (30 g) diced cooked pork
¼ cup (50 g) diced raw or cooked shrimp (optional)

2 tablespoons diced country-style ham, preferably Smithfield
3 or 4 fresh mushrooms, trimmed, wiped clean and chopped
2 green onions (scallions), sliced
¼ cup (25 g) fresh bean sprouts, ends trimmed
Unsalted roasted peanuts, for garnish

Makes 2–3 servings

Noodles Mien

Like rice, wheat has been a staple crop in China for thousands of years. Wheat, along with millet and barley, became one of the primary crop in the cool, dry regions of northern China. The origin of noodles is widely disputed. It has always been assumed that the noodle was a Chinese invention, and that Marco Polo introduced it to Europe after his travels to the Far East in the thirteenth century. Some anthropological clues suggest that noodles may have originated in Central Asia, and that the Etruscans had noodles as early as 1000 BC. There are also a few scholars who believe that the Arabs were the

first to make them. Wherever they came from, there is no doubt that noodles take the place of rice in areas of Northern China, and they rank second to rice in the rest of China, as well as in other countries in Asia.

Many varieties are used, among them wheat-flour noodles, which are readily available. *Laomien* means "tossed and mixed noodles." Noodles are parboiled and then mixed together with meat and vegetables that have already been stir-fried. *Chaomien*, which means "fried noodles," usually refers to parboiled noodles that are fried like a pancake and then topped with, but not stirred into, a meat and vegetable combination.

Parboiled Wheat Noodles

12 oz (100 g) fresh wheat noodles or 8 oz (75 g) dried noodles
½ to 1 tablespoon sesame oil or other vegetable oil

1. Bring a large pot of water to a boil. Gradually add the noodles, keeping the water boiling vigorously. Stir the noodles from time to time and cook until barely

done—the outside should be tender, the inside firm and hard. Test for doneness by biting into a single strand. Cooking time for noodles will vary depending on thickness of the noodle.

2. Drain the noodles and mix with a little oil to keep them from sticking together. Set aside until needed or keep warm in the top of a double boiler.

Makes 2 servings

Noodles Tossed with Garlic, Pork and Vegetables

Zhurou Laomien

Pork is the meat of choice in Chinese cooking, but don't hesitate to substitute beef, chicken or shrimp. This is a perfect one-dish meal, and a good way to use leftovers.

8 oz (225 g) dried wheat noodles

Sauce

¼ cup (50 ml) unsalted chicken stock or water

1-2 tablespoons reduced-sodium soy sauce

½ teaspoon sugar

Freshly ground black pepper, to taste

• • •

1 tablespoon oil

2 large cloves garlic, crushed

8 oz (225 g) cooked pork, cut into thin bite-size strips (see note above, right for instructions on using uncooked pork, beef, chicken or shrimp)

8 oz (200 g) Chinese (napa) cabbage, celery cabbage or bok choy, trimmed and cut into narrow 2-in (5-cm) pieces

4 fresh mushrooms, trimmed and sliced

½ can bamboo shoots, cut into narrow, bite-size strips (optional)

2 green onions (scallions), sliced, for garnish

1. Parboil the noodles (see recipe on pages 28–29 or follow package directions) and keep warm. Combine the sauce ingredients in a small bowl and set aside. Prepare the remaining ingredients and place within easy reach of the stove.

2. Heat a nonstick wok or skillet over high heat. Add the oil. When hot, stir-fry the garlic for 3–4 seconds. Add the pork and stir-fry 30 seconds to 1 minute.

3. Add the cabbage, mushrooms and bamboo shoots and stir-fry 2 minutes. Mix in the sauce and bring to a boil.

4. Add the reserved noodles, stirring and turning briskly until heated through. Add more stock if the mixture seems dry. Garnish with the sliced green onions. Serve extra soy sauce and chili sauce at the table.

NOTE: To substitute uncooked pork, beef, chicken or shrimp, you may wish to coat the raw meat with a small amount of soy sauce and/or wine and stir-fry it a little longer in Step 2 before you add the vegetables. Also, don't hesitate to substitute other vegetables you may have on hand for the ones listed here. The results will be equally good.

Makes 2–3 servings

Pan-Fried Noodles with Chicken and Vegetables

Jirou Chaomien

In this recipe, the noodles are pan-fried, like a pancake, and the other ingredients are stir-fried and served on top.

8 oz (225 g) dried wheat noodles

Sauce

¼ cup (50 ml) unsalted chicken stock or water

1 teaspoon reduced-sodium soy sauce

1-2 teaspoons oyster sauce

½ teaspoon sugar

Freshly ground black pepper

• • •

2 tablespoons vegetable oil

2 large cloves garlic, crushed

8 oz (125 g) cooked chicken, cut into bite-size pieces

2 ribs celery, sliced into short, narrow strips

8 oz (200 g) fresh bean sprouts, ends trimmed

4 fresh mushrooms, sliced

2 green onions (scallions), sliced for garnish

1. Parboil the noodles (see recipe on pages 28–29 or follow package directions) and keep warm. Combine the sauce ingredients in a small bowl and set aside. Prepare the remaining ingredients and place within easy reach of the stove.

2. Heat a nonstick skillet over medium heat. Add 1–2 teaspoons of the oil. When hot, add the noodles and arrange them in a flat, round cake-form. Cook until the bottom side is lightly browned. Add another teaspoon of oil and turn the noodles over to brown the other side. (If you wish, you may divide the noodles into 2 or 4 portions and make individual "pancakes" instead of just one. Remove and keep warm in the oven.

3. Heat the wok over high heat. Add the remaining tablespoon of oil. When hot, stir-fry the garlic for 3–4 seconds. Add the chicken and stir-fry 30 seconds.

4. Add the celery, bean sprouts and mushrooms and stir-fry 2 minutes. Mix in the sauce and bring to a boil, stirring to blend flavors.

5. Remove the hot noodle cake (or cakes) from the oven and pour the sauce mixture on top. Garnish with sliced green onions (scallions). Extra soy sauce and chili sauce may be served at the table.

VARIATION: *Cooked pork or beef may be substituted for chicken. For instructions on using uncooked meats, see the note at the end of the recipe for* Noodles Tossed with Garlic, Pork and Vegetables *(page 29).*

Makes 2 servings

Chicken  Chaoji

Chicken Stir-Fry with Snow Peas
Xuedou Songzi Ji

The combination of chicken and pine nuts is delicious. If you don't have snow peas on hand, substitute asparagus or even frozen peas.

8-12 oz (200–300 g) boneless, skinless chicken cut into thin, bite-size strips

1 tablespoon cornstarch

1 teaspoon reduced-sodium soy sauce

1 egg white, lightly beaten

Sauce

> 2 tablespoons Chinese rice wine or pale
>   dry sherry
>
> 1 tablespoon reduced-sodium soy sauce
>
> 2 tablespoons unsalted chicken stock or
>   water
>
> Salt and freshly ground black pepper, to
>   taste
>
> • • •
>
> 1½ tablespoons vegetable oil
>
> 4 tablespoons pine nuts
>
> 8 oz (225 g) fresh snow peas, tips and
>   strings removed
>
> 2 cloves garlic, crushed

1. Start rice. Prepare the ingredients and them place within easy reach of the stove.
2. Place the chicken pieces in a bowl, sprinkle them with the cornstarch and toss to coat lightly and evenly. Add the soy sauce to the beaten egg white and pour over the chicken pieces. Toss again to coat them thoroughly.
3. Combine the sauce ingredients in a small bowl and set aside.
4. In a nonstick wok (or skillet) heat a few drops of oil over low heat and brown the pine nuts until golden, shaking the wok to prevent scorching. Remove and set aside.
5. Heat the same wok over high heat and add half of the oil, rotating the wok to coat the sides. When the wok is very hot, add the snow peas and stir-fry 1–2 minutes. Remove to a warmed platter.
6. Heat the wok again over high heat and add the remaining oil. Stir-fry the garlic for 3–4 seconds. Add the chicken and stir-fry until it begins to brown, about 2 minutes.
7. Return the snow peas and the sauce to the wok, stirring and tossing until heated through. Do not overcook the chicken or it will dry out. Snow peas should remain green and crisp. Remove to a platter and sprinkle the toasted pine nuts over all. Serve with rice.

VARIATION 1: *12–14 asparagus spears may be substituted for the snow peas. Remove tough ends where they break off naturally, and cut spears on the diagonal into 2-in (5-cm) lengths.*

VARIATION 2: *Shrimp may be substituted for chicken with excellent results.*

Makes 2 servings

Lemon Chicken
Ningmeng Ji

There are many versions of this very popular dish. This one is simplified but still very tasty. Unlike most versions, the chicken is not deep-fried. Prepare a green vegetable to serve with this dish and keep it warm while you cook the chicken.

> 8–12 oz (200–300 g) boneless, skinless
>   chicken, cut into bite-size pieces
>
> 1 tablespoon cornstarch
>
> 1 teaspoon reduced-sodium soy sauce
>
> 1 egg white, lightly beaten

Sauce

> 3–4 tablespoons fresh lemon juice
>
> Grated zest of ½ lemon
>
> 1 tablespoon Chinese rice wine or pale dry
>   sherry
>
> 1 teaspoon reduced-sodium soy sauce
>
> 1 tablespoon sugar
>
> • • •
>
> 1 tablespoon vegetable oil
>
> Sliced green onions (scallions), for
>   garnish

1. Start rice. Prepare the ingredients and place them within easy reach of the stove.
2. Place the chicken pieces in a bowl, sprinkle them with the cornstarch and toss to coat lightly and evenly. Add the soy sauce to the beaten egg white, pour over the chicken pieces and toss again to coat them thoroughly.
3. Combine the sauce ingredients in a small bowl and stir to dissolve sugar. Set aside.
4. Heat a nonstick wok (or skillet) over high heat. Add the oil and rotate the wok to coat the sides. When very hot, stir-fry the chicken about 2 minutes or until it begins to brown. Remove to a serving bowl and keep warm.
5. Discard any excess oil from the wok and reduce heat to medium. Pour the sauce into the wok and bring to a boil. Return the chicken to the wok and stir until heated through. Add 2 or 3 tablespoons of stock or water to prevent scorching if the mixture seems dry. Garnish with green onions (scallions) and serve with rice and a cooked vegetable.

Makes 2 servings

Chicken with Leeks and Oyster Sauce
Jiangbao Dacong Ji

Oyster sauce does not taste fishy nor does it taste like oysters. However, it is especially good with chicken.

8-12 oz (200–300 g) boneless, skinless chicken breast cut into bite-size cubes
1 tablespoon cornstarch
1 egg white, lightly beaten

Sauce

1-1½ tablespoons oyster sauce
1 teaspoon sugar
1 tablespoon Chinese rice wine or pale dry sherry
2-4 tablespoons unsalted chicken stock or water
Freshly ground black pepper and ground red pepper, to taste

• • •

1½ tablespoons vegetable oil
8 young leek stalks, cut into 1-in (2 ½-cm) sections
2 cloves garlic, crushed
1 tablespoon grated fresh ginger

1. Start rice. Prepare the ingredients and place them within easy reach of the stove.
2. Place the chicken pieces in a bowl, sprinkle them with the cornstarch and toss to coat lightly and evenly. Pour the beaten egg white over the chicken pieces and toss again to coat them thoroughly.
3. Combine the sauce ingredients in a small bowl and set aside.
4. Heat a nonstick wok (or skillet) over high heat until very hot. Add ½ tablespoon of the oil and rotate the wok to coat the sides. When very hot, stir-fry the leeks about 1 minute or until they are wilted and slightly browned. Remove from the wok.
5. Heat the wok again over high heat and add the remaining tablespoon of oil. Stir-fry the garlic and ginger for 3–4 seconds. Then add the chicken and stir-fry about 2 minutes or until it begins to brown.
6. Stir in the sauce and mix well with the chicken. Return the leeks to the wok, stirring and tossing until heated through. Serve with rice.

Makes 2 servings

Cantonese Sweet-and-Sour Chicken

Suantien Lichiji

Lychees and pineapples grow abundantly in southern China, where they are used, with their juices, in chicken and pork dishes.

8–12 oz (200–300 g) boneless, skinless chicken cut into bite-size pieces
Ground Sichuan pepper or freshly ground black pepper, to taste
1 tablespoon cornstarch

Sauce

1 tablespoon reduced-sodium soy sauce
3 tablespoons lychee juice
3 tablespoons rice vinegar or other mild vinegar
2 tablespoons sugar
3 tablespoons unsalted chicken stock or water
Ground red chili or chili oil or ground red pepper, to taste

• • •

1 tablespoon vegetable oil
2 large cloves garlic, crushed
1 tablespoon grated fresh ginger
1 green or red bell pepper, cut into 1-in (2½-cm) squares (optional)
2 green onions (scallions), cut into 1-in (2½-cm) lengths
One 8-oz (225-g) can lychees, drained (reserve juice to use in sauce)
1 teaspoon cornstarch, mixed with 1 tablespoon water (optional)

1. Start rice. Prepare the ingredients and place them within easy reach of the stove.
2. Sprinkle the chicken pieces with pepper and dredge in the cornstarch.
3. Mix the sauce ingredients in a small bowl and set aside.
4. Heat a nonstick wok (or skillet) over high heat. Add the oil and rotate the wok to coat the sides. When very hot, add the garlic and ginger and stir-fry a few seconds. Add the chicken and stir-fry about 1 minute or until it is no longer pink.
5. Add the bell pepper, if using, and green onions (scallions) and stir-fry for another minute. Reduce the heat and add the sauce. Bring to a boil and simmer over low heat for 30 seconds.
6. Add the lychees and cook until heated through.
7. Optional Step: Mix in the blended cornstarch and water and stir until the sauce thickens.
8. Serve with rice.

VARIATION: *One or two slices of fresh or canned pineapple, cut into small pieces, may be substituted for the lychees. Substitute pineapple juice for the lychee juice in the sauce.*

Makes 2 servings

Chicken with Sweet Hoisin Sauce

Jiangbao Jiding

Though Sichuan dishes are typically hot, this one is not. Any other green vegetable, such as green beans or asparagus, may be substituted for the broccoli.

8–12 oz (200–300 g) boneless, skinless chicken, cut into bite-size pieces
1 tablespoon cornstarch
2 teaspoons reduced-sodium soy sauce
2 teaspoons Chinese rice wine or pale dry sherry
1 egg white, lightly beaten
1½ tablespoons vegetable oil
8 oz (175 g) broccoli florets, cut into bite-

China

size pieces, or Chinese broccoli, cut
    into 1-in (2 ½-cm) lengths
2 large cloves garlic, crushed
1 tablespoon grated fresh ginger
1-1½ tablespoons hoisin sauce
½ teaspoon sesame oil (optional)

1. Start rice. Prepare the ingredients and place them within easy reach of the stove.
2. Place the cornstarch in a bowl; add the chicken pieces and toss them about until they are lightly coated. Mix in the soy sauce and wine, and then add the egg white, stirring until the chicken is well coated.
3. Heat a nonstick wok (or skillet) over high heat. Add half of the oil and rotate the wok to coat the sides. When hot, stir-fry the broccoli for 1–2 minutes, coating well with the oil. Add 2 tablespoons of water to the wok, cover and steam for 30 seconds to 1 minute, or until broccoli is tender but crisp. Remove, with the juices, to a plate.
4. Wipe the wok dry. Heat it again over high heat and add the remaining oil. Stir-fry the garlic and ginger for 3–4 seconds. Then add the chicken and stir-fry 1–2 minutes or until the chicken begins to brown.
5. Add the hoisin sauce and sesame oil, if using, and stir-fry about 30 seconds to blend flavors.
6. Return the broccoli, with juices, to the wok with the chicken. Stir and toss for half a minute or so or until heated through. Serve with rice.

Makes 2 servings

Hunan-Style Chicken Salad

This is a favorite Hunan combination. Create other combinations to suit your own taste.

8-12 oz (200-300 g) cooked chicken, cut
    into thin bite-size slices
1-2 small cucumbers, peeled, cut in half
    lengthwise, seeded and cut into thin
    slices
Lettuce leaves
2 green onions (scallions), cut into 1-in
    (2 ½-cm) lengths
1 tablespoon sesame seeds, lightly toasted
    (optional)

Dipping sauce

1 tablespoon reduced-sodium soy sauce
2 teaspoons grated fresh ginger
1 clove garlic, crushed
½ teaspoon sugar
2 tablespoons rice vinegar
1 teaspoon sesame oil
3 tablespoons unsalted chicken stock or
    water
1 teaspoon chili sauce, chili oil, or ground
    red pepper, to taste

1. Arrange lettuce leaves on a platter. Combine the chicken and cucumbers, and arrange on top of the lettuce leaves. Top with the sliced green onions (scallions).
2. Heat a dry wok over medium heat and quickly toast the sesame seeds, if using, while shaking the wok to avoid scorching. Set aside.
3. Combine the sauce ingredients and stir until well blended. Divide into two small bowls to be used as a dipping sauce at the table, or pour over the salad. Sprinkle the salad with the toasted sesame seeds, if using. Serve with rice or crusty bread.

Makes 2 servings

Chicken with Red and Green Bell Peppers

Qinghong Lajiao Chaoji

Colorful, light and elegant, this dish is delicious and eye pleasing. I especially like it with nuts, which add another flavorful dimension to the dish.

> 8–12 oz (200–300 g) boneless, skinless chicken breast meat, cut into thin bite-size pieces
> 1 tablespoon cornstarch
> 1 egg white, lightly beaten

Sauce

> 1 tablespoon soy sauce
> 2 tablespoons Chinese rice wine or pale dry sherry
> ½ teaspoon sugar
> Freshly ground black pepper, to taste
> 2–3 tablespoons unsalted chicken stock or water
>
> • • •
>
> 1½ tablespoons vegetable oil
> 1 red bell pepper, seeded and cut into 1-in (2½-cm) squares
> 1 green bell pepper, seeded and cut into 1-in (2½-cm) squares
> 2 large cloves garlic, crushed
> ¼ cup walnut halves or blanched almonds (optional)

1. Start rice. Prepare the ingredients and place them within easy reach of the stove.
2. In a large bowl, sprinkle the chicken pieces with the cornstarch so that they are coated evenly and lightly. Then coat the pieces thoroughly with the egg white.
3. Combine the sauce ingredients in a small bowl and set aside.
4. Heat a nonstick wok (or skillet) over high heat. Add half of the oil and rotate the wok to coat the sides. Stir-fry the bell peppers for about 1 minute. Remove from the wok.
5. Heat the wok again over high heat. Add the remaining oil and, when hot, stir-fry the garlic 3–4 seconds. Add the chicken and stir-fry 1–2 minutes or until it begins to brown. Add the sauce and stir-fry another minute, mixing the sauce well with the chicken.
6. Return the peppers to the wok. Toss everything another minute or so or until heated through. Garnish with nuts and serve with rice.

Makes 2 servings

Broiled Drumsticks with Sesame Seed Glaze

Jiangzhi Jituei

This is simple and hearty. To save on cleanup time, line the pan under the broiler with aluminum foil. Prepare a vegetable or salad to go with the chicken while the drumsticks broil.

> 6 chicken drumsticks

Marinade

> 2 tablespoons Chinese rice wine or pale dry sherry
> 2 tablespoons reduced-sodium soy sauce
> 1½ teaspoons sugar
> 2 teaspoons rice vinegar or other mild vinegar
> 4 slices peeled fresh ginger
> Freshly ground black pepper, to taste
>
> • • •
>
> ¼ cup (25 g) sesame seeds

1. Start rice.
2. Combine the marinade ingredients and coat the chicken pieces. Leave the chicken in the marinade 5–20 minutes; the longer the better.
3. Preheat the broiler to medium.

4. Dredge the marinated chicken in sesame seeds and broil 5–10 minutes on each side, depending on size of drumsticks. Serve with rice and a cooked vegetable or salad.

Makes 2 servings

Chicken with Fresh Bean Sprouts
Yacai Chaoji

No soy sauce is used in this dish. Its goodness depends on the natural flavor of the chicken and sprouts.

    8-12 oz (200-300 g) boneless, skinless
        chicken breast, cut into very thin
        slices, about 2 in (5 cm) long and ⅛ in
        (½ cm) wide
    1 tablespoon cornstarch
    1 egg white, lightly beaten
    1 tablespoon Chinese rice wine or pale dry
        sherry
    1½ tablespoons vegetable oil
    8 oz (200 g) fresh bean sprouts, ends trimmed
    1 clove garlic, crushed
    Salt and freshly ground black pepper, to taste

1. Start rice. Prepare the ingredients and place them within easy reach of the stove.
2. In a large bowl, sprinkle the chicken pieces with the cornstarch so that they are coated lightly and evenly. Then coat the pieces thoroughly with the egg white.
3. Heat a nonstick wok (or skillet) over high heat and add half of the oil. Rotate the wok to coat the sides. Stir-fry the bean sprouts for about 1 minute, coating them well with the oil. Remove to a platter.
4. Heat the wok again over high heat and add remainder of the oil. Stir-fry garlic a few seconds. Add the coated chicken and stir-fry for

about 1 minute or until it begins to brown.
5. Return the bean sprouts to the wok and stir-fry gently with the chicken to reheat and blend flavors. Sprinkle with salt and pepper. Serve immediately with rice.

Makes 2 servings

Spicy Peanut Chicken with Bok Choy
Xiaobaicai Chaoji

In this recipe the chicken and vegetable are stir-fried with a robust hot sauce and topped with peanuts. Adjust the amount of chiles to your tolerance for spicy foods.

    8-12 oz (200-300 g) boneless, skinless
        chicken, cut into bite-size pieces
    1 tablespoon cornstarch
    1 egg white, lightly beaten

Sauce
    1½ tablespoons reduced-sodium soy sauce
    1 tablespoon Chinese rice wine or pale dry
        sherry
    1 tablespoon rice vinegar
    ½ teaspoon to 1 tablespoon hot chili sauce
    1 teaspoon sugar
    3-4 tablespoons unsalted chicken stock
        or water
                    • • •
    1½ tablespoons vegetable oil
    1 small young bok choy (8-12 oz/125 g),
        trimmed and cut into ½-in (1¼-cm)
        lengths
    4 large cloves garlic, crushed
    1-4 dried chiles, seeded and chopped, or
        dried red pepper flakes, to taste
    3-4 tablespoons roasted peanuts

1. Start rice. Prepare the ingredients and place them within easy reach of the stove.

2. In a large bowl, sprinkle the chicken pieces with the cornstarch so that they are coated lightly and evenly. Then coat the pieces thoroughly with the egg white.

3. Combine the sauce ingredients in a small bowl and set aside.

4. Heat a nonstick wok (or skillet) over high heat. Add half of the oil and rotate the wok to coat the sides. Stir-fry the bok choy for about 1 minute, or until it begins to wilt. Remove from the wok.

5. Heat the wok again over high heat and add the remainder of the oil. Stir-fry the garlic and dried peppers for a few seconds. Add the chicken and stir-fry a minute or two or until it begins to brown.

6. Add the sauce and stir constantly to mix ingredients together well. Return the bok choy to the wok, stirring and tossing to heat through and blend flavors. Remove to a platter and sprinkle with the peanuts. Serve with rice.

Makes 2 servings

Chicken with Sweet Bean Sauce

Doubanjiang Chaoji

Chinese cooks prefer dried mushrooms to fresh ones because the drying process concentrates their smoky flavor, but dried mushrooms must be soaked in water before they are cooked. If time is limited, use fresh ones instead.

> 8-12 oz (200-300 g) boneless, skinless chicken breast, cut into bite-size pieces
> 1 tablespoon cornstarch
> 1 egg white, lightly beaten

Sauce
> 1 tablespoon brown bean sauce
> 1 tablespoon Chinese rice wine or pale dry sherry
> 1 teaspoon reduced-sodium soy sauce
> 2 tablespoons mushroom soaking water, unsalted stock or water

• • •

> 1½ tablespoons vegetable oil
> 4 dried black mushrooms, soaked 25-30 minutes in hot water, drained, stemmed and sliced, or use fresh mushrooms
> 1 green bell pepper, seeded and cut into 1-in (2½-cm) squares
> ½ cup (75 g) sliced canned bamboo shoots
> 2 large cloves garlic, crushed

1. Start rice. Prepare the ingredients and place them within easy reach of the stove.

2. In a large bowl, sprinkle the chicken pieces with the cornstarch so that they are lightly and evenly coated. Then coat the pieces thoroughly with the egg white.

3. Combine the sauce ingredients in a small bowl and set aside.

4. Heat a nonstick wok (or skillet) over high heat. Add half of the oil and rotate the wok to coat the sides. Stir-fry the mushrooms for about 2 minutes. Add the green pepper and bamboo shoots and stir-fry for another minute. Remove from the wok.

5. Heat the wok again over high heat and add the remaining oil. Stir-fry garlic for about 3–4 seconds. Add the chicken and stir-fry for about 2 minutes or until it begins to brown.

6. Stir in the sauce and mix well. Return the green pepper and bamboo shoots to the wok, stirring and tossing about 1 minute or until heated through. Serve with rice.

Makes 2 servings

Dipping Sauces

Pick up a roasted chicken at the supermarket and serve with any one of these easy sauces. If you find any of the sauces are too strong for your taste, increase the amount of stock or water to dilute them somewhat.

Sesame-Soy Sauce

1 tablespoon sesame oil
¼ cup (50 ml) reduced-sodium soy sauce
2 tablespoons unsalted chicken stock or water

Combine and mix well.

Rice Wine-Soy Sauce

2 tablespoons Chinese rice wine or pale dry sherry
2 tablespons reduced-sodium soy sauce
1 tablespoon rice vinegar or other mild vinegar
½ teaspoon sugar

Combine and stir until sugar dissolves.

Mustard-Soy Sauce

¼ cup (50 ml) reduced-sodium soy sauce
1 teaspoon powdered mustard
1-2 tablespoons unsalted chicken stock or water

Combine and blend well.

Garlic-Soy Sauce

2-3 large cloves garlic, minced
¼ cup (50 ml) reduced-sodium soy sauce
¼ teaspoon sugar
2 tablespoons unsalted stock or water
Ground red pepper, to taste

Combine and stir until sugar dissolves.

Recipes make enough dipping sauce for 2–3 servings.

Five-Spice Chicken with Braised Zucchini

Wuxiang Ji

The number five makes reference to the five tastes—sweet, sour, salty, bitter and spicy. The importance placed on balancing these elements is related to the belief that the universe is also composed of five elements—water, fire, earth, wood and metal—and that a natural harmony exists between them. The spice is a combination of cinnamon, star anise, fennel, cloves and Sichuan peppercorns, and is available at most major supermarkets.

8-12 oz (200–300 g) boneless, skinless chicken, cut into bite-size pieces
1 teaspoon five-spice powder
1-2 tablespoons reduced-sodium soy sauce
1½ tablespoons vegetable oil
2 small zucchini or yellow squash, sliced into thin rounds
1 tablespoon Chinese rice wine or pale dry sherry (optional)
3 tablespoons unsalted chicken stock
½ teaspoon sugar
1 teaspoon cornstarch mixed with 1 tablespoon water (optional)
Chopped fresh coriander leaves leaves (cilantro) or parsley, for garnish

1. Start rice. Prepare the ingredients and place them within easy reach of the stove.
2. Put the chicken pieces in a bowl, rub them with the five-spice powder, then coat with the soy sauce. Let stand 5 minutes, or longer if there is time.
3. Heat a nonstick wok (or skillet) over high heat and add half of the oil. Rotate the wok to coat the sides. When hot, add the zucchini or yellow squash and stir-fry gently

until it begins to soften but is still firm. Remove from the wok.

4. Heat the wok again over high heat and add the remaining oil. Stir-fry the chicken for 1–2 minutes or until it begins to brown.

5. Return the squash to the wok and add the wine, if using, stock, sugar and any soy sauce that may be left from marinating the chicken. Stir in more stock or water if the mixture seems dry and bring to a boil.

6. Optional Step: Add the cornstarch mixture, turn the heat down to low and simmer a minute or so, or until the sauce begins to thicken.

7. Garnish with coriander leaves (cilantro) or parsley and serve with rice.

VARIATION: *Substitute 8–12 oz (225–350 g) flank steak, cut across the grain into very thin slices. Instead of squash, you may substitute another vegetable.*

Makes 2 servings

■ **Beef** ■

Beef with Tomato, Onion and Green Pepper

Fanqiz Niurou

Pre-sliced beef is sold in most major super-markets, but if you have to do it yourself, remember that meat is easier to slice when it is partially frozen.

8-12 oz (200-300 g) flank steak, cut across the grain into thin slices, about ⅛ in (3 mm) thick

1 tablespoon cornstarch

1 tablespoon Chinese rice wine or pale dry sherry

1 tablespoon reduced-sodium soy sauce

Sauce

1 tablespoon Chinese rice wine or pale dry sherry

1 tablespoon reduced-sodium soy sauce

3-4 tablespoons unsalted chicken stock or water

½ teaspoon sugar

Freshly ground black pepper

• • •

1½ tablespoons vegetable oil

2 large cloves garlic, crushed

1 tablespoon grated fresh ginger

2 small onions, thinly sliced

2 green bell peppers, seeded and cut into 1-in (2 ½-cm) squares

2 tomatoes, quartered and cut into thin wedges

1. Start rice. Prepare the ingredients and place them within easy reach of the stove.

2. In a large bowl, sprinkle the beef slices with the cornstarch so that they are coated evenly and lightly. Then combine the wine and soy sauce and coat the pieces thoroughly with the mixture.

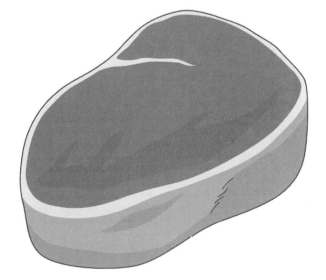

3. Combine thee sauce ingredients in a small bowl and set aside.

4. Heat a nonstick wok (or skillet) over high heat. When hot, add half of the oil and stir-fry the garlic and ginger for 3–4 seconds. Add the beef and stir-fry about 1 minute or until it loses its red color. Remove to a platter with juices.

5. Heat the wok again over high heat, add the remaining oil, and stir-fry the onions and peppers about 2 minutes, or until they soften but still retain some crispness.

6. Add the tomatoes and sauce. Toss lightly until the mixture begins to boil and the tomatoes soften, about 1–2 minutes.

7. Return the beef to the wok and stir-fry about 30 seconds with the vegetables, until heated through. Serve with rice.

Makes 2 servings

Beef with Tender-Crisp Asparagus

Luxun Niurou

This is a very lightly seasoned dish that relies on the natural flavors of the ingredients. If asparagus is not in season, substitute snow peas. Total cooking time for this dish is about 2 minutes, so use only high quality, tender beef, very thinly sliced.

> 8-12 oz (225–350 g) flank steak, cut across the grain into very thin slices (partially frozen meat is easier to slice)
> 1 tablespoon cornstarch
> 2-3 tablespoons Chinese rice wine or pale dry sherry
> 1½ tablespoons vegetable oil
> 14 asparagus spears, tough ends trimmed where they break off naturally, spears

> cut on the diagonal into 1½-in (4-cm) lengths
> 1 teaspoon sugar
> ½ to 1 tablespoon reduced-sodium soy sauce
> 2 tablespoons unsalted chicken stock or water

1. Start rice. Prepare the ingredients and place them within easy reach of the stove.

2. In a large bowl, sprinkle the beef slices evenly and lightly with the cornstarch. Then coat the meat with 1 tablespoon of the wine.

3. Heat a nonstick wok (or skillet) over high heat. Add half of the oil. When it is very hot, add the beef slices and stir-fry about 30 seconds, stirring rapidly to separate the pieces if they stick together. Remove to a platter and keep warm.

4. Heat the wok again over high heat and add the remaining oil. Stir-fry the asparagus about 10 seconds.

5. Return the beef to the wok, and stir-fry quickly while sprinkling with the sugar. Stir in the remaining tablespoon of wine, the soy sauce and stock. Serve immediately with rice.

Makes 2 servings

Beef with Leeks

Dacong Niurou

This is another dish with a cooking time of about 2 minutes, so use only the highest quality, most tender cut of beef and very young leeks. The leek, which tastes like a strong green onion, is a biennial plant and is best in its first year; in its second year it is too tough to eat.

> 8-12 oz (225–350 g) flank steak, cut across the grain into very thin slices
> 1 tablespoon cornstarch

1 egg white, lightly beaten

1½ tablespoons vegetable oil

8–12 oz (125–200 g) young leeks, most of
the green part removed, stalks cut in
half lengthwise, then into 1-in (2 ½-cm)
sections

2 tablespoons Chinese rice wine or pale
dry sherry

1 tablespoon reduced-sodium soy sauce

Freshly ground black pepper, to taste

1. Start rice. Prepare the ingredients and place them within easy reach of the stove.
2. In a large bowl, sprinkle the beef slices lightly and evenly with the cornstarch. Then coat the pieces thoroughly with the egg white.
3. Heat a nonstick wok (or skillet) over high heat. Add half of the oil. When hot, add the beef and stir-fry about 30 seconds, stirring rapidly to separate the pieces if they stick together. Remove to a platter.
4. Heat the wok again over high heat and add the remaining oil. Stir-fry the leeks for about 20 seconds.
5. Return the beef to the wok. Add the wine, soy sauce and black pepper and stir-fry quickly to reheat and blend flavors. Serve immediately with rice.

Makes 2 servings

Beef with Savory Black Bean Sauce

Jiangbao Niurou

Fermented black beans are black soybeans preserved in salt. They give dishes a rich, savory flavor.

Sauce

1 tablespoon fermented black beans

1 tablespoon reduced-sodium soy sauce

3–4 tablespoons unsalted beef broth or
water

½ teaspoon sugar

• • •

1½ tablespoon vegetable oil

8–12 oz (200–300 g) Chinese (napa)
cabbage, shredded

2 large cloves garlic, crushed

8–12 oz (225–350 g) tender beef, cut on
the diagonal into very thin slices, then
into thin strips (partially frozen meat is
easier to slice)

1 teaspoon cornstarch mixed with 1
tablespoon water (optional)

1 teaspoon sesame oil (optional)

1. Start rice. Prepare the ingredients and place them within easy reach of the stove.
2. Put the fermented black beans in a small strainer and rinse under cold running water for 1 minute to rid them of excess salt. Drain and mash with a fork. Combine the beans, soy sauce, water and sugar and set aside.
3. Heat a nonstick wok (or skillet) over high heat and add half of the oil. Add the cabbage and stir-fry for 1 minute or until wilted. Remove to a platter.
4. Heat the wok again over high heat and add the remaining oil. When hot, stir-fry the garlic for a few seconds. Add the beef and stir-fry, tossing and turning about 1 minute or until it loses its red color.
5. Pour the bean sauce mixture over the beef, stir well and bring to a boil. Simmer a minute or so to blend flavors.
6. Return the cabbage to the wok and stir another 30 seconds, or until heated through. Add another tablespoon or two of the stock or water to prevent scorching if the mixture seems dry.

7. Optional Steps: Add the cornstarch mixture and stir until the sauce begins to thicken. Stir in sesame oil.

8. Serve immediately with rice.

Makes 2 servings

Sichuan Beef

Sichuan Niurou

As you would expect from its title, this recipe is a spicy dish, though the heat can be adjusted to personal preference. This dish should be cooked until all of the juices are absorbed.

> 2 tablespoons reduced-sodium soy sauce
> 2 tablespoons Chinese rice wine or pale dry sherry
> 1 teaspoon sugar
> 1 tablespoon grated fresh ginger
> 8–12 oz (225–350 g) flank or boneless sirloin steak, cut on the diagonal into very thin slices
> 1½ tablespoons vegetable oil
> 2–3 (or more) fresh or dried red chiles, seeded and sliced
> 2 small carrots, scraped and cut into matchsticks
> 2 celery ribs, cut into matchsticks
> 1 handful fresh coriander leaves (cilantro), chopped

1. Start rice. Prepare the ingredients and place them within easy reach of the stove.

2. Combine the soy sauce, wine, sugar and ginger in a bowl. Add the beef and mix thoroughly. Set aside.

3. Heat a nonstick wok (or skillet) over high heat. Add half of the oil and stir-fry the chiles for half a minute.

4. Add the carrots and celery and stir-fry 1–2 minutes. Remove to a platter and keep warm.

5. Heat the wok again over high heat and add the remaining oil. Add the beef and stir-fry briskly until it is nicely browned. Add the remaining marinade and continue to stir-fry to blend flavors.

6. Return the vegetables to the wok, stirring constantly, until heated through and dry. Serve garnished with the chopped coriander leaves.

Makes 2 servings

Beef with Hoisin-Glazed Vegetables

Qingjiao Niurou

Hoisin sauce, which gives this dish its distinct flavor, is made from soybeans blended with flour, sugar, vinegar and spices. It has a lower sodium content than most other Chinese condiments.

> 8–12 oz (225–350 g) flank or boneless sirloin steak, cut on the diagonal into very thin slices, then into thin strips (partially frozen meat is easier to slice)
> 1 tablespoon cornstarch
> 1 tablespoon reduced-sodium soy sauce
> 1 tablespoon Chinese rice wine or pale dry sherry
> 1 teaspoon sesame oil (optional)
> 1½ tablespoons vegetable oil
> 1 onion, cut in half and thinly sliced
> 2 green bell peppers, seeded and cut into 1-in (2½-cm) squares
> 2 large cloves garlic, crushed
> 1 tablespoon grated fresh ginger
> 1 tablespoon hoisin sauce
> ½ teaspoon sugar
> Freshly ground black pepper, to taste

1. Start rice. Prepare the ingredients and place them within easy reach of the stove.

2. Place the beef slices in a bowl,

sprinkle them with the cornstarch and toss to coat lightly and evenly. Combine the soy sauce, wine and sesame oil, if using. Add to the beef slices, tossing to coat them thoroughly.

3. Heat a nonstick wok (or skillet) over high heat. Add half of the vegetable oil and rotate the wok to coat the sides. Stir-fry the onion slices about 1 minute. Add the peppers and stir-fry another minute or so, or until the onions have softened but the peppers are still crisp. Remove to a platter and keep warm.

4. Heat the wok again over high heat and add the remaining oil. When hot, stir-fry the garlic and ginger 3–4 seconds. Add the beef and stir-fry briskly about 1 minute or until it begins to brown. Mix in the hoisin sauce, sugar and black pepper and stir well to blend flavors. Stir in the remaining marinade.

5. Return the vegetables to the wok, stir-frying about 1 minute or until heated through. If the mixture seems dry, add a tablespoon or two of stock or water and mix well. Serve with rice.

Makes 2 servings

Ginger Beef with Fresh Peas

Laojiang Chouniurou

If possible, use young, tender, and newly harvested ginger, available in the spring and summer months.

> 1 tablespoon Chinese rice wine or pale dry
>   sherry
> 1 tablespoon reduced-sodium soy sauce
> 8-12 oz (225-350 g) flank steak, cut across

the grain into very thin slices (partially frozen meat is easier to slice)

Sauce

> ½ teaspoon sugar
> 2 teaspoons low-sodium soy sauce
> 1 tablespoon Chinese rice wine or pale dry
>   sherry
> 2 tablespoons unsalted beef or chicken
>   stock or water
>
> • • •
>
> 1 tablespoon plus 1 teaspoon vegetable oil
> 4 tablespoons very thinly sliced fresh
>   ginger
> 8 oz (150 g) fresh or frozen green peas or
>   snow peas, tips and strings removed
> Chopped fresh coriander leaves (cilantro)
>   or parsley, for garnish

1. Start rice. Prepare the ingredients and place them within easy reach of the stove.

2. In a bowl, blend together the wine and soy sauce. Add the beef slices to the bowl; toss them to coat well.

3. Combine the sauce ingredients in a small bowl and set aside.

4. Heat a nonstick wok (or skillet) over high heat. When hot, add 1 teaspoon of the oil and stir-fry the ginger for 5–10 seconds. Be careful not to scorch the ginger. Remove from the wok and set aside.

5. Heat the wok again over high heat and add the remaining tablespoon of oil. Add the beef and stir-fry briskly 1 minute, separating pieces if they stick together. Add the peas and stir-fry 30 seconds.

6. Return the ginger to the wok and pour the sauce mixture over all, stirring constantly until heated through. Sprinkle with chopped coriander leaves or parsley. Serve with rice.

Makes 2 servings

Beef and Snow Peas in Oyster Sauce

Xianggu Chaoniurou

Tender slices of flank steak combine with snow peas, mushrooms and oyster sauce to make this beautiful stir-fry. Dried mushrooms add more flavor to the dish, but must be soaked in hot water for 25–30 minutes before cooking.

8-12 oz (225–350 g) flank steak, cut across
    the grain into very thin slices (partially
    frozen meat is easier to slice)
1 tablespoon cornstarch
1 tablespoon reduced-sodium soy sauce

Sauce
½ teaspoon sugar
1 tablespoon oyster sauce
1 tablespoon Chinese rice wine or pale dry
    sherry
2-3 tablespoons mushroom soaking liquid,
    unsalted stock or water

• • •

1 tablespoon vegetable oil
4 large fresh or dried mushrooms, sliced
12 fresh snow peas, tips and strings removed
2 large cloves garlic, crushed
1 teaspoon cornstarch mixed with 1
    tablespoon water

1. Start rice. Prepare the ingredients and place them within easy reach of the stove.

2. Place the beef slices in a bowl, sprinkle them with the cornstarch, and toss to coat lightly and evenly. Then coat the slices thoroughly with soy sauce.

3. Combine the sauce ingredients in a small bowl and set aside.

4. Heat a nonstick wok (or skillet) over high heat. When hot add half of the oil and rotate the wok to coat the sides. Add the mushrooms and snow peas and stir-fry about 1–2 minutes. Remove from the wok and set aside.

5. Heat the wok again over high heat and add the remaining oil. Stir-fry the garlic a few seconds. Add the beef slices and stir-fry briskly 1 minute, or until they lose their red color, separating pieces if they stick together.

6. Pour the sauce into the wok and stir well. Return the vegetables to the wok and bring to a boil, sstirring continually. Add more mushroom liquid or stock to prevent scorching if the mixture seems dry. Add the cornstarch mixture and stir until the sauce begins to thicken. Serve with rice.

Makes 2 servings

■ Pork ■

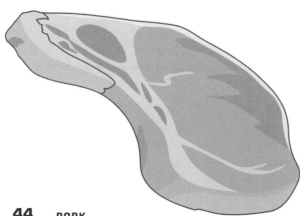

Stir-Fried Pork with Cauliflower

Huacai Chaoniurou

When you tire of using cauliflower, try the botanical combination of broccoli and cauliflower called "broccoflower." It is excellent in this dish.

8-12 oz (200–300 g) lean, boneless pork, cut
   across the grain into thin, bite-size slices
1 tablespoon cornstarch
2 tablespoons low-sodium soy sauce
1 tablespoon Chinese rice wine or pale dry
   sherry
1-1½ tablespoons vegetable oil
2 large cloves garlic, crushed
8-12 oz (100–150 g) cauliflower florets,
   separated into bite-size pieces

1. Start rice. Prepare the ingredients
   and place them within easy reach of
   the stove.
2. In a large bowl, sprinkle the pork
   slices lightly and evenly with the
   cornstarch. Combine the soy sauce
   and wine; add this mixture to the
   pork and toss until thoroughly
   coated.
3. Heat a nonstick wok (or skillet) over
   high heat. Add half of the oil and
   rotate the wok to coat the sides.
   Add 1 clove garlic and stir-fry a few
   seconds. Then add the cauliflower
   and stir-fry 1 minute. Add 2 tablespoons of water; cover and steam a
   few seconds or until cauliflower is
   tender but still crisp. Do not overcook. Remove from the wok.
4. Wipe the wok dry with paper
   towel. Heat the wok again over
   high heat and add the remaining
   oil. Stir-fry the remaining garlic
   a few seconds. Add the seasoned
   pork and stir-fry briskly until it
   begins to brown. Add the remaining marinade. Stir well to blend
   flavors.
5. Return the cauliflower to the wok
   with its juices. Toss with the pork
   until heated through. Be sure the
   pork is completely cooked. If the
   mixture seems dry, add a tablespoon or two of chicken stock or
   water to prevent scorching. Serve
   with rice.

Makes 2 servings

Hunan Sweet-and-Sour Pork with Bok Choy
Suantienrou

North Chinese sweet-and-sour pork
is very simple, as it does not contain
the elaborate seasonings, fruits and
vegetables that Cantonese cooks use.

Sauce
   1 tablespoon reduced-sodium soy sauce
   2 tablespoons sugar
   2 tablespoons rice vinegar or cider vinegar
   Freshly ground black pepper, to taste

   • • •

   1 tablespoon plus 1 teaspoon vegetable oil
   2 large cloves garlic, crushed
   1 tablespoon grated fresh ginger
   8-12 oz (200–300 g) boneless pork loin,
      cut into thin, bite-size slices
   2 large cloves garlic, crushed
   1 young bok choy (8-12 oz/200–300 g),
      trimmed and cut into ½-in (1¼-cm)
      lengths
   Salt and freshly ground black pepper, or a
      little soy sauce, to taste
   Chopped fresh coriander leaves (cilantro),
      for garnish

1. Start rice. Prepare the ingredients
   and place them within easy reach
   of the stove.
2. Combine the sauce ingredients in
   a small bowl, stirring well to dissolve sugar, and set aside.
3. Heat a nonstick wok (or skillet)
   over high heat. Add 1 tablespoon
   of the oil and rotate the wok to
   coat the sides. When hot, stir-fry
   the garlic and ginger for 3–4 seconds. Add the pork and stir-fry
   about 2 minutes, or until it and
   begins to brown.
4. Mix in the sauce. Stir-fry about 2
   minutes or until flavors blend and
   pork is cooked through. Remove
   the pork to a heated platter and
   keep warm.

5. Heat the wok over high heat. Add 1 teaspoon of the oil and stir-fry the garlic a few seconds. Add the bok choy and stir-fry briskly for about 2 minutes, or until tender but still crunchy. Add seasoning to taste.

6. Remove the bok choy to the platter with the pork; garnish with coriander leaves and serve with rice.

Makes 2 servings

Ginger-Braised Pork Chops

Zhupai

No chopping of meat is required here. This is a very simple and delicious way to cook pork chops.

> 2 teaspoons reduced-sodium soy sauce
> 1½ tablespoons Chinese rice wine or pale dry sherry
> 4 thin pork chops

Sauce
> 1 tablespoon reduced-sodium soy sauce
> ½ teaspoon rice vinegar or other vinegar
> 3 slices fresh ginger
> ½ teaspoon sugar
> 2 tablespoons unsalted beef or chicken stock or water
> Freshly ground black pepper, to taste
>
> • • •
>
> 1 tablespoon vegetable oil
> Fresh coriander leaves (cilantro) or parsley, for garnish

1. Start rice. Prepare the ingredients and place them within easy reach of the stove.

2. Combine the soy sauce and wine in a shallow bowl. Place the chops in the mixture, turning to coat. Marinate a few minutes.

3. Combine the sauce ingredients in a

small bowl and set aside.

4. Heat a nonstick skillet over medium-high heat. Add the oil and pan-fry the pork chops for 3–4 minutes on each side or until nicely browned.

5. Reduce heat to low. Pour the sauce over the chops. Mix well. Cover and simmer 2–3 minutes to blend flavors. Cook through, but be careful not to overcook. Garnish with coriander leaves or parsley. Serve with rice.

Makes 2 servings

VARIATION: *For a spicy version of this recipe, using lamb and green onions (scallions), substitute the pork with 8–12 oz (200–300 g) of boneless, lean lamb (preferably from the leg), cut across the grain into bite-sized pieces, and substitute the ginger with 1/2 teaspoon chili paste or sauce, or dried red pepper flakes. Stir-fry the lamb for about 2 minutes, or until the meat loses its red color. Then add the white and green parts of 6 green onions—cut in half lengthwise, then into 1-in (2 ½-cm) lengths—and stir-fry for about 30 seconds. As with the Ginger-Braised Pork Chops,* the sauce is then added for a minute or so to heat through and blend flavors.

Ham and Cabbage Stir-Fry

Chaolarou

In this delicious and easy stir-fry, bok choy may be substituted for the cabbage.

> 1 tablespoon vegetable oil
> 8-12 oz (200-300 g) Chinese (napa) cabbage, shredded
> 2 green onions (scallions), thinly sliced

½–1 tablespoon reduced-sodium soy sauce

1 tablespoon Chinese rice wine or pale dry
sherry

½ teaspoon sugar

Freshly ground black pepper, to taste

Ground red pepper, to taste

6 oz (150 g) country-style ham, preferably
Smithfield, cut into matchsticks

1. Start rice. Prepare the ingredients
and place them within easy reach
of the stove.
2. Heat a nonstick wok (or skillet)
over high heat. Add the oil and

stir-fry the cabbage about 2 minutes, or until wilted but still crisp.
Add the green onions and cook
another 30 seconds.
3. Add the soy sauce, wine, sugar,
black pepper and ground red pepper. Mix well.
4. Stir in the ham and cook 30 seconds or until heated through.
Serve with rice.

Makes 2 servings

■ Seafood ■

Seared Scallops with Asparagus

Luxun Chaoxianbei

Scallops are delicate. One must be
careful not to overcook them or they
will become tough and rubbery and
lose all flavor. If asparagus is out of
season, substitute snow peas or
green peas.

Sauce

1 tablespoon reduced-sodium soy sauce

1 tablespoon Chinese rice wine or pale dry
sherry

½ teaspoon sugar

Salt and freshly ground black pepper, to
taste

• • •

1–1½ tablespoons vegetable oil

14 asparagus spears, tough ends trimmed
where they break off naturally, spears cut
on the diagonal into 2-in (5-cm) lengths

2 tablespoons seafood stock or water

1 tablespoon grated fresh ginger

3 green onions (scallions), white part only,
chopped

8–12 oz (200–300 g) scallops, cut into
¼-in (¾-cm) slices if large, or cut in
half if small

1. Start rice. Prepare the ingredients and
place them within easy reach of the
stove.
2. Combine the sauce ingredients in a
small bowl and set aside.
3. Heat a nonstick wok (or skillet)
over high heat. When very hot,
add half of the oil and stir-fry the
asparagus for 1 minute. Add 2
tablespoons stock or water, cover
the wok and steam 30 seconds
or until nearly tender but crisp.
Remove from the wok with juices.

4. Wipe the wok dry with paper towel. Heat the remaining oil over high heat. Add the ginger and green onions and stir-fry 3–4 seconds. Add the scallops and stir-fry gently for about 1 minute. Blend in the sauce. Cook for about 30 seconds.

5. Return the asparagus with juices to the wok. Stir gently until heated through. Do not overcook. Serve with rice.

Makes 2 servings

Stir-Fried Cod with Bok Choy and Mushrooms
Qingai Chaoyu

Fish fillets are fragile and tend to fall apart when stir-fried with a vegetable. In this recipe, the same wok is used for both, but they are only combined on the serving platter. Cod, snapper or other white-fleshed fish may be used.

1½ tablespoons Chinese rice wine or pale dry sherry
1½ tablespoons reduced-sodium soy sauce
8–12 oz (225–350 g) cod or other white-fleshed fish fillets, cut into 4 or 6 pieces
1 tablespoon cornstarch
1½ tablespoons vegetable oil
2 large cloves garlic, crushed
4 fresh or dried Chinese mushrooms, stemmed and cut in half (dried mushrooms must be soaked 25–30 minutes in hot water)
8–12 oz (200–300 g) young bok choy, trimmed and cut into bite-size pieces
1 tablespoon grated fresh ginger
Lemon wedges, for garnish

1. Start rice. Prepare the ingredients and place them within easy reach of the stove.

2. Combine the wine and soy sauce in a bowl, and coat the fish with the mixture. Then sprinkle both sides of the fillets lightly and evenly with the cornstarch and set aside.

3. Heat a nonstick wok (or skillet) over high heat. When hot, add half of the oil and stir-fry 1 garlic clove 3–4 seconds. Add the mushrooms and stir-fry 1–2 minutes or until softened. Then add the bok choy and stir-fry another minute or two, until tender but crisp. Sprinkle with the salt and pepper. Remove to a platter and keep warm.

4. Heat the remaining oil over high heat. Add the remaining garlic clove and ginger and stir-fry a few seconds. Add the fish fillets and stir-fry 1–2 minutes, until nicely browned on both sides. Handle carefully to keep fillets from breaking apart. Serve on a platter with vegetables. Garnish with the lemon wedges and serve with rice.

Makes 2 servings

Stir-Fried Fish Fillets with Oyster Sauce
Chao Yu Pien

Haddock, sea bass or halibut are especially tasty in this recipe, though other firm-fleshed white fish will also work. Oyster sauce, made from oysters, is a thick, brown sauce with a rich flavor. It is available in jars in most supermarkets.

1 tablespoon vegetable oil
3 large cloves garlic, crushed
8–12 oz (225–350 g) firm-fleshed fish fillets, cut into 4 or 6 pieces
6 green onions (scallions), cut into 1-in (2½-cm) lengths
1 tablespoon oyster sauce

1 teaspoon Chinese rice wine or pale dry
    sherry
2 tablespoons fish stock or water

1. Start rice. Prepare the ingredients and place them within easy reach of the stove.
2. Heat a nonstick wok (or skillet) over high heat and add the oil. Stir-fry the garlic for 3–4 seconds. Add the fillets and cook for about 1 minute on each side, until nicely browned. Test with a fork for doneness. Do not overcook. Remove to a warmed platter and keep warm.
3. Maintaining high heat, add the green onions and stir-fry about 1 minute. Stir in the oyster sauce, wine and water and mix well. Cook for 1 more minute to blend flavors. Pour over the fish and serve with rice.

Makes 2 servings

Shrimp and Vegetable Stir-Fry

Chaoxia

With its bright colors, this dish is beautiful yet simple to prepare.

Sauce

    1 tablespoon reduced-sodium soy sauce
    1 tablespoon Chinese rice wine or pale dry
        sherry
    2 tablespoons mushroom soaking water or
        fish stock or water

• • •

    1½ tablespoons vegetable oil
    2 large cloves garlic, crushed
    1 tablespoon grated fresh ginger
    8–12 oz (200–300 g) medium shrimp, shelled
        and deveined, leaving tails intact
    14 fresh snow peas, tips and strings
        removed

    1 red bell pepper, seeded and cut into 1-in
        (2 ½-cm) squares
    4 small fresh or dried Chinese mushrooms,
        stemmed, left whole or cut in half
        (dried mushrooms must be soaked in
        hot water for 25–30 minutes)

1. Start rice. Prepare the ingredients and place them within easy reach of the stove.
2. Combine the sauce ingredients in a small bowl and set aside.
3. Heat a nonstick wok (or skillet) over high heat. When hot, add half of the oil and rotate the wok to coat the sides. Add 1 clove garlic and the ginger and stir-fry 2–3 seconds. Add the shrimp and stir-fry briskly until they begin to turn pink, about 1 minute. Remove to a platter and keep warm.
4. Maintaining high heat, add the remaining oil. Stir-fry the remaining garlic for 3-4 seconds. Add the snow peas, bell pepper and mushrooms and stir-fry about 2 minutes. Vegetables should be tender but still crisp and keep their bright color.
5. Return the shrimp to the wok. Mix in the sauce and stir-fry briskly for about 1 minute or until heated through. Do not overcook. Serve with rice.

Makes 2 servings

Sichuan Shrimp

Lawei Xia

For more flavor, some cooks prefer to cook shrimp with the shells on and do the shelling at the table. This method also saves prep time. Hot bean sauce (or paste) is available in jars and cans in the Asian section of many supermarkets.

1½ tablespoons vegetable oil

8–12 oz (300–450 g) medium shrimp, unshelled or shelled and deveined, leaving tails intact

2 cloves garlic, crushed

1 tablespoon grated fresh ginger

1 can bamboo shoots, cut into bite-size pieces

2 tablespoons unsalted seafood stock or water

1 tablespoon Sichuan hot bean sauce

1 tablespoon reduced-sodium soy sauce

1 tablespoon Chinese rice wine or pale dry sherry

1 teaspoon cornstarch mixed with 1 tablespoon water (optional)

2 green onions (scallions), sliced, or fresh coriander leaves (cilantro), for garnish

1. Start rice. Prepare the ingredients and place them within easy reach of the stove.
2. Heat a nonstick wok (or skillet) over high heat, add the oil and rotate the wok to coat the sides. When hot, add the shrimp and stir-fry briskly, until they become opaque, about 1 minute. Do not overcook or they will toughen. Remove from wok.
3. Heat the wok again and add the garlic and ginger. Stir-fry 3–4 seconds. Add the bamboo shoots and stock or water, and stir-fry 10 seconds. Add the bean sauce, soy sauce and wine. Stir together about 1 minute to blend ingredients.
4. Return the shrimp to the wok and heat through, stirring about 30 seconds. Add another tablespoon or two of stock or water to keep the mixture from scorching if it seems dry.
5. Optional Step: Add the cornstarch mixture and stir until the sauce begins to thicken.
6. Garnish with the green onions or coriander leaves. Serve with rice.

VARIATION: *Fish fillets may be substituted for the shrimp.*

Makes 2 servings

Pan-Fried Fish with Ginger-Wine Sauce
Jiangpien Yu

Sole or flounder fillets, whole butterfish, porgies or any small fish of your choice will work in this recipe.

8–12 oz (225–350 g) fish fillet, cut into 4 pieces

1 tablespoon cornstarch

1½ tablespoons vegetable oil

2 tablespoons grated fresh ginger

2 green onions (scallions), chopped into ¼-in (6-mm) pieces

3 tablespoons Chinese rice wine or pale dry sherry

1 tablespoon reduced-sodium soy sauce

1–2 tablespoons unsalted seafood stock or water

Freshly ground black pepper, to taste

1. Start rice. Prepare the ingredients and place them within easy reach of the stove.
2. Dredge the fish lightly in cornstarch.
3. Heat a nonstick wok (or skillet) over medium heat. Add the oil and swirl to coat the wok. Pan-fry the fish for 1–2 minutes on each side, depending on thickness, until nicely browned. Remove to a serving platter and keep warm.
4. To the same wok add the ginger and green onions and stir-fry a few seconds. Add the wine, soy sauce, stock or water, and pepper. Bring to a boil and pour over the fish. Serve with rice.

Makes 2 servings

Ginger-Garlic Shrimp

Yan Xu Xia

For this dish, usually the shrimp is deep-fried in a light batter. This recipe is simpler to cook, lower in fat, and still very tasty. To save preparation time, leaves the shells on the shrimp to be peeled at the table.

8-12 oz (300–450 g) medium shrimp, unshelled or shelled and deveined, leaving tails intact
1½ tablespoons vegetable oil
2 tablespoons grated fresh ginger
4 large cloves garlic, minced
Fresh coriander leaves (cilantro) or parsley sprigs, for garnish

1. Start rice. Prepare a salad and set aside.
2. Heat a nonstick wok (or skillet) over high heat and add the oil. Rotate the wok to coat the sides. Add the ginger and garlic and stir-fry 3–4 seconds to flavor the oil and to release their fragrance.
3. Add the shrimp and stir-fry until they begin to turn pink, 1–2 minutes, depending on their size. Remove to a warm platter and garnish with coriander leaves or parsley sprigs. Serve with rice and a salad.

Makes 2 servings

Steamed Fish with Ginger and Green Onions

Jiangpien Zhengyu

If you don't own a steamer, improvise one in your wok (or skillet). Use a tuna can (top and bottom removed) as a stand under a heatproof dish.

1 whole fish, cleaned and scaled, about 1 lb (450 g) or larger
2 tablespoons Chinese rice wine or pale dry sherry

Sauce

¼ teaspoon vegetable oil
2 tablespoons grated fresh ginger
1 tablespoon reduced-sodium soy sauce
1 tablespoon Chinese rice wine
1 teaspoon vinegar
2 tablespoons fish stock or water
½ teaspoon sugar
½ teaspoon cornstarch mixed with 1 tablespoon of water
2 green onions (scallions), green part only, thinly sliced, for garnish

1. Rinse the fish in cold water and dry with a paper towel. Place the fish on a heatproof plate and pour wine over it. Put the plate in a steamer and add boiling water. Do not allow water to get onto the plate with the fish. Cover and steam. To determine cooking time, measure the fish at the thickest part and cook 8–10 minutes to the inch, or until it flakes when prodded with a fork.
2. While the fish is cooking, heat the oil in a small wok over medium heat and stir-fry the ginger about 10 seconds. Add the remaining ingredients, bring to a boil and cook half a minute or so, or until the sauce begins to thicken. Pour over the steamed fish and sprinkle with green onions.

Makes 2 servings

Shrimp with Cashews

Yao Kuo Xiaren

In this recipe, the shrimp is usually coated with batter and deep-fried.

Typically, the cashews are also deep-fried. Omitting these steps simplifies the recipe and reduces fat considerably without compromising taste.

Sauce

  1 tablespoon Chinese rice wine or pale dry sherry
  1 tablespoon reduced-sodium soy sauce
  ½ teaspoon sugar
  2 tablespoons fish stock or water
  Freshly ground black pepper or dried red pepper flakes, to taste

• • •

  1 tablespoon vegetable oil
  ¼ cup (40 g) cashew nuts, preferably unsalted
  1 tablespoon grated fresh ginger
  1 large clove garlic, crushed
  8–12 oz (300–450 g) shrimp, shelled and deveined, leaving tails intact
  8 oz (150 g) fresh or frozen green peas or snow peas, tips and strings removed

1. Start rice. Prepare the ingredients and place them within easy reach of the stove.
2. Mix the sauce ingredients in a small bowl and set aside.
3. Heat a nonstick wok (or skillet) over medium heat. Add a little of the oil and stir-fry cashews about 1 minute. Drain on paper towels.
4. Heat the wok over high heat. Add the remaining oil and rotate the wok to coat the sides. Stir-fry the ginger and garlic for 3–4 seconds. Add the shrimp and stir-fry about 30 seconds, or until they begin to turn pink.
5. Add the peas and cook for 1 minute. Peas should remain green and crisp.
6. Stir in the sauce and cook for another minute. Mix in the cashews and serve with rice.

Makes 2 servings

■ Soups ■

Crab and Tofu Soup
Xierou Doufu Tang

When in season, crab may be bought already cooked from your fish market. If you use canned crabmeat, rinse well and drain. If you don't have watercress, almost any quick-cooking vegetable may be substituted. Serve with some crusty bread and a salad for a quick, light meal.

  2 egg whites mixed with 1 tablespoon water, beaten until frothy
  About 3 cups (700 ml) unsalted chicken stock
  1 tablespoon Chinese rice wine or pale dry sherry
  6 oz (100 g) cooked crabmeat, flaked

½ block (6 oz/175 g) soft or firm tofu, cut
    into ½-in (1¼-cm) cubes
1 bunch watercress, trimmed and cut into
    1-in (2½-cm) lengths, or 1 small bunch
    spinach, stemmed
1 tablespoon reduced-sodium soy sauce
Freshly ground black pepper, to taste
1 teaspoon cornstarch mixed with 1
    tablespoon water (optional)

1. Beat the egg whites and set aside.
2. Bring the chicken stock to a boil.
   Add the wine, crabmeat, tofu,
   watercress, soy sauce and pepper.
   Simmer 2–3 minutes.
3. Optional Step: Add the cornstarch
   mixture, stirring constantly to prevent lumps.
4. Beat the egg whites again if they
   are no longer frothy. Turn the
   heat off and immediately pour
   egg whites into the soup in a thin
   stream, stirring once or twice.
   Serve immediately.

Makes 2–3 servings

Ham and Corn Chowder
Xumitang

Corn was unknown outside the New
World before 1492. Seed grains of
Indian maize, brought to Europe and
Africa by 16th-century explorers,
were planted and eventually thrived
throughout most of the world,
including China. Field corn is usually
used in this soup, not sweet table
corn. Notwithstanding, this elegant
soup is very easy to make with
ingredients you probably already
have in your pantry.

2 egg whites mixed with 1 tablespoon
    water
About 3 cups (700 ml) unsalted chicken
    stock

One 17-oz can (500 g) cream-style sweet
    corn, no salt added
1 tablespoon Chinese rice wine or pale dry
    sherry
1 teaspoon grated fresh ginger
Generous dash of freshly ground white or
    black pepper
4-6 oz (75-100 g) cooked ham, preferably
    Smithfield, cut into thin strips
1 teaspoon cornstarch mixed with 1
    tablespoon water (optional)
Snipped chives, sliced green onions
    (scallions) or fresh coriander leaves
    (cilantro), for garnish

1. Beat the egg whites and water
   until frothy and set aside.
2. In a medium saucepan, bring the
   chicken stock to a boil. Add the
   corn, wine, ginger, pepper and
   ham. Simmer on low heat for 2–3
   minutes.
3. Optional Step: Add the cornstarch
   mixture, stirring constantly to
   prevent lumps.
4. Beat the egg whites again if they
   are no longer frothy. Turn the
   heat off and immediately pour
   the egg whites into the soup in
   a thin stream, stirring once or
   twice. Quickly remove from the
   heat, garnish with chives, green
   onions or coriander leaves and
   serve immediately. For a complete meal, serve with some
   crusty bread and a salad.

VARIATION 1: *4 oz (100 g) tofu,
either soft or firm, cut into 1/2-in
(1¼-cm) cubes may be added with
the ham.*

VARIATION 2: *Fresh or canned
crabmeat may be substituted for the
ham.*

Makes 2–3 servings

Tofu ■ Doufu

Most commonly known in the West by its Japanese name tofu, bean curd, called *doufu* by the Chinese, has been a protein staple of Asian diets for 2,000 years. It became known as "meat without bones" because it is highly nutritious and rich in protein. Unlike meat, it is inexpensive, very low in calories and saturated fats, and contains no cholesterol. Tofu has a light, creamy texture and its bland taste blends well with other foods.

The process of making tofu is relatively simple. Dried soybeans are soaked, ground to a puree, mixed with water and strained to form soybean milk. The bean milk is heated, a coagulant is added, and the mixture is poured into a square mold and pressed. There are four types of tofu: soft (or silken), medium, firm and extra-firm. The difference in the varieties of tofu is the result of the size of the weight used and the length of pressing time. In many supermarkets, tofu is sold in just two forms—soft, which is used in cold dishes and soups, and firm, which is used for stir-frying and stewing.

Tofu and Mushroom Stir-Fry

Donggu Doufu

Dried mushrooms work best in this dish, as they have a smoky flavor that complements the blandness of the tofu.

Sauce
- 1½ ½tablespoons reduced-sodium soy sauce
- 2 teaspoons oyster sauce
- 3–4 tablespoons mushroom soaking liquid or unsalted stock or water
- 1 tablespoon Chinese rice wine or pale dry sherry
- ¼ teaspoon sugar
- Salt and freshly ground black pepper, to taste

• • •

- 2 tablespoons oil
- 4 green onions (scallions), cut into 1-in (2½-cm) pieces
- 6 dried Chinese black mushrooms, soaked in hot water for 25–30 minutes, stems removed, caps cut in half, or fresh mushrooms
- 1 block, about 14 oz (400 g), firm tofu, cut into 2-in (5-cm) squares
- 1 teaspoon cornstarch mixed with 1 tablespoon water (optional)

1. Start rice. Prepare the ingredients and place them within easy reach of the stove.

2. Mix the sauce ingredients in a small bowl and set aside.

3. Heat a nonstick wok (or skillet) over high heat. Add 2 teaspoons of the oil and stir-fry the green onions and mushrooms 30 seconds to 1 minute. Remove from the wok and keep warm.

4. Add the remaining 4 teaspoons of oil and the tofu. Stir-fry, turning the pieces gently to cook on both sides so that they heat through evenly and begin to brown, 3–4 minutes.

5. Add the sauce and stir gently until the mixture comes to a boil. Return the mushrooms and green onions to the wok and cook for a minute or so to blend flavors. Add more stock or water if the mixture seems dry.

6. Optional Step: Mix in dissolved cornstarch to thicken the sauce while stirring constantly to prevent lumps.

7. Serve with rice.

VARIATION: *To make a tofu stir-fry with red peppers, substitute the mushrooms with 2 red bell peppers, seeded and cut into 1-in (2 ½-cm) squares, and 1 clove crushed garlic.*

Makes 2–3 servings

Ma Po Tofu

This is an abbreviated version of a well-known Sichuan dish. It is named after its creator, whose face was scarred with pockmarks. Thus the name "Grandmother Pockmark's Tofu." It is usually cooked with pork, but you may substitute chicken, if you wish. Some cook this dish with soft tofu to provide the palate with a creamy respite from the hot chili paste.

2 teaspoons vegetable oil

2 large cloves garlic, minced

1 tablespoon grated fresh ginger

4 oz (125 g) lean ground pork or chicken or turkey

2–3 teaspoons chili paste or sauce (adjust amount to suit degree of heat desired)

1 tablespoon reduced-sodium soy sauce

½ cup unsalted chicken stock or water

1 teaspoon sesame oil (optional)

1 block, about 14 oz (400 g), firm tofu cut into ½-in (1¼-cm) pieces

4 green onions (scallions), thinly sliced

1. Start rice. Prepare the ingredients and place them within easy reach of the stove.

2. Heat a nonstick wok (or skillet) over high heat. Add the oil and stir-fry the garlic and ginger for 3–4 seconds. Add the pork and stir-fry for 1–2 minutes, separating pieces if they stick together.

3. Mix in the chili paste, soy sauce, chicken stock, sesame oil, if using, and most of the sliced green onions, reserving some for garnish. Bring to a boil and simmer 1 minute.

4. Reduce heat and add the tofu, stirring gently to keep pieces intact. Cook over low heat for 2–3 minutes, uncovered. Add more stock or water if the mixture seems dry. Garnish with the remaining green onions and serve with rice.

Makes 2 servings

Eggs

Egg Foo Yung

Eggs, nature's best-known fast food, are seldom served alone in Chinese cooking as they are in the West— for example, soft boiled or fried. However, they are used to give body to certain foods, or to bind other ingredients as in *foo yung* and omelet dishes. Though Chinese restaurants usually deep-fried Egg Foo Yung, the version given here is pan-fried. The filling is stir-fried first, then cooled and mixed into the beaten eggs. The combination is then cooked together like a wokcake. The variations on the fillings are limitless, and an excellent way to use leftovers. The proportion is about 1 to 1 ¼ cups meat and vegetables to 3 eggs.

Since yolks are high in fat (5 g per yolk) and dietary cholesterol (272 mg per yolk), but the white is fat- and cholesterol-free, you can make an acceptable omelet by using 1 whole egg with extra whites. There is even a Cantonese dish—chicken foo yung— that is made with egg whites only.

3 whole eggs or 1 whole egg and 4 whites
1 tablespoon or more vegetable oil

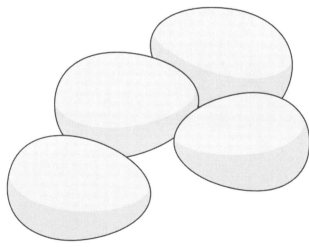

½ cup (about 4 oz/100 g) cooked or raw chicken meat, shredded
½ green bell pepper, finely chopped
2 fresh mushrooms, finely chopped
1 green onion (scallion) or 1 or 2 sprigs fresh parsley or chives, finely chopped

Seasoning

1 teaspoon Chinese rice wine or pale dry sherry (optional)
½–1 teaspoon reduced-sodium soy sauce
¼ teaspoon sugar
Freshly ground black pepper, to taste

Note: You may divide the mixture and make 4 small individual omelets instead of one large one.

1. Beat the eggs lightly with a fork and set aside.
2. Heat a nonstick wok (or skillet) over high heat until very hot. Add a teaspoon of the oil and stir-fry the chicken, bell pepper, mushrooms and green onions or herbs briskly for about 30 seconds to 1 minute. Stir in the seasoning ingredients and stir-fry another 30 to 40 seconds. Let cool.
3. Add the cooled chicken mixture to the beaten eggs and mix well.
4. Heat the wok again over high heat and add the remaining oil. Pour the egg and chicken mixture into the wok and fry until the omelet is lightly browned and set, about 1 minute. Turn over and cook on the other side.

VARIATION: *To make a vegetarian omelet, eliminate meat and increase the quantity of vegetables. Include eggplant and tomatoes, coarsely chopped, and stir-fry well. Then combine with the beaten eggs.*

Makes 2 servings

Serving Suggestions

Serve on a warm platter. Some like to sprinkle a few drops of soy sauce on top of the omelet, or eat it with a little chili sauce. Have a bottle of each at the table. Instead of rice, you may wish to serve the omelet with some crusty bread and a salad.

Stirred Eggs

Choujidan

Unlike scrambled eggs, the eggs in this dish are seldom cooked alone. Various combinations of cooked seafood, meats or vegetables are mixed into the beaten eggs before they are stirred (scrambled). I think some foods are best stir-fried for a few seconds in the skillet to soften them a bit before the eggs are poured over them. This dish makes an excellent lunch, brunch or light dinner, and is a good way to use leftovers.

> 3 whole eggs or 1 whole egg and 4 egg whites
> ⅛ teaspoon sugar
> ½ teaspoon Chinese rice wine or pale dry sherry
> 2 teaspoons vegetable oil
> ¼ teaspoon grated fresh ginger (optional)
> 1-2 green onions (scallions), thinly sliced
> ½ cup (75 g) cooked country-style ham, preferably Smithfield, shredded

1. Beat the eggs in a bowl. Add the sugar and wine and set aside.

2. Heat a nonstick skillet over medium heat and add the oil. Stir-fry the ginger, if using, green onions and ham for about 1 minute.

3. Add the egg mixture. As the eggs begin to set, use a spoon to push them gently away from the edges of the skillet toward the center. Do not turn over to cook the other side. Eggs should remain creamy and soft, not fried brown and crisp. Serve immediately with some crusty bread and a salad. If desired, sprinkle cooked eggs with a little soy or oyster sauce.

VARIATION: *Vegetarian Stirred Eggs. Leave meat out and add shredded zucchini and a coarsely chopped tomato in Step 2. You may also wish to add a teaspoon of soy sauce. Vegetables should be cooked until nearly done before adding the eggs in Step 3.*

Makes 2 servings

additions for omelets and stirred eggs

Leftovers, cooked or uncooked:

pork • shrimp • ham
crabmeat • turkey

as well as vegetables, such as:

fresh or dried mushrooms
water chestnuts • bamboo shoots
tomatoes • bean sprouts • onions

Use approximately 1 to 1 ¼ cups of combined meat and vegetables to 3 eggs.

Vegetables ■ Sucai

To save time, most of the recipes in this book combine meat, chicken, or seafood with a vegetable and call for cooking them in the same wok. For the dishes that do not include a vegetable, the following are some recipes for stir-frying vegetables as an accompaniment to a meat or fish dish. Stir-frying, the most typical Chinese cooking technique, calls for the vegetable to be tossed quickly in a small amount of hot oil flavored with garlic or ginger, and then to finish cooking in its own juices or in liquid, which is added later. The wok must be very hot before the oil is added. When the oil begins to sizzle, the vegetable is quickly stir-fried until it becomes coated with oil. If the oil is not hot enough, the vegetables will become limp and watery.

Soft vegetables, such as tomatoes, bean sprouts, spinach and other leafy vegetables, have a lot of water in them naturally and usually need no additional liquid. Some soft vegetables, like mushrooms and zucchini, need no liquid, but benefit from being covered for half a minute or so after stir-frying, to cook in their own juices.

Harder vegetables do not give off juices in the cooking process, and most Chinese cooks steam or parboil them before stir-frying. This adds another step and another utensil to meal preparation. To save time, I have found that after a quick stir-frying, they may be steamed briefly in a little liquid added to the wok, and then stir-fried again with their seasonings, all accomplished in the same wok. The harder the vegetable, the longer it should steam. Hard vegetables include broccoli, cauliflower, carrots, green beans and celery. Snow peas and asparagus are also hard, but they require very little time to steam, if any at all. The result should be tender but still crisp and crunchy.

Stir-Fried Spinach
Chao Bocai

Use this recipe as a guide to cook almost any vegetable of your choice. Heat the oil, flavor it with garlic or ginger, and stir-fry the vegetable quickly until it is tender but still crisp. Add a little soy sauce.

½ tablespoon vegetable oil
2–3 large cloves garlic, thinly sliced
1 lb (450 g) fresh spinach, stemmed and
    washed
1 teaspoon reduced-sodium soy sauce, or
    to taste
¼ teaspoon sugar
Freshly ground black pepper, to taste

1. Heat a nonstick wok (or skillet) over high heat. Add the oil and rotate the wok to coat the sides. When hot, stir-fry the garlic for 3–4 seconds to brown the pieces lightly. Add the spinach and stir-fry to coat the leaves with the oil. Cover the wok for 3–4 seconds.

2. Remove the cover and sprinkle soy sauce over all. Then add the sugar and pepper and stir-fry for a few seconds. Serve immediately.

VARIATION: *Add 3 or 4 sliced fresh mushrooms in Step 1 and stir-fry for 1 minute until mushrooms soften, before adding the spinach. Garnish the finished dish with sesame seeds, almonds or walnuts. If you like, toast sesame seeds or nuts in a small, dry skillet over low heat. Shake the wok while toasting to avoid scorching.*

Makes 2–3 servings

Ginger-Garlic Broccoli
Chao Jielan

Chinese broccoli differs from Western broccoli in that it has longer, thinner stems, the florets are smaller and the flavor has a slightly bitter edge. Either variety may be used.

Sauce
1 teaspoon reduced-sodium soy sauce, or
    to taste
1 tablespoon Chinese rice wine or pale dry
    sherry
¼ teaspoon sugar
Freshly ground black pepper

• • •

About 1 lb (450 g) broccoli
½ tablespoon vegetable oil
2 cloves garlic, crushed
½ tablespoon grated fresh ginger
2 tablespoons unsalted chicken or
    vegetable stock or water

1. Combine the sauce ingredients and set aside.

2. Cut the florets from the stems and divide into bite-size pieces. Cut the stems diagonally to make thin slices 1 inch (2½ cm) long and ⅛ inch (½ cm) thick. If using Chinese broccoli, cut away the tough outer skin and separate the florets. Cut stems diagonally into 1-inch (2½-cm) lengths.

3. Heat a nonstick wok (or skillet) over high heat. Add the oil and rotate the wok to coat the sides. When hot, stir-fry the garlic and ginger for 3–4 seconds. Add the broccoli stems and stir-fry 30 seconds. Add the florets and stir-fry 30 seconds. Add the stock or water. Cover the wok and steam for about 1 minute, or until tender but still crisp. The broccoli should remain bright green. Overcooking spoils the color and texture.

4. Remove the cover. Add the sauce and stir until the mixture comes to a boil. Serve immediately.

Makes 2–3 servings

Green Beans with Garlic

Chao Doujiao

In this dish Asian seasonings accent and enhance tender, crisp green beans.

1 tablespoon vegetable oil

3 large cloves garlic, thinly sliced

1 lb (450 g) Chinese yard-long beans
   or green beans, trimmed and cut
   diagonally into 2-in (5-cm) lengths

2 tablespoons unsalted stock or water

1 teaspoon reduced-sodium soy sauce, or
   to taste

2 teaspoons rice vinegar

½ teaspoon sugar

1. Heat a nonstick wok (or skillet) over high heat. Add the oil and rotate the wok to coat the sides. When hot, stir-fry the garlic for 3–4 seconds. Add the beans and stir-fry about 1 minute, tossing to coat with the oil. Add the water, cover the wok and cook for another 2 minutes or longer, until beans are almost done. Test for doneness.

2. Remove the cover. Continue to stir-fry briskly. Sprinkle with the soy sauce and vinegar and continue to stir while adding the sugar. Stir-fry a few seconds longer to dissolve the sugar.

Makes 3–4 servings

Japan

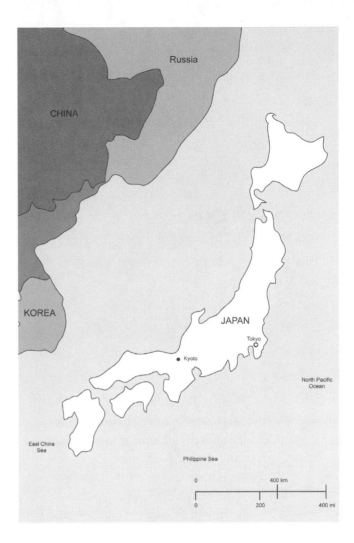

Japan is the first Asian country to develop a technologically advanced industrial economy, and although possessed of few industrial raw materials, it is the world's second leading economic power after the United States. Large-scale trade with the entire world has exposed the Japanese to influences from the West and the East, and has resulted in the development of an international perspective in every aspect of Japanese life. The miracle is that this astonishing development has taken place in such a short time—since the end of World War II.

Yet despite these foreign influences and the pressure of rapid change, the Japanese have managed to preserve much of their cultural heritage and to keep their customs and their cuisine intact, while also borrowing and adapting from other parts of the world.

Like the culinary habits of other nations, those of Japan are a reflection of the country's climate and geography, its ethnic inheritances, history and religious beliefs. While their origin is uncertain, it is believed that most of Japan's early settlers were probably immigrants from the arid, wind-blown steppes of northern Asia. When they crossed the water from Siberia or from Korea, they found islands with green vegetation, a temperate climate and coastal waters teeming with fish. Some believe that the gratitude that these early settlers must have felt helped create a general reverence for nature and a desire to live in harmony with it.

Eventually this evolved into a religion known as Shinto, "the Way of the Gods," which is still widely practiced today. Essentially, Shinto

is a simple animism, a religion of thankfulness for the bounty and beauty of nature. This ancient respect for the sacredness of nature and of food still prevails, as centuries-old celebrations give thanks for the fertility of the land and for plentiful harvests. Humankind is seen not as a lord of nature but as part of it. In keeping with this idea, Shinto shrines and Buddhist temples are conceived and built to be part of nature, blending harmoniously with their physical surroundings.

Since only a small proportion of Japan's mountainous terrain is suitable for agriculture, the earliest Japanese diet was sparse and simple, consisting mainly of rice, fish, seaweed and vegetables. Other nations with natural resources as limited as Japan's have compensated by importing the things they lacked. But the Japanese, an insular people relatively isolated from their neighbors by a strip of sea

three times wider than the English Channel, pursued a policy of either enthusiastically accepting ideas from the outside world, or shutting the world out entirely for centuries at a time. This vacillating policy affected not only Japanese eating habits but their life in general. When they opened their doors to the outside world, they borrowed only what they found useful and attractive. When they closed their doors, they blended and reshaped what they borrowed to fit into their very refined way of life.

Although Chinese culture had influenced Japan even during the prehistoric period, it was not until the introduction of Buddhism that the entire Japanese civilization became permeated with Chinese culture. It began with the arrival in 552 of a mission from the Korean kingdom of Paekche (Kudara), which brought Buddhist images and scriptures along with a message from their king about the teachings of Buddhism. They were followed in succeeding years by other images, as well as monks, scholars and craftsmen. All these missionaries came from Korea, which has a long history as a cultural bridge across which Chinese culture was transmitted to Japan and Japanese influences reached the mainland.

Perhaps the most important culinary innovation acquired from China was the soybean, which the Japanese transformed to suit their own taste. The use of chopsticks was also acquired, as was tea, which was transformed into a uniquely Japanese art. Zen Buddhist monks in China drank tea ceremonially during their devotions, but it was the Japanese in the fifteenth century who raised these rituals to the fine art of the Tea Ceremony.

When the T'ang Dynasty collapsed in the middle of the ninth century, Japan once again closed its doors to outsiders, and began to refine its borrowings and adapt them to Japanese civilization. The dynasty began in Nara and moved to Heian-Kyo (Kyoto). The four hundred years following the city's founding in 794 are known as the golden age of Japanese culture. Though the imperial court was ultra-refined, its cuisine remained austere and simple. The diet contained no meat because the Buddhist religion forbad it, but in keeping with the past, it consisted of rice, fish, vegetables and fruit, all savored in the season when each article of food was at its prime.

This golden age of Heian courtiers came to an end as a warrior class called the samurai rose to power. Although these were times of violent civil strife, the warriors adopted the imperial court's elegant table etiquette and its artful presentation of foods. Since their ranks included men of noble and lesser birth, refined practices began to reach lower levels of Japanese society.

Toward the middle of the sixteenth century, a new culinary influence came to Japan, this time from the West. They were the Portuguese who had come to begin trade between Chinese and Japanese ports in the south. The Japanese regarded them as harmless barbar-

ians—pale, long-nosed people who ate with their fingers and showed their feelings with little self-control. But the Portuguese left a recipe for deep-fried foods, which has become one of the most important dishes in Japanese cuisine. They were good Catholics, and could not eat meat on Friday, during Lent, or on the Ember Days. Ember Days, which constituted any Wednesday, Friday, or Saturday in four designated weeks of the year, are called, in Latin, *Quatuor Tempora*, the "four times" of the year. The Portuguese ate seafood instead, usually shrimp, and so the Latin word for *times* became *tempura,* the word for shrimp fried in batter.

But the tempura of the Portuguese bears no resemblance to what the Japanese prepare today. Not only has it been adapted to include other foods, but the batter has been miraculously transformed to produce a light, lacy coating. The secret is the combination of the freshest ingredients, the lightest cooking oil and perfect timing. As anyone who has eaten tempura in Japan knows, deep-fried Japanese food has a delicacy no other country can match. The Japanese also prepare a mackerel dish in the *nan-ban*, or "southern barbarian" style, reflecting the Portuguese influence. The fish is dredged in cornstarch, deep fried until crisp, then marinated in a spicy vinegar sauce.

When the Portuguese, Spanish, and Dutch traders and missionaries began invading territories in Asia, the Japanese felt threatened and, in 1638, expelled all Westerners. They locked their doors once more until the arrival of Commodore Perry more than two centuries later. In the Meiji period (1868–1912), the country again opened to the West and the court was moved from Kyoto to Edo (Tokyo). Intrigued by the dynamic civilization of the West, the Japanese rushed headlong into learning all they could about Western ways, including art, literature, music, science and technology, as well as Western food styles—such as the eating of meat.

People gradually abandoned the dietary restrictions of the Buddhist religion, and chicken, pork and beef were added to the Japanese menu. Before long, the Japanese were raising some of the world's finest beef cattle, again improving and refining existing techniques. Kobe beef is world-renowned, and beef is the principal ingredient in the most internationally famous dish in Japanese cuisine—sukiyaki. Other adoptions include ice cream, bread, fried eggs, hamburgers, spaghetti with tomato sauce and curry, as well as coffee—full bodied, freshly brewed, and served with cream. Yet, however complete the acceptance of foreign culture has been, the country at heart remains true to its own traditions and continues to preserve its own identity.

Whatever critics may say about Japan's modernization, Japanese cuisine still stands apart from all

Japanese cuisine still stands apart from all other Asian cuisines because of its subtlety, its simplicity, and its meticulous preparation.

other Asian cuisines because of its subtlety, its simplicity, and its meticulous preparation. Great emphasis is placed on the freshness of the ingredients, on their quality and especially on foods in season. The first of any seasonal food is always greatly prized. There are strawberries in February, the huge matsutake mushroom in the fall, and the early moist rice (*shinmai*) in November. That is when rice, fresh from harvest, tastes best. Only the simplest cooking methods are needed to preserve a fresh food's intrinsic flavor. While other cuisines tend to meld many ingredients in one dish, or rely on herbs and exotic spice blends, Japanese cuisine is rather sparse in its use of seasonings. Another difference is that many Japanese dishes are cooked in or steamed over water, while other cuisines commonly use oil as a cooking medium.

As important as the preparation of the food itself is its presentation. Nothing in the Western world can compare with the role that aesthetics have played in Japanese life. More than in any other Asian country, a sense of aesthetics—tranquil and understated—plays an important part in Japanese culture, whether it be in the presentation of food, table settings or gardens. It is no accident that the Japanese make the most beautiful ceramics and lacquerware in the world. They are made not only as art objects to be exhibited, but for everyday use, and great care is taken in choosing the right bowl or dish in which to serve food in order to enhance its visual appeal. This refined aesthetic sense, as well as the simplicity of Japanese cooking styles, has influenced the direction of cuisines internationally.

Equally important to Japan's haute cuisine stature are the many health benefits associated with it. Since it is lower in calories and fat than any other Asian cuisine, many nutritionists believe that Japanese cuisine is the best diet for good health and long life. Consider these statistics. American men live an average of seventy-five years; American women, eighty. In Japan the age is seventy-eight for men and eighty-five for women. This is the highest in the world. What do the Japanese eat? A lot of rice, fish, vegetables, soybean products and seaweed, and only a very small amount of meat and fat.

Japanese Pantry

*To keep shopping to a minimum, and to speed preparation and
cooking time, it is helpful to keep these Japanese staples
on hand in your kitchen.*

Ingredients with a Long Shelf Life

dashi, instant variety

ginger, pickled (*beni shoga*)

kombu (dried kelp)

mirin

miso (soy bean paste), white
(*shiro*) or red (*aka*)

nori (dried seaweed)

rice, short or medium grain

rice vinegar

sake

sansho powder (Japanese
pepper)

sesame seeds, black or white

seven-spice powder (*shichimi
togarashi*)

shiitake mushrooms, dried

soy sauce (*shoyu*)

teriyaki sauce

Fresh Ingredients

daikon (giant white radish)

garlic

ginger

green onions (scallions)

onions

■ Rice ■

In Japanese and Korean cooking, a slightly glutinous short- or medium-grain rice, cooked so that it is moist but not firm, is generally preferred. As with long-grain rice, opinions differ as to whether rice should be washed before cooking. To preserve its nutrients, I tend to side with the nonwashers, and the Japanese rice that I use plainly says WASHING NOT NECESSARY on the package. The best way to make perfect rice is to use an automatic rice cooker.

Boiled Rice, Japanese Style

Gohan

Because of the differences in the many varieties of Japanese rice on the market, use this recipe as a guide only, and follow the cooking instructions on the rice package.

> 1 cup (225 g) short- or medium-grain
>   Japanese rice
> 1¼ cups (300 ml) cold water

1. In a medium saucepan, combine the rice and water. Bring to a rolling boil over high heat.
2. Reduce the heat to low, cover and simmer for 25 minutes. Do not remove the lid at any time during cooking.
3. Remove from the heat and fluff lightly with a spoon before serving. For softer, clingier rice, increase the amount of water slightly. Reduce water for firmer rice.

Makes about 3 cups or 2–3 servings

Rice with Peas

Ao-mame Gohan

For an accompaniment to a main dish, rice can be cooked with almost any vegetable. A popular Japanese combination is rice with peas.

> 6 oz (125 g) fresh or frozen green peas
> 1 cup (225 g) short- or medium-grain
>   Japanese rice
> Salt

1. Blanch the fresh peas in boiling water for 30 seconds. Drain immediately. If you're using frozen peas, simply pour boiling water on them and drain them immediately. Add salt to taste.
2. After the rice has cooked for 20 minutes, uncover the pot and stir the peas into the rice. Cover the pot again and keep warm.

Makes 2 servings

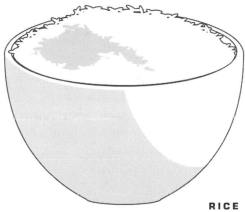

Donburi

Donburi means bowl, but it also means a ceramic bowl with a cover, about twice as large as a rice bowl, filled with plain boiled rice and topped generously with slivers of flavorfully cooked meat, fish or vegetables, garnishes and condiments. Donburi, falling in the same general category as noodle dishes, is one of Japan's original fast foods. A great number of donburi chains may be found in Japan's urban centers, and there are even a growing number outside of Japan, at least in San Francisco. Almost any type of food may be served over the rice, which makes it a favorite way to use leftovers.

Note: Cooked noodles can replace rice in any of the donburi recipes.

Chicken and Eggs Over Rice

Oyako Donburi

This is one of the most popular donburi combinations, containing chicken and eggs. *Oyako* means mother and child, a poetic reference to the chicken and egg spread over the rice.

1 cup (225 g) short- or medium-grain Japanese rice

Donburi broth

1¼ cups (300 ml) dashi, or unsalted chicken stock

1 tablespoon mirin

2 tablespoons reduced-sodium soy sauce

½ teaspoon sugar

• • •

6-8 oz (175-200 g) boneless, skinless chicken, cut into bite-size pieces

2 green onions (scallions), sliced into 1-in (2 ½-cm) pieces

½ cup (75 g) fresh or frozen green peas

2 eggs

Sansho powder or freshly ground black pepper, to taste

1 sheet nori, toasted over a flame and crumbled (optional)

1. Start rice.
2. While the rice is cooking, combine the stock, mirin, soy sauce and sugar in a pan. Bring to a gentle boil over medium heat and add the chicken. Reduce the heat to medium-low, cover the pan and simmer for 2–3 minutes. Skim off any froth. Add the green onions and green peas and cook for 30 seconds longer.
3. Break the eggs in a small bowl and stir with a fork or chopsticks just long enough to combine the yolks and whites. Stir in the pepper and pour the eggs into the simmering chicken mixture. Cover and cook another minute or two, or until the eggs are just set. Do not overcook.
4. Divide the cooked rice into 2 large bowls. With a large spoon, spread the chicken and egg mixture over the rice. Pour enough sauce over the donburi to add flavor without making it soupy.
5. Optional Step: Garnish with the crumbled nori.

Chicken, Mushrooms and Eggs Over Rice
Oboro Donburi

1. Add 4 fresh mushrooms, preferably shiitake, to the ingredients in the Oyako Donburi recipe on page 68. Cut them in half and add them in Step 2. Follow directions above through Step 2. Then go to Step 3 below.
3. Beat eggs slightly and cook in a large, lightly greased skillet to make 2 or 3 large, flat, thin omelets, taking care not to brown them. Place the cooked eggs on a flat surface and cut into narrow strips, about ½ inch (1½ cm) wide and 2 inches (5 cm) long.
4. Divide the hot chicken pieces over top of the rice in reserved bowls, and spoon the liquid, in which the chicken was cooked, over the rice. Arrange the mushrooms and peas over chicken. Decorate top with omelet strips.

Makes 2 servings

VARIATION 1: *Beef Donburi.*
Substitute 12 ounces (225 g) lean, boneless sirloin for the chicken in the above recipes. Leave out the eggs and mushrooms.

VARIATION 2: *Yakitori Donburi.*
Prepare donburi broth (page 68) and bring to a boil. Prepare Chicken and Vegetable Yakitori *(page 73), remove from skewers and serve over rice with donburi broth.*

VARIATION 3: *Shrimp Donburi.*
Prepare donburi broth (page 68) and bring to a boil. Prepare Shrimp Skewers *(page 79), remove from skewers and serve over rice with donburi broth.*

■ Noodles ■

Soba with Tofu and Mushrooms

Noodles are as important in Japanese cuisine as rice. Eaten hot during the winter and cold in the summer, they are cooked in a variety of ways to make for satisfying one-dish meals. Usually noodles are served in a very large bowl with lots of broth. Cold noodles are often served with dipping sauce. Simplified recipes for two kinds of hot noodles are given here—one for soba, a brownish-gray buckwheat noodle, and another for udon, a round or flat white wheat noodle similar to spaghetti. Either noodle may be used in both recipes. Noodle ingredients and broths are infinitely variable. Change them to suit seasonal availability of foods and, of course, your own taste. The noodle broth is

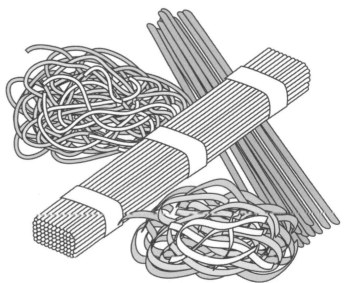

important. Taste it and experiment by adding more or less seasoning to it. The recipe below is on the mild side.

If the package of the noodles you buy includes directions, follow them. Otherwise, use the basic method in this recipe. The noodles should be drained when they are still quite firm.

Noodle broth (kake-jiru)

3 cups (24 oz/700 ml) fresh or instant dashi or unsalted chicken stock

1½ tablespoons reduced-sodium soy sauce

1½ tablespoons mirin

• • •

4 fresh mushrooms, preferably shiitakes, wiped, trimmed and cut in half, or 4 dried mushrooms soaked in hot water for 25–30 minutes, trimmed and sliced

8 oz (225 g) soft or firm tofu, cut into bite-size cubes

8 oz (75 g) dried soba or udon noodles

2 green onions (scallions), thinly sliced

1 sheet nori, toasted over a flame and crumbled

Seven-spice powder (*shichimi togarashi*) or freshly ground black pepper

1. Bring 2 quarts of water to a rolling boil in a large pot. Also, bring a kettle of water to a boil to rinse noodles after they cook. While these two are coming to a boil, prepare the noodle broth.

2. Put the prepared dashi, soy sauce and mirin in a saucepan and bring to a boil. Reduce the heat and simmer for 1–2 minutes. Add the mushrooms and simmer for another minute. Add the tofu cubes, let the stock come to a boil again, then lower the heat to keep it warm while you boil the noodles.

3. When the water in the large pot begins to boil, add the soba noodles and cook until tender but still firm. Test frequently for doneness by biting into a noodle. Pour into

a strainer and rinse with boiling water. Drain the noodles and place in large bowls, either 1 serving bowl or 2 large individual bowls.

4. Pour the hot broth with mushrooms and tofu over the soba. Garnish with green onions and nori. Season with the seven-spice powder or black pepper.

Makes 2 servings

Udon with Chicken, Shrimp and Vegetables
Nabeyaki Udon

This can be a wonderfully appetizing combination of ingredients cooked in one pot. It is essential that a heatproof casserole be used if the egg added at the end is to be briefly simmered. Again, as in the previous recipe, the ingredients are variable. Leave out the egg if you wish, or substitute other meats. Either udon or soba noodles may be used for this recipe.

Noodle broth (*Kake-jiru*)

3 cups (24 oz/700 ml) fresh or instant dashi, or unsalted chicken stock

1½ tablespoons reduced-sodium soy sauce

1½ tablespoons mirin

• • •

4 oz (100 g) boneless, skinless chicken, cut into bite-size pieces

2 fresh mushrooms, preferably shiitake, wiped, trimmed and cut in half, or 2 dried mushrooms soaked in hot water for 25–30 minutes

4 medium shrimp, shelled and deveined leaving tails intact

4 oz (100 g) fresh spinach, stemmed and washed

2 green onions (scallions), cut into 1-in (2½-cm) lengths

8 oz (75 g) dried udon or soba noodles

2 eggs

Seven-spice powder (*shichimi togarashi*) or freshly ground black pepper

1. Bring 2 quarts of water to a rolling boil in a large pot. Also, bring a kettle of water to a boil to rinse the noodles after they cook. While these two are coming to a boil, prepare the noodle broth.

2. Put the prepared dashi, soy sauce and mirin in a saucepan and bring to a boil. Reduce the heat and simmer for 1–2 minutes. Add the chicken, mushrooms and shrimp; let the stock come to a boil again and simmer for 1–2 minutes. Add the spinach and green onions and lower the heat to keep warm.

3. When the water in the large pot begins to boil, add the udon noodles and cook until just done but still firm. Test frequently for doneness by biting into a noodle.

Pour into a strainer and rinse with boiling water. Drain and place in heatproof bowls, either 1 large serving bowl or 2 individual bowls. Arrange the chicken, mushrooms, shrimp, spinach and green onions on top of the noodles and ladle the hot broth over all. Cover and place on the stove. Bring to a boil over medium heat.

4. Using the back of a large spoon, make an indentation in the noodles in which to cook the eggs. Crack the eggs and drop them into the indentation. Cover and simmer for 1–2 minutes or until the eggs are set but the yolks are not quite firm. Sprinkle lightly with seven-spice powder or black pepper and serve immediately. You may wish to serve soy sauce at the table for stronger flavor.

Makes 2 servings

■ Sauces ■

Teriyaki Sauce

Teriyaki, a common type of Japanese cuisine, refers to meat or fish that is broiled or grilled after being marinated in teriyaki sauce. The sauce (or marinade) is composed of a soy sauce and mirin (rice wine) base, often seasoned with other ingredients such as garlic, ginger and sugar. Chicken stock may be added to the sauce for a more delicate result.

3 tablespoons reduced-sodium soy sauce

3 tablespoon mirin

2 teaspoons sugar

1 clove garlic, crushed (optional)

1 tablespoon grated fresh ginger (optional)

1 tablespoon fresh lemon juice, sake, or chicken stock (optional)

Combine the ingredients in a small bowl and mix until the sugar is dissolved.

Makes about 4 tablespoons

Chicken

Teriyaki Chicken

Tori Teriyaki

Teriyaki means broiling or grilling in a soy sauce marinade. If you do not wish to make your own teri-yaki sauce, it is available in bottles like soy sauce. Remember to line your broiler pan with foil to reduce cleanup time. Most teriyaki recipes may also be cooked on a hibachi or charcoal grill. Vegetables may also be dipped in the sauce and broiled along with the meat. I recommend Japanese eggplant, zucchini or yellow squash, cut in half lengthwise, as well as green or red bell peppers, seeded, and cut into quarters.

Note: One pound (450 g) of chicken parts with bone in may substituted for boneless chicken, though it will take more time to cook—probably a full 20 minutes—depending on size. Cut parts into small pieces for faster cooking.

- 3 tablespoons reduced-sodium teriyaki sauce, such as Kikkoman, or mix your own (see recipe on page 71)
- 8-12 oz (200-300 g) boneless and skinless chicken cut into serving pieces

1. Start rice and prepare a salad or vegetable of your choice.
2. Preheat the broiler to high.
3. Put the teriyaki sauce in a large bowl. Dip the chicken pieces into the sauce, coating them well. Broil the chicken about 3 inches from the heat for 2–3 minutes, or until golden brown. Turn them over and cook for 2–3 minutes on the other side, basting occasionally. If you're using chicken parts with the bone in, broil longer on each side, 5–10 minutes, depending on thickness.

Serving Suggestion

Serve with rice. Some like to serve the teriyaki chicken with mustard sauce. Mix 2 teaspoons dry mustard with just enough water to make a thick paste.

VARIATION: *Lean, boneless beef, such as flank or sirloin, may be substituted for the chicken.*

Makes 2 servings

Chicken and Vegetable Yakitori

One of the most common restaurant foods in Japan is *yakitori*, skewered pieces of chicken and chicken liver grilled over a charcoal fire. Four or five small pieces are impaled on a bamboo skewer *(kushi)* and brushed with teriyaki sauce before grilling. To fit into the schedule of a hurried home cook, the skewers may be broiled with equally impressive results. Japanese cooks prefer the thigh or leg meat of the chicken because it is juicier than breast meat.

> Bamboo skewers
> 8–12 oz (200–300 g) skinless and boneless chicken, cut into 1-in (2 ½-cm) squares
> 2 green bell peppers, cut into 1-in (2 ½-cm) squares
> 4 green onions (scallions), cut into 2-in (5-cm) lengths
> 8 fresh mushrooms, preferably shiitake, cut in half
> 4 tablespoons reduced-sodium teriyaki sauce, such as Kikkoman, or mix your own (see recipe on page 71)
> Sansho powder or freshly ground black pepper, to taste

1. Start rice.
2. Preheat the broiler to high.
3. Skewer the chicken pieces, alternating them with the vegetables. Brush the skewers with the teriyaki sauce, coating them well.
4. Broil the skewers 3 inches from the heat for 2–3 minutes, or until brown. Baste them with the sauce again and grill on the other side for an additional 2 minutes, or until done. Sprinkle with a little sansho powder or black pepper. If desired, leftover sauce may be brought to the table as a dipping sauce. Serve with rice.

VARIATION: *Chicken livers cut in half are often combined with chicken in this recipe. Thread them on separate skewers.*

Makes 2 servings

Sesame Chicken
Tori no Goma Yaki

Sesame seeds are used extensively by Japanese, Korean and Chinese cooks. They are also used in sweets in Southeast Asia.

> 3 tablespoons sake
> 1 tablespoon reduced-sodium soy sauce
> 8–12 oz (200–300 g) boneless, skinless chicken breast, cut into serving pieces
> Seven-spice mixture (*shichimi togarashi*), sansho powder or freshly ground black pepper
> 2 tablespoons white sesame seeds
> 1 tablespoon vegetable oil
> Parsley sprigs, for garnish

Note: 1 pound (450 g) of chicken parts with bone in may substituted for boneless chicken, though it will take more time to cook—probably a full 20 minutes—depending on size. Cut parts into small pieces for faster cooking.

1. Start rice and make a salad or vegetable of your choice.
2. Combine the sake and soy sauce in a shallow bowl. Sprinkle the chicken generously with the seven-spice mixture and place in the bowl, turning the pieces over to cover both sides with the soy sauce and sake.
3. In a dry, nonstick skillet, toast the sesame seeds over very low heat, stirring constantly until they are golden. Take care that they do not burn. Remove and set aside.
4. Heat the same skillet over high heat and add oil. Cook the

chicken pieces about 2 minutes on each side until golden brown. Reduce heat and cook a minute or two longer, or until they are done. Sprinkle with the sesame seeds, garnish with the parsley and serve with rice.

Makes 2 servings

Chicken and Vegetables Simmered in Dashi
Iridori

This is a light dish of chicken and vegetables stir-fried, then simmered in a sweetened sauce. This recipe uses vegetables more familiar than those typicallly included—for example, *gobo* (burdock root).

> 8–12 oz (200–300 g) boneless, skinless chicken thigh meat, cut into bite-size pieces
> 1–1½ tablespoons vegetable oil
> 2 small carrots, scraped and cut into thin slices
> 4 fresh mushrooms, preferably shiitakes, wiped, trimmed and cut in half, or 4 dried mushrooms, soaked for 25–30 minutes in hot water, trimmed and cut in half
> About 3-in (8-cm) long fresh bamboo shoot, or canned bamboo shoots, cut into thin slices
> ¾ cup (175 ml) fresh or instant dashi or unsalted chicken stock
> 1–2 tablespoons reduced-sodium soy sauce
> 1–2 teaspoons sugar
> 4 oz (75 g) fresh or frozen snow peas, tips and strings removed, or green peas

1. Start rice. Prepare the ingredients and place them within easy reach of the stove.
2. Heat a nonstick wok (or skillet) over high heat. When hot, add

half of the oil and stir-fry the chicken about 2 minutes, or until it is lightly browned. Remove from the wok.
3. Heat the remaining oil and add the vegetables, except the peas, one at a time. Stir-fry 1–2 minutes.
4. Stir in the dashi, soy sauce and sugar and simmer 2–3 minutes until vegetables are tender-crisp.
5. Return the chicken to the wok and add the peas. Cook for another minute or so, until heated through. The peas should remain bright green and crisp. Serve with rice.

Makes 2–3 servings

Broiled Chicken and Leeks, Yuan Style
Tori no Yuanyaki

Unlike yakitori, *Tori no Yuanyaki* is made using large pieces of boneless chicken (usually leg meat), which are marinated, impaled on long skewers and broiled over hot coals. Use whole pieces of chicken, whether they are bone-in or boneless pieces.

Marinade
> 3 tablespoons reduced-sodium soy sauce
> 2 tablespoons sake
> 2 tablespoons mirin
> Grated zest of 1 lemon
>
> • • •
>
> 8–12 oz (200–300 g) skinless, boneless chicken, preferably from the leg, or about 1 lb (450 g) chicken parts
> 2 small leeks or 4 green onions (scallions), cut into 2-3-in (5-8-cm) lengths
> Lemon wedges

1. Start rice and make a salad or vegetable of your choice.

2. Combine the marinade ingredients in a large bowl.

3. Pierce the chicken in a few places to allow the marinade to penetrate. Place the chicken pieces and leeks or green onions in the marinade, turning them until they are well coated. Allow the chicken and leeks to marinate for a few minutes before broiling.

4. Preheat the broiler to high.

5. Broil the chicken about 4 minutes on each side, basting occasionally. The thickness of the chicken pieces will determine how long they need to cook. Broil the leeks until they begin to brown.

6. To serve, cut the chicken crosswise into ½-in (1¼-cm) slices and arrange on a platter with the broiled leeks. Garnish with the lemon wedges and serve with rice.

Makes 2 servings

■ Seafood ■

Seared Scallops in Teriyaki Sauce

Hotategai Teriyaki

Scallops are a natural fast food that cook in seconds. Using the washed, bagged spinach available in most supermarkets cuts preparation time considerably. To save even more time, use commercially prepared teriyaki sauce.

> 2 tablespoons reduced-sodium teriyaki sauce, such as Kikkoman, or mix your own (see recipe on page 71)
> 8-12 oz (225-350 g) small scallops, sliced in half
> 1 tablespoon vegetable oil
> 1 lb (450 g) fresh spinach, stemmed and washed (do not dry)

1. Start rice. Prepare the ingredients and place them within easy reach of the stove.

2. Put the teriyaki sauce in a bowl. Add the scallops to the bowl, turning them over to coat with the sauce. Let them marinate 10 minutes.

2. Heat a nonstick wok (or skillet) over medium heat, and add the oil.

Drain the scallops, reserving the marinade. Cook briefly, about 30 seconds to 1 minute on each side or until they become opaque. As soon as the scallops are done, promptly remove them from the pan or they will toughen. (If more convenient, scallops may be broiled.)

3. Add the spinach and stir-fry about 30 seconds. Cover the wok and steam about 1 minute or until leaves are wilted but still green and crisp.

4. Reduce the heat to low. Move the spinach to one side and return the scallops to the wok. Add the remaining marinade and cook for another minute, turning the scallops in the wok until heated through. Serve with rice.

VARIATION: *Salmon or any fish fillet may be prepared in the same way. Other vegetables, such as asparagus, Chinese cabbage or snow peas, may be substituted.*

Makes 2 servings

Fish in Vinegar Sauce with Salad

Sakana Nanban Zuke

Nanban refers to the "Southern Barbarians," or the Portuguese, who introduced the Japanese to deep-frying and to chiles. In this dish, the fish is usually deep fried, then marinated with the vegetables for several hours, thus making it too complicated for a hurried dinner. This simplified version has a milder flavor and is lower in fat.

Sauce

¼ cup (50 ml) rice vinegar
1 tablespoon reduced-sodium soy sauce
1 teaspoon sugar

Salad

1 small carrot, scraped and sliced into thin rounds
2 small green or red bell peppers or one of each, seeded and cut into thin rings
1-3 small dried red chiles, seeded and chopped, or dried red pepper flakes or ground red pepper, to taste (optional)

• • •

8-12 oz (225–350 g) mackerel or large smelts or other whole fish or fish fillet
Cornstarch or flour, for dredging fish

1 tablespoon vegetable oil
Fresh parsley sprigs and lemon wedges, for garnish

1. Start rice. Prepare the ingredients and place them within easy reach of the stove.
2. Combine the sauce ingredients in a large bowl. Add the sliced vegetables and chiles and mix well.
3. Dredge the fish in the cornstarch or flour. Use a paper towel or wrapping paper as a dredging surface to reduce cleanup time. Heat a nonstick skillet over medium heat and add the oil. Add the fish and brown lightly on both sides. Depending on the thickness of the fillet or whole fish, this should take 1–2 minutes per side. Test for doneness with a fork at the thickest part of the fish. Do not overcook.
4. While fish is cooking, drain the vegetables thoroughly, reserving the marinade.
5. Add the marinade to the fish, turning over to coat both sides. Cook for a half minute or so, or until hot. Garnish with the parsley and lemon wedges. Serve with rice alongside the bell pepper and salad.

Makes 2 servings

Simple Pan-Fried Halibut

Sakana Nanban Yaki

Here is another quick and easy *nanban*-style recipe. It works well with whatever fish happens to be in season. Thin fish fillets will take less time than a fish steak.

1 tablespoon vegetable oil
8-12 oz (225–350 g) halibut steak
1 tablespoon rice vinegar

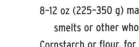

1 tablespoon mirin
1 tablespoon reduced-sodium soy sauce
2 green onions (scallions), thinly sliced
Lemon wedges and fresh mint or parsley
    sprigs, for garnish

1. Start rice. Prepare a salad or vegetable of your choice.

2. Heat a nonstick skillet over medium-high heat and add the oil. Brown the fish on both sides, until done. This should take about 1–3 minutes per side, depending on the thickness of the fish. Test for doneness with a fork, and do not overcook. Transfer to a warm plate.

3. Add the vinegar, mirin, and soy sauce to the skillet and cook a few seconds. Stir in the green onions and pour the sauce over the fish. Garnish with the lemon wedges and mint leaves or parsley sprigs. Serve with rice.

Makes 2 servings

Steamed Fish and Vegetables with Ponzu Sauce

Sakana Mushiyaki

If you don't own a steamer, one can be easily improvised using a wok or a skillet with a tight lid. Place the food in a shallow heatproof bowl, using a tuna can (top and bottom removed) as a stand under the bowl. Select a firm-fleshed fish, such as lingcod, salmon or halibut.

Ponzu sauce
2 tablespoons fresh lemon or lime juice or
    a mixture of both
2 tablespoons reduced-sodium soy sauce
3 tablespoons dashi, unsalted chicken
    stock or water
1 teaspoon mirin

• • •

8-12 oz (225–350 g) fish fillet, cut into 4 pieces
4 fresh mushrooms, preferably shiitake,
    wiped and sliced in half, or dried
    shiitake mushrooms soaked in hot
    water for 25–30 minutes
12 large spinach leaves, or several stems
    watercress, washed and cut into 3-in
    (7½-cm) lengths
4 thin lemon slices
¼ cup (50 ml) sake
1 tablespoon reduced-sodium soy sauce

1. Start rice.

2. Combine the sauce ingredients in a small bowl and set aside.

3. Place the fish in a heatproof bowl. Place the sliced mushrooms on top of the fish. Arrange the spinach over the mushrooms. Top with the lemon slices. Combine the sake and soy sauce and sprinkle over all.

4. Pour boiling water in the bottom of the steamer and place the heatproof bowl in the center. Be sure water docs not get into the bowl. Cover the steamer and cook for 5–10 minutes, depending on the thickness of the fish. Test with a fork at the thickest part for doneness. Remove and serve immediately with ponzu sauce—either drizzle the sauce over the fish or divide it into 2 small bowls and use as a dipping sauce at the table. Serve with rice.

Makes 2 servings

Teriyaki Salmon

Sakana Teriyaki

Salmon is best when it is cooked just long enough to be done but not so long as to become dry. If you do not wish to take the time to make your own teriyaki sauce, it is available commercially bottled, like soy sauce.

2 tablespoons reduced-sodium teriyaki
   sauce, such as Kikkoman, or mix your
   own (see recipe on page 71)
2 salmon steaks, about 6 oz (175 g) each
Lemon wedges and fresh parsley or mint
   leaves, for garnish

1. Start the rice and make a salad or
   a vegetable of your choice.
2. Preheat the broiler to high.
3. Coat the salmon on both sides
   with the teriyaki sauce. If there is
   time, let the fish stand in the sauce
   a few minutes. The longer it marinates the stronger the flavor.
4. For easy cleanup, place a sheet
   of aluminum foil in a baking pan
   under the broiler. Grill the steaks
   under the broiler or on the grill,
   basting once or twice during cooking. The rule for grilling fish is to
   measure it at its thickest part and
   to cook it 8–10 minutes to the inch,
   turning once. Do not overcook.
   Test for doneness with a fork.
5. Garnish with the lemon wedges and
   parsley or mint leaves and serve
   with rice.

VARIATION: *To pan-fry the fish, heat
a nonstick skillet over medium heat
and add a tablespoon vegetable oil.
Brown the fish 1–2 minutes on each
side, depending on thickness. Do not
overcook. Test with fork for doneness.*

Makes 2 servings

Baked Fish and Vegetables
Sakana Gingami Yaki

You can bake this delicious dish in a
neat package, with no pans to wash
afterwards. Salmon, sea bass, yellowtail
and trout are all good cooked this way.

Marinade

2 tablespoons sake
1–2 teaspoons reduced-sodium soy sauce
1–2 teaspoons fresh ginger juice or 1
   tablespoon grated ginger

• • •

8–12 oz (225–350 g) fish fillets
1 small onion, thinly sliced
1 green bell pepper, seeded and cut into
   thin slices
2 small carrots, scraped and cut into thin
   rounds
Vegetable oil
Lemon wedges, for garnish

1. Start rice.
2. Preheat
   the oven
   to 375°F
   (190°C).
3. Combine
   the marinade
   ingredients in
   a shallow bowl.

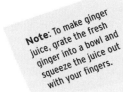

Note: To make ginger juice, grate the fresh ginger into a bowl and squeeze the juice out with your fingers.

4. Place the fish in
   the marinade bowl,
   coating both sides well. Let stand
   while you slice the vegetables.
5. Cut 2 large sheets of heavy-duty
   aluminum foil—large enough
   to wrap each serving securely.
   (If you're using thin aluminum
   foil, use double sheets to prevent
   leakage.) Brush the foil with oil.
   Place each serving of fish in the
   center of the foil, reserving the
   marinade. Arrange the sliced
   vegetables over fish and pour
   the marinade over all. Wrap into
   a neat, secure package, keeping
   the seam side on top. Bake for
   15–20 minutes. Open to test the
   fish with a fork for doneness.
   Place the packages on individual
   plates and garnish with the lemon
   wedges. Serve with rice.

Makes 2 servings

Broiled Tuna Steaks with Stir-Fried Greens

Fresh tuna makes an elegant presentation when prepared this way. I'm told that some people like their tuna rare, and that the Japanese method to achieve this result is to put steaks in the freezer an hour before cooking.

Marinade

- 2 tablespoons reduced-sodium soy sauce
- 2 tablespoons mirin
- 2 tablespoons fresh lemon juice
- 1 tablespoon grated fresh ginger
- 1 large clove garlic, crushed
- 1 teaspoon sugar
- Seven-spice powder (*shichimi togarashi*)

• • •

- 2 tuna steaks, about 6 oz (175 g) each
- 1-2 tablespoons vegetable oil
- 1 lb (450 g) washed and stemmed fresh greens, such as baby bok choy, spinach, dandelion greens or Swiss chard
- Salt and freshly ground pepper, taste
- Pickled ginger (*beni shoga*), for garnish

1. Start rice.
2. Combine the marinade ingredients in a shallow bowl and add the tuna, coating both sides well. Let stand at least 5 minutes. The longer it marinates, the stronger the flavor. Be sure the fish is at room temperature when you cook it.
3. Preheat the broiler to high. Line your broiler pan with aluminum foil to save on cleanup time.
4. Heat a large nonstick wok (or skillet) over high heat and add half of the oil. When hot, stir-fry the greens for 1–2 minutes, coating well with the oil. Add the salt and pepper, cover and cook another minute, or until the greens are just tender but still bright green. Set the wok aside and keep warm.
5. Drain the tuna steaks. Brush with the remaining oil and broil until well browned on the outside. If you want the tuna to be pink in the center, broil it for about 1–2 minutes on each side. If you prefer it to be cooked through, broil it about for 2–4 minutes on each side, or until just done, but not a moment more. Test for doneness with a fork.
6. Divide the greens between two plates. Place a piece of tuna over the greens and top with pickled ginger. Serve with rice.

Makes 2 servings

Shrimp Skewers
Ebi Kushiyaki

Shrimp are one of nature's most delicious fast foods. They may be either broiled in the oven or over a charcoal grill.

- 2 tablespoons reduced-sodium soy sauce
- 2 tablespoons mirin
- 8-12 oz (300–450 g) medium shrimp, shelled and deveined, leaving tails intact
- Bamboo skewers

1. Preheat the broiler to high.
2. Mix the soy sauce and mirin in a bowl.
3. Place the shrimp on skewers, piercing from the front end toward the tail. Brush the sauce over both sides of the shrimp. Broil 2–3 minutes while turning and brushing with additional sauce. Serve with rice, or in Shrimp Donburi (page 69).

Makes 2 servings

Note: For ease in cleanup, place a sheet of aluminum foil on the baking pan under the broiler.

Japan

Scrambled Tofu

Iridofu

Similar in preparation and appearance to scrambled eggs, this dish may be made with or without vegetables. With vegetables, it needs only rice to make a complete meal. Browned ground chicken may also be added.

Egg mixture

1 egg, lightly beaten

1 tablespoon reduced-sodium soy sauce

1 teaspoon sugar

• • •

14 oz (400 g) tofu, preferably extra-firm

1 tablespoon vegetable oil

½ small carrot, scraped and cut into thin matchsticks

½ small zucchini or green bell pepper, finely chopped

2 small fresh mushrooms, preferably shiitake, finely chopped

1 teaspoon grated fresh ginger

1 tablespoon sake

2 green onions (scallions), cut into ½-in (1½-cm) lengths

Seven-spice mixture (*shichimi togarashi*) or freshly ground black pepper, to taste

1. Start rice.
2. In a small bowl combine the egg mixture and stir until sugar dissolves. Set aside.
3. Cut the tofu into small pieces and place in a large strainer over a bowl. Using a fork or the back of a large spoon, crumble the tofu to expel as much water as possible. Drain.
4. Heat a nonstick wok (or skillet) over medium-high heat and add the the oil. Stir-fry the carrot, zucchini, mushrooms and ginger until barely tender, about 3 minutes.
5. Turn the heat down to medium and add the crumbled tofu. Stir-fry 3–4 minutes, or until completely heated through. Stir in the sake.
6. Add the beaten egg mixture and stir gently until the egg is set. Stir in the green onions and sprinkle lightly with the seven-spice mixture or black pepper. Serve with rice.

VARIATION: *4 ounces (100 g) ground chicken or turkey may be stir-fried lightly for about 2 minutes in Step 3 before the vegetables are added.*

Makes 2–3 servings

Stir-Fried Tofu and Vegetables

Yakidofu

In this simple yet flavorful dish, slices of tofu are stir-fried, topped with vegetables and served with green garnishes.

1-2 tablespoons vegetable oil

1 small Japanese eggplant (unpeeled), cut in half lengthwise and sliced very thin

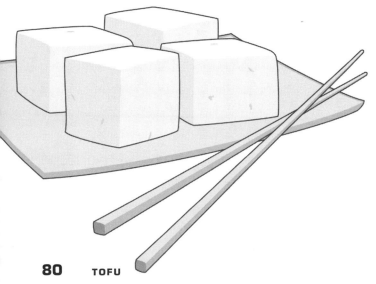

1 small green bell pepper, cut into quarters
    and sliced into thin strips
1 or 2 small tomatoes, quartered and thinly
    sliced
1–2 tablespoons reduced-sodium soy sauce
1 tablespoon mirin
14 oz (400 g) extra-firm tofu, cut into 6 equal
    slices and placed on paper towels to dry
Seven-spice mixture (*shichimi togarashi*),
    for garnish
Watercress and green onions (scallions), cut
    into 2-in (5-cm) lengths, for garnish

1. Start rice.
2. Heat a nonstick wok (or skillet) over medium-high heat. Add half of the oil and stir-fry the eggplant for 1–2 minutes. Add the green pepper and tomato, and continue to stir-fry until the vegetables are tender. Stir in the soy sauce and mirin and cook another minute. Remove from the wok and keep warm.
3. Heat the remaining oil over medium heat and fry the tofu slices until they are lightly browned on both sides. Spread the vegetable mixture over the tofu and cover the wok to steam about 1 minute, or until heated through. Serve with rice and the garnishes.

Makes 2–3 servings

Tabletop Cookery

Seafood and Vegetable Hot Pot

Yosenabe

A warm and colorful dish, *Yosenabe* means "a gathering of everything" and is adapted from the repertory of *nabemono*—one-pot dishes in which the cooking is done at the table. The uncooked food is sliced and arranged on a platter in advance, as is the dipping sauce. It is probably the easiest kind of cooking that a home cook can do. The choice of ingredients may be as simple or as elaborate as you wish, and since portions are adjustable, extra diners may easily be accommodated. All that is required is that you buy the food, cut it up and arrange it attractively on a platter. For good health, use twice the volume of vegetables as meat or fish, and cut everything to a fairly uniform size so that each food will have about the same cooking time.

Set the heating unit and its cooking pot in the center of the table and bring the broth to a boil. Adjust the heat so that the liquid simmers throughout the meal. Provide each diner with a large shallow soup bowl, a small bowl of dipping sauce, and

chopsticks or a long-handled fork. Each diner selects his or her own food from the platter and cooks it in the simmering broth. Leftover broth may be served as soup.

Ingredients for *nabemono* may be varied according to season and availability. But it is best to avoid any meat or fish that is excessively fatty. For healthful eating, any vegetable that complements the meat or seafood may be used. Think of the ingredients that follow as suggestions. Use as few or as many as you wish and don't hesitate to make additions or substitutions.

Ponzu dipping sauce

¼ cup (50 ml) reduced-sodium soy sauce
¼ cup (50 ml) fresh lemon or lime juice

Broth

3 cups (24 oz/700 ml) instant dashi or
    unsalted chicken stock, fresh or canned
One 2-in piece of kombu, to flavor the
    broth (optional)

• • •

2 small carrots, scraped and sliced into
    thin rounds
6-8 medium shrimp, peeled and deveined,
    leaving tails intact
12-16 oz (300-400g) fillet of a firm-fleshed
    fish, cut into 1-in (2 ½-cm) squares
4 cherrystone clams, shucked, or mussels
    (optional)
6 fresh mushrooms, preferably shiitake,
    halved
1 or 2 leeks or 4 green onions (scallions)
    cut into ¾-in (2-cm) pieces
6-8 oz (175-225 g) fresh spinach or other
    green leafy vegetable, stemmed and
    washed
16 snow peas, tips and strings removed
8 cherry tomatoes
6 oz (175 g) tofu, cut into 1-in (2 ½-cm)
    squares

1. Start rice.
2. Combine the dipping sauce ingredients and divide into small bowls.

If you wait until the cooking begins, you may use a tablespoon or two of broth from the soup to dilute the soy–lemon juice combination for a subtler taste.
3. Following the instructions in the introduction, place the broth ingredients in a pot and bring to a boil. If your tabletop heat source is not strong enough, you may have to bring the pot to a boil on the kitchen stove. Lower the heat so that the broth simmers gently throughout the meal.
4. With chopsticks, each diner selects and cooks his or her own food to taste, and dips it into the dipping sauce to flavor it before eating. Add stock or water to the pot when needed to maintain an adequate amount of liquid. At the end of the meal, the broth may be seasoned with a little dipping sauce and eaten as soup.

Makes 3–4 servings

Tofu Hot Pot
Yudofu

This is a vegetarian dish from the tabletop cooking repertory of *nabemono*. Instructions from the previous recipe, Yosenabe, also apply here, but the ingredients in this recipe are so few that it might be just as easy to cook the soup in the kitchen and serve it in large soup bowls.

Dipping sauce

⅓ cup (75 ml) reduced-sodium soy sauce
1½ tablespoons mirin or pale dry sherry
1 teaspoon grated fresh ginger (optional)

Broth

3 cups (24 oz/700 ml) dashi, fresh or
    instant, or unsalted vegetable stock

One 2-in (5-cm) piece kombu, to flavor the
  broth (optional)

• • •

14 oz (400 g) firm tofu, cut into ¾-in
  (2- cm) cubes
6 fresh mushrooms, preferably shiitake,
  halved
8 oz (225 g) fresh spinach, stemmed and
  washed, or snow peas with tips and strings
  removed, or other green vegetable
4 green onions (scallions), cut into ¾-in
  (2-cm) lengths
1 sheet nori, toasted and crumbled, for
  garnish (optional)

1. Start rice.
2. Combine the sauce ingredients and
   divide into small bowls. If you wait
   until the cooking begins, you may
   use a tablespoon or two of broth
   from the soup to dilute the dipping
   sauce for a subtler taste.
3. Following the instructions in the
   introduction to Yosenabe (page
   81), place the broth in a pot and
   bring to a boil. Lower the heat so
   that the broth simmers constantly
   throughout the meal. Add the tofu,
   mushrooms and spinach and cook
   for 2–3 minutes. Do not overcook the tofu. Garnish with green
   onions and crumbled nori, if using.
4. Serve immediately with the dipping sauce. The broth may be seasoned with a little dipping sauce
   and enjoyed as soup at the end of
   the meal.

Makes 2–3 serving

Serving Suggestion

Serve with rice and, if you
wish, Pickled Cucumbers (page
88); they combine very well
with this dish.

Teppanyaki

This is another recipe in which no
time at all is spent cooking in the
kitchen. Meat and vegetables are
browned at the table in a nonstick
electric skillet or on a griddle. The
diners do all the work. Since the
portions are flexible, it is easy to
accomodate extra diners without
harrying the cook. The only work
is making the sauce and slicing and
arranging the food on a platter. In
restaurants specializing in this dish,
the *teppan* (iron sheet) is either a
large griddle built into the dining
table or counter that has been turned
into an enormous griddle. (*Yaki*
means broiling or grilling.) In the
United States, teppanyaki was made
famous by the Benihana restaurant
chain.

The following ingredients lend
themselves nicely to being cooked this
way, but you may add, subtract, or
substitute other foods in season. For
example, fresh ears of corn cut in half
or thirds are delicious browned in a
skillet, but they must be boiled for
about 2 minutes first. Keep in mind
that meat is easier to slice when it is
partially frozen.

1 lb (425 g) tender, boneless beef, pork or
  chicken, cut into thin slices
8 medium shrimp, peeled and deveined,
  leaving tails intact
6 fresh mushrooms, preferably shiitake,
  halved
1 onion, thinly sliced
2 green or red bell peppers, seeded and
  cut into quarters
1 small Japanese eggplant, unpeeled, cut
  into thin slices
1 sweet potato, peeled and cut crosswise
  into thin slices
1-2 tablespoons vegetable oil

Ponzu dipping sauce

¼ cup (50 ml) reduced-sodium soy sauce
¼ cup (50 ml) fresh lemon or lime juice
Up to ¼ cup (50 ml) dashi or unsalted
    chicken stock or water to dilute sauce

Optional ingredients for guests to mix into dipping sauce

2 green onions (scallions), thinly sliced
Peeled and grated daikon (Japanese white
    radish)
Grated fresh ginger
Seven-spice mixture (*shichimi togarashi*)

1. Start rice. If you have an electric rice cooker, plug it in next to the dining room table.
2. Arrange the meat and vegetables on a platter (insert a toothpick in the onion slices to hold them together).
3. Prepare the dipping sauce and divide into individual bowls.

Prepare the optional ingredients for dipping, if using.

4. At the table, plug in an electric nonstick griddle or skillet and turn to high heat. Add a few drops of the oil to the griddle. Using a piece of cloth or paper towel, spread the oil evenly across the surface of the griddle. Using chopsticks or a long-handled fork, lay a few pieces of the food on the griddle to test the temperature and cook them, turning once, until done. Be careful not to overcook anything. You may need to turn the heat down to medium once the meal has started.
5. Serve a platter of meat and vegetables with dipping sauce, rice, and optional dipping ingredients, if using. Diners can select food from the platter and cook items throughout the meal.

Makes 3–4 servings

■ Beef ■

Ground Beef, Eggplant and Peppers with Miso

Japanese eggplants are small and not usually peeled because they are so tender. If you are using the large globe variety, its coarser skin should always be peeled, though a few strips of purple might be left on to add color to the finished dish. Eggplant has a tendency to absorb a lot of oil, but less is absorbed if a nonstick pan is used and the pan and oil are very hot.

Sauce

1 tablespoon miso, either white (*shiro*) or
    red (*aka*)
1 tablespoon reduced-sodium soy sauce
1 tablespoon sake
1 teaspoon sugar

2 tablespoons dashi or unsalted stock or
   water

• • •

1-2 tablespoons vegetable oil
I small onion, quartered and sliced
1 tablespoon grated fresh ginger
1 clove garlic, crushed
8-12 oz (225-350 g) ground lean beef,
   chicken or pork
2 Japanese eggplants, or 1 small globe
   variety eggplant, cut into thin slices
1 green bell or red bell pepper, seeded and
   sliced

1. Start rice.
2. Combine the sauce ingredients in
   a small bowl and set aside.
3. Heat a nonstick wok (or skillet)
   over high heat and add half of
   the oil. Stir-fry the onion about
   1–2 minutes, or until softened.
   Add the ginger and garlic and
   stir-fry for a few seconds.
4. Add the ground meat and stir-fry
   2–3 minutes or until the meat
   begins to brown. Separate pieces
   of the meat if they stick together.
5. Add the eggplant and stir-fry 3-4
   minutes or until nearly done.
6. Add the green pepper and stir-fry
   1–2 minutes more. The peppers
   should remain crisp and bright
   green.
7. Add the sauce and stir until the
   mixture begins to boil. Add more
   liquid if the mixture seems dry.
   Reduce the heat and simmer a
   minute or two to blend flavors.
   Serve with rice.

VARIATION: *4–6 ounces (100-
175 g) firm tofu, cut into 1-inch
cubes (2½-cm), may be added after
Step 5, and stirred gently for an
additional 2 minutes. You may wish
to use less ground meat when adding tofu.*

Makes 2–3 servings

Beef Steak with Soy-Ginger Sauce
Bifuteki Shoga Tare

Many still look forward to a juicy
steak once in a while, and often
cook it with no seasoning at all.
This will be just as quick and quite
delicious. The secret to a good
steak is to sear it over very high
heat. A charcoal grill is best, but
pan-broiling also produces very
good results. If you broil the steak,
be sure to preheat the broiler to the
highest temperature.

Serve it with a cooked vegetable
that can be made while the steak is
broiling, or just a salad. Instead of
rice, you might want to take another
easy way out. Canned beans are a
very acceptable convenience food. I
suggest a can of small white beans,
rinsed well and dressed with vinegar,
oil, and a clove of minced garlic.
Garnish the white beans with chopped
green onions or red bell pepper.

Marinade
2 tablespoons reduced-sodium soy sauce
2 tablespoons sake
½ teaspoon sugar
1 teaspoon grated fresh ginger

• • •

8-12 oz (225-350 g) flank steak or any
   other beef steak of your choice, at
   room temperature
Pickled ginger (*beni-shoga*) and parsley
   sprigs, for garnish

1. Start rice. Prepare a salad or vegetable of your choice.
2. To broil the steak, follow this step
   and Steps 3 and 4. To pan-sear the
   steak, follow Steps 3 and 5. To broil
   the steak, preheat the broiler to high.
   Line the broiler pan with aluminum
   foil to cut down on cleanup time.

3. Combine the marinade ingredients in a shallow bowl, stirring well to dissolve the sugar. Add the steak, coating both sides well.

4. Remove the steak from the marinade and place on the broiler pan, 2 inches (5-cm) from the heat source. Cook to desired tenderness—rare, medium, or well-done—turning once. Brush occasionally with marinade.

5. To pan-sear the steak, preheat a heavy, nonstick skillet over high heat for about a minute. Add a small amount of oil and sear the steak quickly, no more than 1–2 minutes on each side. Reduce the heat to medium, then cook to the desired degree of doneness, turning once.

6. Serve with rice and garnish with the pickled ginger and parsley.

Makes 2 servings

■ Pork ■

Pork Teriyaki with Chinese Cabbage

Butaniku no Teriyaki

Meat is easier to cut when it is partially frozen; easier still is to buy it already sliced. For quicker preparation, Kikkoman Less Sodium Teriyaki Marinade and Sauce may be substituted for the sauce in this recipe.

4 tablespoons reduced-sodium teriyaki sauce, such as Kikkoman, or mix your own (see recipe on page 71)
1 tablespoon vegetable oil
8 oz (225 g) Chinese (napa) cabbage, trimmed and cut into small pieces
8-12 oz (225–350 g) lean boneless pork (or beef) cut across the grain into thin 1-in (2 ½-cm) strips
2 green onions (scallions), sliced

1. Start rice. Prepare the ingredients and place them within easy reach of the stove.

2. Prepare the teriyaki sauce, stirring the sauce ingredients in a bowl until the sugar dissolves.

3. Heat a nonstick wok (or skillet) over high heat and add half of the oil. Add the cabbage and stir-fry 1–2 minutes or until it begins to wilt. Remove from the wok to a serving platter.

4. Heat the remaining oil and stir-fry the pork (or beef) until it begins to brown, about 2–3 minutes. Add the teriyaki sauce and stir until the pork is well done.

5. Return the cabbage to the wok and stir-fry another minute or until it heats through. (Watch carefully if you're using beef since it will be done sooner than pork.) Stir in the sliced green onions. Serve with rice.

Makes 2–3 servings

Pork Cutlet

Tonkatsu

Ton means pork and *katsu* is the Japanese word for cutlet. This is one of the most popular meat dishes in Japan, deriving from the German schnitzel. It is usually accompanied by Tonkatsu sauce—a thick sauce similar to Worcestershire that is available in many supermarkets. *Tonkatsu* is usually served on a bed of shredded raw cabbage.

Serving Suggestion

Serve with rice and commercially prepared *Tonkatsu* sauce or Worcestershire sauce. Wasabi (Japanese horseradish) would also be appropriate. Mix 4 teaspoons wasabi powder with about 2 tablespoons of water, added a little at a time to make a thick paste. Let stand for 5 minutes.

1 small head of young cabbage
2 slices, 4–6 oz (100–150 g) each, boneless
    pork loin or tenderloin
Freshly ground black pepper
Cornstarch or flour, for dredging
1 egg, lightly beaten
1 cup fresh or dried bread crumbs
1 tablespoon vegetable oil
Lemon wedges, for garnish
1 green onion (scallion), sliced, for garnish

1. Start rice.
2. Shred enough cabbage on 2 plates to form a bed on which to lay the chops.
3. Sprinkle the pork with black pepper and dredge lightly in the corn-
starch. Dip into the beaten egg and then in the breadcrumbs, pressing them firmly into the meat.
4. Heat a nonstick skillet over medium-high heat and add the oil. Brown the breaded pork for about 3–5 minutes on each side, depending on thickness. Test for doneness. Be sure the pork is cooked through and no pink remains. Drain on paper towels. Cut into slices and place on the bed of cabbage, garnished with the lemon wedges and sliced green onions.

Makes 2 servings

■ Salads ■

Sunomono and Aemono

*S*unomono (vinegared foods) and *aemono* (combined, dressed foods) may be thought of as Japanese-style salads. Served in beautiful bowls, they are small dishes meant to accompany and complement main dishes. In sunomono, practically any vegetable, raw or partially cooked, as well as many kinds of fish and shellfish, steamed, grilled, or fried, may be served with a sprinkling of lemon or vinegar dress-

ing. Aemono consists of several raw or cooked ingredients—vegetables, poultry or fish—which may also be dressed with a vinegar-based dressing. These mixed salads are also served with thicker dressings to which egg yolk, miso, puréed tofu or grated ginger is sometimes added.

As there is great scope for creativity in their preparation, sunomono and aemono are perfect vehicles for meals that must be prepared in a hurry. For example, roasted chickens and cooked shrimp are available in many grocery stores. These can be effortlessly incorporated into a salad with vegetables of your choice and dressed with a simple Japanese-style dressing.

Crab and Cucumber Salad

Kani Kyuri no Sunomono

This crab and cucumber combination makes a good light dinner or lunch all by itself. Fresh cooked crab can be found in many grocery stores, or use canned crab (though fresh is best).

> 2-3 small Japanese cucumbers or
>   1 large one, peeled lengthwise, leaving
>   ¼-in (6-mm)-wide green strips to
>   add color
> Lettuce leaves
> 8-12 oz (125-200 g) fresh cooked (or
>   canned) crabmeat, shredded, cartilage
>   and bits of bone removed
> Pickled ginger (*beni shoga*), for garnish
> 1 green onion (scallion), thinly sliced, for
>   garnish

Dressing (*Sanbaizu*)
> 2½ tablespoons rice vinegar
> 4 teaspoons sugar or mirin
> 2 teaspoons reduced-sodium soy sauce
> 2½ teaspoons dashi or unsalted stock or
>   water, or to taste

1. Optional Step: (If you have the time, follow this step. Otherwise go to Step 2.) Mix 1 tablespoon of salt into the sliced cucumbers and let them stand for 5–10 minutes. Rinse the cucumbers well under running water and drain. This process will make the cucumbers wilt.
2. Line two shallow serving bowls with the lettuce. Divide and arrange the cucumbers and crabmeat on top.
3. Combine the dressing ingredients, stirring to dissolve the sugar. Divide the dressing into small bowls and serve as dipping sauce. Or, if you prefer, pour the dressing on top of the salad. Garnish with chopped green onion and serve with the pickled ginger and some crusty bread.

Makes 2 servings

Pickled Cucumbers

Kyuri no Sunomono

Different versions of cucumber salad are common in many Asian cuisines. Crisp, cool and quick to prepare, they go well with almost any main course.

> 1 large or 2-3 small Japanese cucumbers,
>   peeled lengthwise, leaving some strips
>   of green skin to add color
> About ⅓ cup Dressing (*Sanbaizu*), see
>   recipe at left

1. Optional Step: (If you have the time, follow this step. Otherwise go to Step 2.) Mix a tablespoon of salt into the sliced cucumbers and let them stand for 5–10 minutes. Rinse the cucumbers well under running water and

drain. This process will make the cucumbers wilt.

2. Combine the dressing, stirring to dissolve the sugar. Add to the cucumbers and mix well.

VARIATION: *For a more elaborate salad, add thinly sliced carrots, celery and shredded lettuce to the cucumbers.*

Makes 2 servings

Bean Sprout and Bell Pepper Salad

Moyashi Sanbaizu

Bean sprouts and bell peppers are a tasty combination with *Sanbaizu*—a classic sweet-and-sour dressing—to which I've added the bright flavor of fresh grated ginger.

Dressing

2 ½ tablespoons rice vinegar

1-2 teaspoons sugar or mirin

2 teaspoons reduced-sodium soy sauce

2 tablespoons dashi or unsalted vegetable stock or water, or to taste

1 teaspoon grated fresh ginger

• • •

1 small carrot, cut into thin matchsticks

6 oz (175 g) fresh bean sprouts, trimmed

1 green bell pepper, seeded and sliced into thin strips

1. Combine the dressing ingredients in a small bowl and set aside. You may not need all of the dressing; the remaining dressing can be stored in the refrigerator.

2. Bring 2 cups water to a boil. Add the carrots and cook for 1 minute. Add the bean sprouts and bell pepper to blanch for 30 seconds. Drain, toss with dressing and serve immediately.

VARIATION: *Green beans are excellent with this dressing. They will need to be cooked about 5 minutes, until tender.*

Makes 2 servings

Daikon and Carrot Salad

Namasu

This very simple salad, or semi-pickle, is a traditional dish in Japanese cooking. Unlike most salads, it may be kept a day or two in the refrigerator without spoiling.

8 oz (225 g) daikon (Japanese white radish), peeled and cut lengthwise into thin matchsticks

1 large carrot, scraped and cut into thin matchsticks

Dressing

¼ cup (50 ml) rice vinegar

1 tablespoon fresh lemon juice (optional)

1 tablespoon sugar

1. Optional Step: (If you have the time, follow this step. Otherwise go to Step 2.) Mix a tablespoon of salt into the daikon and carrots and let them stand for 5–10 minutes. Rinse them well under running water and drain before adding the dressing. This process will make the vegetables wilt.

2. Combine the dressing ingredients, stirring to dissolve the sugar, and pour over the vegetables. It is best if the salad is allowed to stand for a few minutes before serving. Drain excess dressing before serving.

Makes 2–4 servings

Spinach with Toasted Sesame Seeds

Horenso no Goma-ae

This is a delicious way to cook spinach. And since it may be prepared ahead and set aside to be served at room temperature, it's easy on the cook.

> 2 tablespoons black or white sesame seeds
> 1 lb (450 g) fresh spinach, stemmed and washed

Dressing
> 2 tablespoons dashi or unsalted vegetable stock or water
> 1 tablespoon reduced-sodium soy sauce
> ¼–½ teaspoon sugar

1. Toast the sesame seeds in a dry skillet over medium heat, stirring constantly and shaking the skillet to avoid scorching. Set aside.
2. In a large saucepan, bring 1 cup of water to a boil. Add the spinach, cover tightly and cook over high heat until the upper leaves begin to wilt. Drain the spinach in a colander and rinse with cold water. Drain and squeeze out moisture. (Some cooks prefer to steam vegetables, which also may be done here.) Place the spinach in a large serving bowl, or in two individual bowls.
3. Combine the dressing ingredients and stir to dissolve the sugar. Pour over the spinach and sprinkle with the toasted sesame seeds.

VARIATION: *Any mild green vegetable, such as savoy cabbage or Swiss chard, may be prepared this way.*

Makes 2–3 servings

Lemon Asparagus with Toasted Sesame Seeds

Asparagasu no Goma-ae

Asparagus is especially tasty when accented with mirin, soy sauce and lemon juice.

> 1 teaspoon black or white sesame seeds
> 12 thin stalks of asparagus, hard ends cut off

Dressing
> 2 teaspoons reduced-sodium soy sauce
> 2 teaspoons mirin
> 2 teaspoons fresh lemon juice

1. Toast the sesame seeds in a dry skillet over medium heat, stirring constantly and shaking the skillet to avoid scorching. Remove from the pan and set aside.
2. Parboil or steam the asparagus until tender but still crisp and green, 2–3 minutes. Rinse in cold water. Drain and arrange on a serving plate.
3. Combine the soy sauce, mirin and lemon juice and pour over the asparagus. Sprinkle with the toasted sesame seeds.

Makes 2 servings

Korea

Korea, a peninsula just 600 miles long in the northern part of Asia, is situated between China and Japan, with Russia to the north. Because of its location, it has a long history as a cultural bridge across which Chinese culture was transmitted to Japan, and Japanese influences reached the mainland. Buddhism and all other aspects of Chinese culture, especially Confucian learning and the written language, were introduced to Korea in about the fourth century. In turn, Korean missionaries introduced Buddhism to Japan in the sixth century, and Korean artisans were sent to Japan to give the Japanese the professional training necessary to make Buddhist art. The plain and often coarse style of Korean pottery was highly influential in Japan, stimulating the development of new kinds of pottery characterized by simplicity in contrast to the highly finished products of China.

Korean culture was greatly enriched by contact with its neighbors—and vice versa—and yet, because of its vulnerable geographic location, it has endured a continuous flow of conquerors, including Chinese, Japanese, Mongolian and Western. Though Korea was a kind of Chinese protectorate until the mid-seventeenth century, the period of China's strong influence ended at the close of the sixteenth century with the Japanese invasion. In the nineteenth century, Korea was the center of a struggle between China, Japan and Russia, and was officially annexed to Japan. Sadly, its modern history continues to be troubled with its division into two rival governments. Nevertheless, the Koreans have maintained their identity as a separate and distinct people, and the extent to which they have done so is remarkable indeed.

Korean cooking, though influenced by Chinese and Japanese cuisine, is generally more hearty than that of its neighbors. It is characterized by thick, warming soups and stews, pickled vegetables and a fondness for beef. Surrounded on three sides by water, Korea has an abundance of fish and seafood, and the diet of Korea, like Japan, consists mainly of products of the sea. Fish is often filleted, coated with batter and fried; made into rich, spicy stews; and sometimes combined with meat or poultry. Fish is also eaten raw, mixed with watercress, cucumbers and white radishes, and seasoned with a vinegar and red pepper paste dressing. The result is far more robust than sashimi, the plain raw fish favored by the Japanese.

The cuisine can be very hot, especially in the southern part of the country. The red chile probably came into use in the sixteenth century with the Portuguese, who brought it from the New World. The Chinese and the Japanese were also introduced to it about the same time, but it was the Koreans who fully embraced it. Red chiles are an ingredient in *koch'ujang*, a very hot soybean paste, which is a staple in Korean cooking. A bean paste similar to Japanese miso is also used. Other soybean products are also staple foods in Korea. But it is red chile, together with garlic, ginger, soy sauce, sesame oil and sesame seeds, that are the main seasonings in Korean cooking. Sesame seeds are toasted and crushed before they are added to marinades or mixed with cooked dishes, giving them a rich nutty flavor. Green onions (scallions) are also a favorite addition to many dishes. Though beef is the most favored meat, pork and chicken are also popular. The Koreans make a banquet stew cooked at the table using the charcoal-heated firepot. This stew includes fish, chicken, liver and beef, but never lamb. This is a puzzle, since the firepot was probably introduced by the Mongols when they conquered China and Korea in about the thirteenth Century (the Chinese use lamb or mutton in their firepot cooking).

Unlike other Asian cuisines, Korean cuisine includes many uncooked vegetables served in the form of salads and pickles. The most famous of these is *kimch'i*, one of Korea's national dishes—a spicy, pungent, sometimes fiery hot combination of pickled cabbage, chiles, ginger, turnip and other seasonable vegetables. Next to rice, kimch'i is considered an indispensable food. It accompanies every meal, including breakfast. In Seoul, there is even a kimch'i museum devoted to its

> Korea has never been a true tea-drinking nation. The beverages that often accompany a Korean meal are barley tea, drunk cold in summer and hot in winter, and corn tea, which has recently become popular.

meaning, its making and especially its taste. There are probably as many versions of kimch'i as there are cooks. According to ancient tradition, the vegetables are cut up, seasoned, placed in crocks, and buried in the earth for the winter in order to ferment. Every house-wife used to make her own, but all that is changing. Women in the cities are too busy keeping pace with modern life to make kimch'i, so they buy it ready-made, packed in vacuum bags or in jars.

Another food that appears frequently on the Korean table is *kim,* the Korean name for the seaweed (called *nori* in Japanese cuisine). These thin sheets of seaweed are lightly toasted with sesame oil and a sprinkle of salt. They are cut into small rectangles and eaten with rice that, unlike the rice used in Japanese sushi, is not seasoned. Kim is also used as a wrapper for a roll known as *kim bap*, containing cooked rice, meat, egg and vegetables. The roll is wrapped tightly and cut into thin bite-size slices, resembling the Japanese *temaki-zushi.*

Rice, of course, as it is almost everywhere in Asia, is the foundation of every meal. Though millet, barley, wheat and noodles are also used, rice is the most venerated of the grains. Like their Japanese neighbors, Koreans prefer short-grain rice over the long-grain varieties preferred in China and in the West. Most often rice is boiled, though it may also be steamed or fried. It is always cooked in just enough water so that by the time the water has been absorbed, the rice will be tender. It is said that the richest part of a pot of rice is at the bottom. Rather than waste the nutrition in the toasty, browned grains that may stick to the pan, a cup or two of water is added after the rice is cooked and served. The water simmers slowly during the meal and the rice tea is served once the meal is over.

Koreans, like the Chinese and Japanese, use chopsticks, but in Korea they are often made of silver. Every person has his or her own rice bowl, often with a lid and made of metal, and the food is served and eaten from bowls, not plates. All the dishes cooked for a meal—rice, soup, kimch'i, and fish, meat and vegetable dishes with sauces—are put on the table at once, and there is usually no dessert. Sometimes fresh fruits are served. There are a number of Korean sweets and confections, but they are usually eaten only as snacks.

Korean Pantry

To keep shopping to a minimum, and to speed preparation and cooking time, it is helpful to keep these Korean staples on hand in your kitchen.

Ingredients with a Long Shelf Life

bean paste, hot
   (*koch'ujang*)

black pepper, ground

chiles

chili sauce or ground
   red chiles

kimch'i (ready-made)

mushrooms, dried

red pepper, ground

rice, short and medium
   grain

rice vinegar

seaweed (*kim*)

sesame oil

sesame seeds

soy sauce

Fresh Ingredients

garlic

ginger

green onions
   (scallions)

onions

■ Rice ■

Plain Rice

To make plain rice, follow the recipe for Boiled Rice, Japanese Style (page 67).

Bi Bim Bop

This is a very simple, flexible recipe for rice with typical Korean seasonings. The hot rice is placed in individual bowls and the stir-fried additions are heaped on top. This recipe uses beef, but tofu, pork or chicken will work just as well. Vegetables can also be varied. Be sure to start cooking the rice (preferably short or medium grain), before you stir-fry the vegetables. Use the recipe for Japanese boiled rice on page 67. The stir-fried mixture need not be highly seasoned during cooking, since strong seasonings may be added to taste at the table.

1 tablespoon sesame or vegetable oil

2 large cloves garlic, finely chopped or crushed

4-6 oz (125-175 g) lean, tender beef, cut into thin bite-size slices

1 red bell pepper, seeded and cut into matchsticks

2 green onions (scallions), thinly sliced

8 oz (100g) fresh bean sprouts, trimmed

1 tablespoon reduced-sodium soy sauce

Freshly ground black pepper or ground red pepper, to taste

2-3 cups (500-750 g) cooked short-grain rice, placed in 2-3 individual bowls and kept warm

1 tablespoon toasted, crushed sesame seeds (*kkaesogeum*, see page 102), for garnish

koch'ujang (a very hot soybean paste) and soy sauce, to be added at the table

1. Start rice.
2. Heat a nonstick wok (or skillet) over medium-high heat. Add the oil and stir-fry the garlic for 3–4 seconds. Add the beef and stir-fry about 1 minute or until it begins to brown.
3. Add the bell pepper and green onions and stir-fry for another minute or two, or until the pepper softens.
4. Add the bean sprouts and stir-fry until they are just heated through. Sprinkle with the soy sauce and back or red pepper and stir for a few seconds until the mixture is blended and very hot. Place on top of the hot cooked rice and sprinkle with the sesame seeds. Serve with *koch'ujang* and soy sauce.

Makes 2–3 servings

■ Noodles ■

Noodle Soup

Kuksu

A delicious noodle soup recipe from my friend Clare You, a Korean scholar at the University of California, Berkeley. For a vegetarian soup, substitute tofu for the chicken and shrimp.

8 oz (225 g) dried wheat vermicelli noodles

2-3 cups (475-700 ml) unsalted chicken or beef stock

1 tablespoon sesame or vegetable oil

1 onion, coarsely chopped

2 large cloves garlic, crushed

4-6 oz (100-150 g) raw or cooked chicken, cut into bite-size pieces

4 fresh mushrooms, preferably shiitakes, wiped, trimmed and sliced, or 4 dried mushrooms soaked in hot water for 25-30 minutes, trimmed and sliced

4 oz (150 g) small or medium shrimp, shelled and deveined, leaving tails intact

1-3 chiles, seeded and chopped, or dried red pepper flakes or ground red pepper, to taste

1 tablespoon reduced-sodium soy sauce, or to taste

3 green onions (scallions), finely chopped, for garnish

1. Bring a large pot of water to a rolling boil. Gradually add the noodles, keeping the water boiling vigorously. Cook about 3 minutes, stirring occasionally, until barely done. The outside of the noodles should be tender, the inside firm and hard. Test for doneness by biting into a single strand. Cooking time will vary, depending on the size and thickness of the noodle. Drain and keep warm.

2. Bring the stock to a boil.

3. While the stock is coming to a boil, heat a nonstick wok (or skillet) over high heat and add the oil. Stir-fry the onion about 1 minute or until softened. Add the garlic and cook for 3–4 seconds. Add the chicken and stir-fry 1–2 minutes or until it becomes opaque. Add the mushrooms and stir-fry until softened. Drop in the shrimp and stir-fry until they turn pink. Mix in the chiles and soy sauce and continue to cook until the mixture is well blended.

4. To serve, divide the noodles into large soup bowls and add the hot broth. Place the stir-fried mixture on top and garnish with the green onions. Serve with kimch'i.

VARIATION: *For a vegetarian soup, use vegetable stock in place of the meat stock, and in place of the chicken and shrimp substitute a block of soft or firm tofu, about 14 oz (400 g), cut into bite-size cubes. Add the tofu at the end of Step 3 and cook for about 2 minutes to heat through.*

Makes 2–3 servings

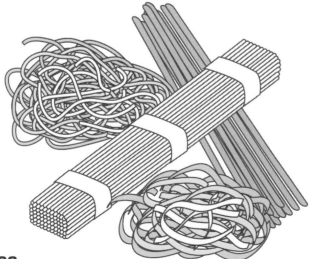

Chicken

Chicken Stewed with Vegetables

Tak Tchim

This simple recipe involves simmering rather than stir-frying. Vegetables may be substituted as you wish, and the amount of soy sauce is also variable. Use less soy sauce to begin and add more to taste. Dried mushrooms add more flavor than fresh, but they must be soaked in hot water first, which adds to preparation time.

1 lb (450 g) chicken parts, cut into very small pieces for faster cooking, or 8–12 oz (200–300 g) boneless, skinless chicken, preferably from the leg, cut into 1-in (2½-cm) cubes

1–3 tablespoons reduced-sodium soy sauce

2 large cloves garlic, finely minced or crushed

1 teaspoon sugar

¼ cup (50 ml) mushroom soaking liquid or unsalted chicken stock or water

4 dried mushrooms (soaked in hot water for 25–30 minutes), stemmed, halved and sliced, or substitute 4 fresh mushrooms

3 green onions (scallions), thinly sliced

1 carrot, scraped and cut into 2-in (5-cm) matchsticks

1 onion, quartered, then thinly sliced

4 celery ribs, cut into 2-in (5-cm) matchsticks

Freshly ground black pepper or dried red pepper flakes or ground red pepper, to taste

1 teaspoon sesame oil (optional)

Fresh green chiles, sliced into matchsticks or sliced green onions (scallions), for garnish

1. Start rice. Prepare the ingredients and place them within easy reach of the stove.
2. In a stewing pot, coat the chicken pieces with the soy sauce. Add the garlic, sugar and the stock, and mix well. Cover the pot, bring to a boil and simmer gently over low heat, about 10 minutes if you're using chicken parts with bones, or for 2–3 minutes for boneless chicken.
3. Add the vegetables, pepper and 3–4 more tablespoons of stock or water. Simmer gently over low heat for 5 minutes, or until the chicken is tender. Do not overcook the vegetables.
4. Stir in the sesame oil. Remove to a shallow serving bowl and garnish with the chiles or green onions. Serve with rice and kimch'i.

Makes 2–3 servings

Chicken Braised with Mushrooms

Tak Beoseot Tchim

In this recipe, the chicken is lightly browned first. Dried mushrooms must be soaked in hot water first, but they add more flavor than fresh mushrooms. If you have time, opt for more flavor.

Marinade

  2-3 tablespoons reduced-sodium soy sauce
  2 large cloves garlic, minced or crushed
  1-2 teaspoons hot chili sauce or ground
    red pepper, or to taste
  2 teaspoons sesame oil

  • • •

  1 lb (450 g) chicken parts, cut into very
    small pieces for faster cooking, or
    8-12 oz (200-300 g) boneless, skinless
    chicken, preferably from the leg, cut
    into 1-in (2-cm) cubes
  1 tablespoon vegetable oil
  1 onion, cut in half and then into 8
    segments
  4 dried Chinese mushrooms soaked in hot
    water for 25-30 minutes, stemmed,
    cut in half and thinly sliced (do not
    discard soaking liquid), or 4 medium-
    sized fresh mushrooms
  4 green onions (scallions), sliced
  4 tablespoons mushroom soaking liquid or
    unsalted chicken stock or water
  1-2 green or red chiles or bell peppers,
    seeded and chopped
  1 tablespoon toasted, crushed sesame
    seeds (*kkaesogeum*, see page 102), for
    garnish

1. Start rice. Prepare the ingredients and place them within easy reach of the stove.
2. Combine the marinade ingredients in a bowl. Add the chicken and rub well with the mixture.
3. Heat a nonstick wok or skillet over medium-high heat. Add the oil. When hot, add the onion and stir-fry 1–2 minutes.
4. Remove the chicken from the marinade, and set the marinade aside. Stir-fry the chicken quickly until lightly browned.
5. Add the mushrooms and stir-fry 1–2 minutes, then stir in the green onions (scallions) and reserved marinade, along with about 4 tablespoons of the mushroom soaking liquid, chicken stock or water. Cover, bring to a boil and simmer gently over low heat for 5–10 minutes, or until the chicken is tender. (If you're using boneless chicken cubes, cook them only 2–3 minutes.) The larger the chicken pieces, the longer they will need to cook.
6. Add the chiles or bell pepper in the last 2 minutes of cooking. Add more stock if the mixture seems dry. Remove to a platter and sprinkle with the sesame seeds. Serve with rice and kimch'i.

Makes 2–3 servings

Broiled Chicken with Sesame Glaze

Tak Kui

The traditional recipe calls for chicken parts, rather than boneless chicken pieces, barbecued over coals. However, boneless chicken cooks much faster. The chicken may be cooked under a broiler or pan-fried.

Marinade

  3 tablespoons reduced-sodium soy sauce
  2 tablespoons toasted, crushed sesame
    seeds (*kkaesogeum*, see page 102)
  2 large cloves garlic, crushed
  One 1-in (2 ½-cm) piece of fresh ginger,
    peeled and minced or grated
  1-2 teaspoons sugar

Freshly ground black pepper and ground
red pepper, to taste
2 teaspoons sesame oil or vegetable oil

• • •

3-4 chicken thighs, scored deeply to allow
marinade to penetrate, or 8-12 oz
(200–300 g) boneless, skinless chicken,
cut into flat slices about 2 in (5 cm)
square
2 green onions (scallions), thinly sliced,
for garnish

1. Combine the marinade ingredients in
a bowl. Stir well to dissolve the sugar.
Coat the chicken pieces thoroughly
and let them stand about 5 minutes.
(Korean cooks usually marinate the
chicken for several hours, but heating

the sauce as described in Step 3 will
make up for short marinating time.)
2. Drain the chicken pieces, reserving
the marianade, and roast them over
coals or under an oven broiler until
brown on both sides. To pan-fry,
add 1 tablespoon of oil to a nonstick wok (or skillet). Cook the
chicken pieces over medium-high
heat until they are browned on
both sides.
3. Add a little water to the remaining
marinade, bring to a boil and pour
over the chicken pieces. Sprinkle
with green onions and serve with
rice and kimch'i.

Makes 2 servings

■ **Beef** ■

Korean-Style Hamburgers

Wanja Jeon

These patties may be either grilled or
pan-fried. Some cooks mix ground
pork with the beef. Though it is not
authentic to Korean cooking, ground
chicken or turkey can also be used.

8-12 oz (225–350 g) ground lean beef
2 tablespoons reduced-sodium soy sauce
2 large cloves garlic, crushed
2 tablespoons toasted, crushed sesame
seeds (*kkaesogeum*, see page 102)
1 (green onion) scallion, thinly sliced
Freshly ground black pepper, to taste
Cornstarch or flour, for dredging
1 egg, slightly beaten
1 tablespoon vegetable oil

1. Start rice. Prepare the ingredients
and place them within easy reach
of the stove.
2. Mix the meat with the soy sauce,

garlic, sesame seeds, green onion
and pepper. Divide into 12 patties. Dredge with the cornstarch or
flour and dip in the beaten egg.
3. Heat a nonstick skillet over
medium-high heat. Add the oil
and, when it is very hot, add the
meat patties. Cook them on both
sides until nicely browned, with no
trace of pink on the inside. Serve
with rice and kimch'i.

Makes 2–3 servings

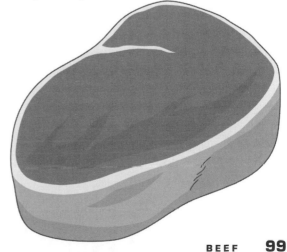

Beef, Vegetable and Noodle Stir-Fry

Chapch'ae

This one-dish meal has a lot of ingredients, but is surprisingly simple to prepare. Transparent (cellophane) noodles are soaked in hot water rather than boiled. Substitute vegetables of your choice, but for a pleasing dish, remember to pick vegetables in a variety of colors.

2-3 oz (50-75 g) Chinese cellophane noodles, soaked in hot water for 20 minutes, then drained and cut into 4-in (10-cm) lengths
2 large cloves garlic, crushed
2 tablespoons reduced-sodium soy sauce
1 teaspoon sugar
8 oz (225 g) flank steak, sliced against the grain into thin bite-size pieces (meat is easier to slice when it is partially frozen)
1½-2 tablespoons vegetable oil
1 onion, quartered, then thinly sliced
1 carrot, scraped and cut into 2-in (5-cm) matchsticks
1 green or red bell pepper or 3 oz (75 g) green beans, cut into 2-in (5-cm) matchsticks
4 dried Chinese mushrooms, soaked in hot water for 25-30 minutes, stemmed, halved and thinly sliced, or 4 medium-sized fresh mushrooms
3 green onions (scallions), cut into 2-in (5-cm) lengths

Garnishes

Freshly ground black pepper or dried red pepper flakes or ground red pepper, to taste
1 tablespoon toasted, crushed sesame seeds (*kkaesogeum*, see page 102)
2 green onions (scallions), thinly sliced

1. Place the noodles in hot water to soak for 20 minutes before using.

After they have soaked, cut them into short lengths. Prepare the remaining ingredients and place them within easy reach of the stove.

2. Combine the garlic, soy sauce and sugar in a bowl and coat the beef pieces.

3. Heat a nonstick wok (or skillet) over medium-high heat and add a little of the oil. Drain the beef, reserving the marinade, and briefly stir-fry until it is lightly browned, about 2 minutes. Remove the beef to a platter and keep warm.

4. Add a little more of the oil and stir-fry the vegetables one at a time until they are tender-crisp. Remove each vegetable as it is cooked and place on the platter with the beef.

5. Add the remaining oil and stir-fry the noodles, tossing to heat evenly. If the mixture seems dry, add a tablespoon or two of water.

6. Return the meat and vegetables to the wok with the noodles. Sprinkle with the pepper and the remaining marinade. Stir-fry a minute or two to heat through and blend the flavors. Remove to a serving platter and sprinkle with the sesame seeds, sliced green onions and additional pepper. Serve with kimch'i and soy sauce.

VARIATION: *Boneless chicken, cut into thin bite-size pieces, may be substituted for the beef. Korean cooks usually prefer the meat from the leg and thigh.*

Makes 2–3 servings

Bulgogi

Bulgogi, barbecued tender beef slices flavored in a soy-sesame marinade, is considered by some to be the national dish of Korea. In restaurants it is cooked at the table by the diner, which can also be done at home on an electric griddle. When the marinated beef slices are stir-fried the dish is called *kogi bokkeum*. There is a third version, as you will see below, called *sangch'i ssam*. Prepared bulgogi marinade is often available in jars where soy sauce is sold, which will shorten preparation time for the hurried cook.

Bulgogi marinade

4 tablespoons reduced-sodium soy sauce

2 tablespoons sul (Korean rice wine) or Chinese rice wine or pale dry sherry (optional)

1 tablespoon sesame oil

One 1-in (2 ½-cm) piece fresh ginger, peeled and finely chopped or grated

2 large cloves garlic, crushed

1 green onion (scallion), thinly sliced

1 tablespoon sugar

Freshly ground black pepper or dried red pepper flakes or ground red pepper, to taste

• • •

12 oz–1 lb (350–450 g) lean, tender flank or sirloin steak, cut across the grain into pieces ¼-in (¾-cm) thick, then into 2 x 1-in (5 x 2½-cm) pieces

1. Start rice.

2. Combine the marinade ingredients in a bowl and stir to dissolve the sugar. Add the beef strips and mix well to coat all sides. Cook immediately or as soon as the rice is finished, or you may let the beef marinate longer.

3. There are three suggested methods for cooking the beef. You may cook the beef on a lightly greased grill about 4 inches above the coals, or under a very hot broiler for about 1 minute on each side, or on a lightly greased electric griddle placed at the table. Do not overcook.

VARIATION 1: *Boneless chicken may also be marinated and cooked Bulgogi style.*

VARIATION 2: *The beef or chicken pieces may be threaded onto bamboo skewers with onions and mushrooms, then charcoal grilled or oven broiled.*

Serving Suggestion

Serve immediately with Sesame Seed Dipping Sauce (below), rice, cucumber salad or another vegetable dish and kimch'i.

Makes 2–3 servings

Sesame Seed Dipping Sauce
Ch'oganjang

2 tablespoons toasted, crushed sesame seeds (*kkaesogeum*, see page 102)

½ –1 teaspoon sugar

3 tablespoons fresh lemon juice or rice vinegar or other mild vinegar

3 tablespoons reduced-sodium soy sauce

1 teaspoon sesame oil (optional)

1-3 tablespoons water, or more, if a subtler taste is desired

1 clove garlic, minced or crushed

1 dried or fresh hot chile or ground red pepper, to taste

1 green onion (scallion), thinly sliced

Combine all the ingredients and stir until sugar dissolves. Divide into individual bowls.

Makes about ⅔ cup

Stir-Fried Beef Strips
Kogi Bokkeum

Cut and marinate the beef as described in the Bulgogi recipe (page 101). Instead of grilling, heat a nonstick wok (or skillet) over high heat and coat with 1 tablespoon oil. Add the beef strips along with 1–2 tablespoons of the bulgogi marinade (page 101). Stir-fry quickly until the meat is browned on both sides, about 2 minutes. Do not overcook. Garnish with some toasted and crushed sesame seeds (right).

Makes 2–3 servings

Vinegar-Soy Dipping Sauce
Ch'ojang

3 tablespoons rice vinegar or cider vinegar
4 tablespoons reduced-sodium soy sauce
1-2 teaspoons sugar or to taste
1 green onion (scallion), thinly sliced

Serving Suggestion

After the beef is stir-fried, divide it on two individual plates. Serve steamed rice and soft lettuce leaves on the plate alongside the beef. To eat, fill a lettuce leaf with meat and rice, and roll up and eat out of the hand. You may wish to serve it with Sesame Seed Dipping Sauce (page 101) or Vinegar-Soy Dipping Sauce (above). In Korean this dish is known as *Sangch'i Ssam*, or beef and rice in lettuce leaves.

Combine the ingredients and stir until the sugar dissolves. Divide into individual bowls. If a subtler taste is desired, a tablespoon or two of water may be added to dilute the mixture.

Makes about ½ cup

Toasted, Crushed Sesame Seeds
Kkaesogeum

This is such an essential seasoning in Korean cooking that it is best to prepare a fair amount in advance and store it in a screw-top jar in the refrigerator. The nutty flavor of sesame seeds is enhanced when the seeds are lightly toasted and crushed.

1 cup (125 g) white sesame seeds
Salt, to taste

1. Place the sesame seeds in a skillet and cook over medium heat for 2–4 minutes, shaking the pan or stirring constantly to prevent scorching. Do not allow the seeds to darken too much or they will turn bitter. Remove from the heat and cool.
2. Sprinkle the seeds with salt and crush them in a pepper grinder or crush them using a mortar and pestle (seeds may also be crushed in a bowl, using the back of a wooden spoon). For low-sodium diets, eliminate the salt. Store in a glass jar.

Makes about 1 cup

Seafood

Pan-Fried Fish

Saengseon Bokkeum

Any fish fillet may be cooked this way—sole, flounder, snapper and salmon—and served with dipping sauce.

> About ½ cup Vinegar-Soy Dipping Sauce
> (*Ch'ojang*, see page 102)
> 8-12 oz (225-350 g) fish fillet, cut into 4
> pieces
> Salt and freshly ground black pepper
> Cornstarch or flour, for dredging
> 1 egg, lightly beaten
> 1 tablespoon vegetable oil
> 1 green onion (scallion), thinly sliced

1. Start rice.
2. Prepare the Vinegar-Soy Dipping Sauce and divide into individual serving bowls.
3. Sprinkle the fish with the salt and pepper, dredge lightly with the cornstarch or flour, and then coat with the beaten egg.

4. Heat a nonstick skillet over medium heat. Add the oil and fry the fish until golden, 1–2 minutes on each side, depending on thickness. Do not overcook. Remove to a warmed platter. Garnish with the sliced green onion and serve with the dipping sauce, rice, salad and kimch'i.

Makes 2 servings

VARIATION: *To make pan-fried shrimp, substitute the fish with 12 large shrimp. Shell and devein the shrimp, leaving the tails intact. Slit the shrimp lengthwise down the back, without cutting all the way through the flesh, and flatten.*

Soups

Fish, Shrimp and Tofu Stew

Saewu Tchigae

A *tchigae* is a peppery hot, chowderlike stew containing a variety of ingredients. This recipe combines fish, shrimp and tofu, but the seafood and vegetable combinations can be used to suit taste and availability of ingredients. A vegetarian tchigae would include only vegetable stock, tofu and vegetables. Tchigae is seasoned with *koch'ujang*, a red bean paste similar to Japanese miso. The

difference is that koch'ujang is laced with hot chiles. If it is not available in your market, miso may be substituted.

2-3 cups (475-700 ml) unsalted chicken or beef stock

2 large cloves garlic, chopped

1 onion, coarsely chopped

3 fresh mushrooms, preferably shiitakes, wiped, trimmed and sliced, or dried mushrooms soaked in hot water for 25-30 minutes, trimmed and sliced

½ small head Chinese (napa) cabbage, leaves cut into 1½-in (4-cm) squares

1 zucchini, sliced

1-2 tablespoons (more or less) Korean bean paste (koch'ujang) or Japanese red miso with ground red pepper added

6 medium shrimp, shelled and deveined, leaving tails intact

6 oz (200 g) firm fish fillet, cut into bite-size pieces

About ½ block (6 oz/175 g) firm tofu, cut into ½-in (1¼-cm) cubes

2 green onions (scallions), green part only, cut into 1-in (2½-cm) lengths

1. Start rice.
2. Place the broth, garlic and onion in a soup pot and bring to a boil. Simmer for about 5 minutes. Add the vegetables and bean paste. It's best to start with a small amount of bean paste because it is very hot. Simmer 10 more minutes, then taste the broth. Stir in more bean paste if desired, or add more broth if the mixture is too spicy.
3. Add the shrimp, fish and tofu and cook for another 2 minutes or until the fish is done. Do not overcook. Add the green onions and serve with rice.

Makes 2–3 servings

Simple Chicken Soup
Tak Kuk

This simple soup may have therapeutic value, if we believe what we read in the newspapers. Chicken soup has been prescribed for colds since Moses Maimonides (AD 1138–1204), a doctor, philosopher and cold researcher, began singing its praises. More recently, the Mayo Clinic and Mount Sinai Medical Center have endorsed chicken soup as a way to soothe cold symptoms and relieve congestion. Another report from a medical center in Los Angeles states that hot pepper and spices are as medicinally valuable as chicken soup. Still other reports promote the use of garlic and ginger. Here is a soup that has all these ingredients. Double the recipe if you want leftovers. It improves overnight.

About 1 lb (450 g) chicken parts, cut into very small pieces for faster cooking (remove the skin for a low-fat soup)

1-2 tablespoons reduced-sodium soy sauce

1 tablespoon vegetable oil

4 large cloves garlic, chopped

4 green onions (scallions), cut into 1-in (2½-cm) lengths

1-3 fresh red or green chiles, seeded and chopped, or dried red pepper flakes, to taste

2-in (5-cm) piece fresh ginger, peeled and cut into thin slices

2-3 cups (475-700 ml) water

Freshly ground black pepper and ground red pepper, to taste

1. Start rice.
2. Coat the chicken pieces with the soy sauce.
3. Heat a heavy-bottomed soup pot over medium-high heat. Add the oil and brown the chicken pieces on both sides. Toss in the garlic

and half of the green onions and fry at the same time.

4. Add the ginger, water and ground black and red pepper; bring to a boil. Skim off the froth. Reduce the heat and cover the pot. Simmer for 15–20 minutes, or until the chicken is tender. Larger pieces of chicken will take longer to cook. Garnish with the remaining green onions and serve with rice.

Makes 2–3 servings

■ Vegetarian Dishes ■

Tofu and Vegetable Stir-Fry

Tubu Bokkeum

Coating the tofu before browning it makes for a richer dish, but the step may be eliminated if you are in a hurry.

> About ½ cup (about 14 oz/400 g) Vinegar-Soy Dipping Sauce (*Ch'ojang*, see page 102)
> 1 block extra-firm tofu (about 14 oz/400 g), cut in half lengthwise, then crosswise into ½-in (1¼-cm)-thick slices
> 1 small Japanese eggplant or small zucchini or both, cut into 2-in (5-cm) matchsticks
> 1 green bell pepper, cored and cut into strips the same size as the eggplant
> 1 onion, quartered, then thinly sliced
> 2 tablespoons vegetable oil
> Cornstarch or flour, for dredging (optional)
> 1 egg, slightly beaten (optional)
> ½ to 1 tablespoon reduced-sodium soy sauce
> 1 green onion (scallion), thinly sliced

1. Start rice. Prepare the ingredients and place them within easy reach of the stove.
2. Make the Vinegar-Soy Dipping Sauce. Divide into individual bowls and set at the table.
3. Optional Step: Dredge the tofu slices lightly in cornstarch or flour and dip in the beaten egg.
4. Heat a nonstick wok (or skillet) over moderate heat. Add half of the oil and rotate the pan to coat the sides. Brown the tofu lightly on both sides, taking care to keep them intact. Arrange on a serving platter and keep warm.
5. Add the remaining oil and stir-fry the vegetables over medium-high heat, one at a time, until tender-crisp. Do not overcook. Mix the vegetables together, stir in a little soy sauce and place on top of the cooked tofu. Sprinkle with sliced green onions and serve with the dipping sauce, rice and kimch'i.

Yield 2–3 servings

Green Onion Pancakes
Phajeon

This tasty snack can be prepared at a moment's notice for a light dinner. Besides green onions (scallions), Korean cooks use many other vegetables in pancakes—watercress, onions, bell peppers, mushrooms, zucchini, lotus root, napa cabbage and even kimch'i. The amount of flour is flexible. Using less flour results in a lighter pancake, more like a French crepe. For non-vegetarian pancakes, try pancakes with beef, liver, oysters and other seafood, or combinations of these ingredients.

4 large eggs
2 tablespoons water
1 teaspoon sesame or vegetable oil
4 tablespoons all-purpose flour
Salt, freshly ground black pepper and
    ground red pepper, to taste
1 carrot, peeled and shredded

6 green onions (scallions), split in half
    lengthwise and cut into 1-in (2½-cm)
    pieces
Oil, for greasing griddle

1. Beat the eggs lightly with water. Add the oil, flour, salt and pepper, and stir until the mixture has the consistency of thick cream. Do not overbeat. Fold in the vegetables.
2. Heat a nonstick griddle or skillet. (Before cooking, test it by letting a few drops of water fall on it. If the water sputters, it is ready to use.) Grease it lightly with a few drops of vegetable oil.
3. Pour enough batter to make a large pancake. When it is brown underneath, turn it with a spatula to brown the other side. Use a few drops of oil for each pancake. Serve with Sesame Seed Dipping Sauce (*Ch'oganjang*, page 101).

Makes 6 large pancakes

■ Salads ■

Kimch'i—a hot and pungent pickle usually made from Chinese (napa) cabbage, but often including head cabbage, turnips, radishes and cucumbers—is such a staple of the Korean diet and appears in so many forms that in Seoul there is a museum that preserves its history and recipes. Kimch'i is perhaps the national vegetable dish. It is served at every meal, even breakfast. It is traditionally made in autumn, in batches large enough to last a family through the following winter and spring. The cabbages are salted overnight. The following day they are rinsed and seasoned with garlic, green onions (scallions), ginger, chiles and anything else the cook thinks will add flavor. The spicy cabbage mixture is then packed in huge earthenware jars and stored underground to ferment. In the villages there are special storerooms built in the ground for this purpose. Many households in large cities have such kimch'i houses, and for apart-

ment dwellers there are communal backyards especially provided for the storing of such jars. A heavy weight must be placed on the lid of the clay jars because once the kimch'i starts to ferment the water drawn by the vegetables "boils" and overflows.

Alas, this process may be a passing art, a victim of our fast-paced lifestyles and mass-produced food. Kimch'i has become one more thing a household can buy commercially prepared at any supermarket, and fortunately it is usually very good. Hotness, pungency and salt content vary from brand to brand. In the United States, every Korean grocery store has its own homemade kimch'i.

Daikon and Pear Salad

Mu Saengch'ae

For the experimental cook, I offer a salad substitute for kimch'i. It's made with Japanese white radish known as daikon, sometimes called Chinese turnip. Hard, crisp Asian pear is added to give a little relief from the pungent radish. Adjust pepper to suit your own taste.

Dressing

2 teaspoons reduced-sodium soy sauce
2–3 tablespoons rice vinegar or other mild
  vinegar
1–2 teaspoons sugar
2 teaspoons sesame oil or vegetable oil
1 large clove garlic, crushed or finely
  chopped (optional)
1 fresh or dried red chile, seeded and finely
  chopped, or ground red pepper, to taste
1 tablespoon toasted, crushed sesame
  seeds (*kkaesogeum*, see page 102)
  (optional)

• • •

1 daikon, about 1 lb (450 g), peeled and cut
  into thin 2-in (5-cm) strips

2 Asian pears or crisp, unripened Western
  pears, cut into the same size pieces as
  the radish
Juice of 1 lemon
2 green onions (scallions), thinly sliced

Combine the dressing ingredients in a serving bowl. Add the daikon, pear and green onions. Mix well.

VARIATION: *For tossed salad, toss your favorite greens with the dressing used for Daikon and Pear Salad.*

Makes 2–3 servings

Blanched Vegetable Salad

Ch'ae and Namul

Simple to make and refreshing to eat, *namul* and *ch'ae* are composed of very briefly cooked vegetables—such as bean sprouts, carrots, cabbage, spinach and watercress—tossed with a soy-sesame dressing. Adjust the proportion of soy sauce to vinegar to suit your own taste, and if the combination seems too strong, dilute it with a little water.

Soy-Sesame dressing

1 tablespoon reduced-sodium soy sauce
1 teaspoon rice vinegar or other mild vinegar
2 teaspoons sesame oil
1 tablespoon toasted, crushed sesame
  seeds (*kkaesogeum*, see page 102)
1 green onion (scallion), thinly sliced
Chili oil or ground red pepper, to taste

Combine the dressing ingredients and stir until the sugar dissolves.

Four suggested salads follow, though any vegetable or combination of vegetables may be blanched and served with soy-sesame dressing.

Spinach Salad
Sigeumch'i Namul

1 lb (450 g) spinach

Discard the roots and tough stems from the spinach and blanch in boiling water for about 1 minute, until wilted but still green. Drain well, squeezing out excess water. Toss with Soy-Sesame Dressing (page 107).

Bean Sprout Salad
Kong Namul

12 oz (350 g) fresh mung or soy bean sprouts, washed and trimmed

Blanch the mung bean sprouts in boiling water for 1 minute and soy bean sprouts, if using, for about 2 minutes. Drain well, dry on paper towels and toss with Soy-Sesame Dressing (page 107).

Carrot and Cabbage Salad
Yangbaech'u Tangeun Ch'ae

3 carrots, scraped and cut into matchsticks
4 oz (100 g) cabbage, preferably Chinese (napa), finely shredded

Blanch the carrot sticks and shredded cabbage in boiling water for about 1 minute. Drain well and mix with Soy-Sesame Dressing (page 107). If you wish, you may eliminate the blanching step and dress the salad as is.

Watercress Salad
Minari Namul

1 large bunch of watercress or 2 small ones, trimmed and cut into 1-in (2½-cm) lengths

Blanch the watercress in boiling water for about 1 minute. Drain well and mix with Soy-Sesame Dressing (page 107). If you wish you may eliminate the blanching step and dress the watercress as is.

Cucumber Salad
Oi Namul

Most Asian cooks, as well as some European ones, salt cucumber and let it stand for half an hour in the brine to wilt before putting it in a salad. If you don't have time for this step, go directly to Step 2.

2 small cucumbers or 1 large one, cut into very thin slices

Dressing
2 tablespoons salt
2 tablespoons rice vinegar
1 teaspoon sugar
1 green onion (scallion), thinly sliced
1 tablespoon toasted, crushed sesame seeds (*kkaesogeum*, see page 102)
Freshly ground black pepper or ground red pepper, to taste

1. Sprinkle the cucumber slices with salt and let stand 30 minutes. Rinse well and drain.
2. Combine the dressing ingredients and mix with the cucumbers. Sprinkle with the sesame seeds.

Makes 2–3 servings

Thailand

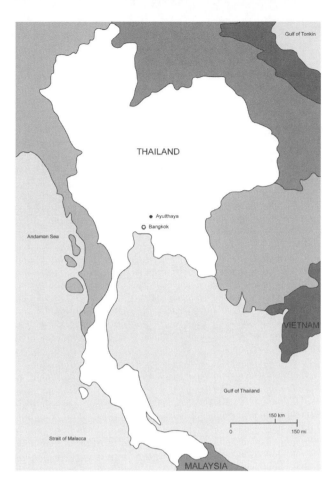

Thailand, like its neighbors in Southeast Asia, has been exposed to many outside influences—cultural, religious and culinary—but it has succeeded in adapting and integrating them more coherently. This is not surprising in view of Thailand's history. Alone among the countries of Southeast Asia, Thailand has never been subject to European colonial rule, and only rarely and briefly has it been overrun by other Asian nations. This long heritage of independence is attributable to an extraordinary succession of scholar-innovator-warrior kings, which can be traced back to the thirteenth century.

The cohesive nature of the monarchy had a profound influence on Thailand's culinary development. Besides carrying out affairs of state, Thai kings encouraged many elegant traditions, including the advancement of culinary arts. They became patrons of the art of cooking, and out of this a royal cuisine developed. It is believed that this cuisine may have originated as a tradition that was practiced when kings had many wives who lived in the palace in their own apartments, each with their own kitchens and a retinue of cooks and servants. They had parties and each wife was expected to furnish one lavish dish, beautifully presented. Actually, these were cooking contests—the king was the judge and he awarded prizes. This was probably the beginning of the creation of the exquisitely carved garnishes the Thai are famous for. It did not take long before many of these palace recipes became known to other classes of Bangkok society.

As in other countries of Southeast Asia, rice is the mainstay of the Thai

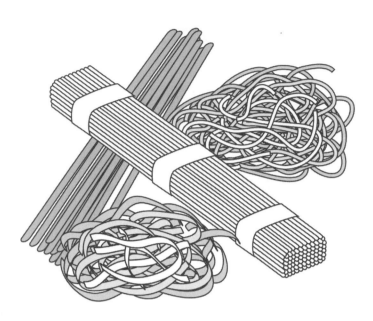

Glutinous or sticky rice is preferred in northeastern Thailand, whose people have more in common with the Laotians, their neighbors to the east who are ethnically Thai, than they do with the Thai of the central plain, who prefer jasmine rice—a long-grain variety also known as fragrant or scented rice. Jasmine rice is also preferred in the southern parts of Thailand. Northern dishes are cooked dry, and the sticky rice is rolled into balls and used in place of an eating utensil to scoop up food. In the South, glutinous rice, also called sweet rice, is used exclusively for sweets and little snacks that are often prepared with coconut milk.

The cuisine of Thailand is a blend of Chinese and Indian culinary influences, expertly integrated into native Southeast Asian specialties. There is a predominance of stir-fried dishes and a spectrum of dishes, from soup to curries, called *kaeng*, which means liquid. This is not surprising since Thai culture has been shaped by both of these influences, and the Chinese comprise by far the largest minority. India exerted its culinary influence as a result of the spice trade with Indonesia, as well as its direct contact with the Khmers in Cambodia. In adapting Chinese stir-fried dishes, the Thai substitute fish sauce (*nam pla*) for soy sauce. Nam pla is so similar to the Vietnamese *nuoc mam* that they may be used interchangeably. Fish sauce is used in Thai cooking as frequently as soy sauce is used in Japanese and Chinese cooking.

diet. It is also the leading agricultural export. It is believed that northeastern Thailand may have been the site of one of the earliest rice cultivations in Asia. It is this extremely fertile central plain that produces two crops of the highest quality rice a year, more than the nation requires to feed its own people. In Thai, even the words for expressing hunger reflect the importance of that food. *Hiu khao* means "I'm hungry for rice." Even when food is referred to in general, the word *khao*, which means rice, is used.

Besides rice, for most of the people who live along the banks of the rivers and canals, freshwater fish is the principal addition to their diet. *Pla tu*, a small mackerel abundant in these waters, is fried and eaten with a bowl of rice and a fiery hot sauce called *nam prik*. Rounding out this diet is the enormous variety of fruits and vegetables that grow year round in the country's lush, tropical climate.

Indian-spiced dishes underwent gradual alteration to meet local tastes, but most dishes called *kaeng*, though they may be described as curries, contain no spices at all. They use garlic and chiles in large quantities, as well as herbs, shallots and *kapi*—a salty, pungent paste made from fermented shrimp, similar to the Indonesian *terasi*. The two exceptions, obviously related to Indian cuisine, are prepared with either beef or chicken. They are *Kaeng Masaman*, or Muslim curry, which contains aromatic spices such as cinnamon and nutmeg, and *Kaeng Kari*, a yellow curry that contains turmeric and cumin. These spices are seldom used in other Thai dishes.

Coconut milk is another important ingredient in Thai cooking, blending together and mellowing stronger flavors. *Kaeng* can also be soup, such as *kaeng chud*, which is a clear, mild broth with chicken,

The cuisine of Thailand is a blend of Chinese and Indian culinary influences, expertly integrated into native Southeast Asian specialties.

squid or vegetables. Other important ingredients in Thai cooking are fresh coriander leaves (cilantro), lemongrass, lime juice, and several varieties of ginger, galangal, mint and basil.

Street food is another important cuisine in the Thai culinary repertory. Rice soup made from chicken or pork broth and sprinkled with fried garlic and red pepper flakes makes a good breakfast. For lunch or at any other time of day, the itinerant noodle vendor makes his appearance with his delicious concoctions. Rice, wheat and egg noodles, either stir-fried or in soups, with combinations of meats and vegetables, are one-dish meals derived from Chinese sources.

Though the majority of the Thai people are Buddhists, there is a small Islamic minority whose food preferences—lamb, for example—are beginning to be incorporated into the Thai cuisine.

Thai Pantry

To keep shopping to a minimum, and to speed preparation and cooking time, it is helpful to keep these Thai staples on hand in your kitchen.

Ingredients with a Long Shelf Life

black pepper, ground

black peppercorns, whole

chiles, dried and whole, or red
   pepper flakes

chili sauce, preferably
   Sriracha brand

coconut milk, unsweetened,
   canned

coriander, ground

curry pastes: green, red, yellow
   and Massaman

fish sauce (*nam pla*)

kaffir lime leaves
   (*bai makrut*)

red pepper, ground

rice, Thai jasmine

rice noodles, flat, dried

rice vinegar

Fresh Ingredients

basil leaves

chiles, preferably small hot Thai
   or bird chiles

coriander leaves (cilantro)

galangal

garlic

ginger

green onions (scallions)

lemongrass

limes

onions

shallots

■ Rice ■

Plain Rice

To make plain sticky rice, follow the recipe for Boiled Rice, Japanese Style (page 67).

To make a drier rice (favored by central and southern Thais), follow the recipe for Plain Rice, Indian Style (page 157), using jasmine or another long-grain rice.

Thai-Style Fried Rice

Khao Phat

Every rice-consuming region in Asia has its own way of using leftover rice to produce the one-pot meal known as fried rice. In this version, tomatoes, tomato ketchup or tomato paste is used as a seasoning, which gives the rice a pinkish color. For best results, the rice should be cold and a day old so the grains have separated and dried out.

1–2 tablespoons vegetable oil

1 small onion, finely chopped

2 large cloves garlic, crushed

8 oz (200 g) lean pork or chicken, cut into bite-size pieces, or 12 medium shrimp, shelled, or use a combination of both

1 large tomato, coarsely chopped

1–2 tablespoons Thai fish sauce (*nam pla*)

1–2 small fresh red Thai chiles, seeded and chopped, or 1 tablespoon Thai chili sauce, preferably Sriracha brand, or dried red pepper flakes, to taste

½–1 tablespoon ketchup

½ teaspoon sugar

1–2 eggs, lightly beaten (optional)

3 cups (750 g) cold cooked rice

2 green onions (scallions), cut into bite-size lengths, for garnish

Chopped fresh coriander leaves (cilantro), for garnish

1. Prepare the ingredients and place them within easy reach of the stove

2. Heat a nonstick wok (or skillet) over medium-high heat. Add half of the oil and rotate the wok to coat the sides. Stir-fry the onion for 1–2 minutes or until it softens. Add the garlic and stir-fry a few seconds longer.

3. Add the pork or chicken and stir-fry until it is nicely browned. If using shrimp, add it now. Stir-fry the shrimp for 1 minute or until it turns pink. Add the tomato and cook for another minute.

4. Stir in the fish sauce, chiles, ketchup and sugar. Stir until the sugar dissolves and the ingredients are well blended.

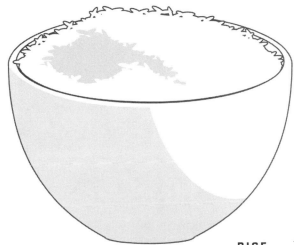

Thailand

5. If using the beaten eggs, make a hole in the center of the mixture and pour them in. Stir gently until they begin to set. Mix in the rice and continue to stir the mixture until the rice heats through and the eggs are completely cooked. Serve garnished with the green onions and chopped coriander leaves.

Makes 2–3 servings

■ Noodles ■

Pad Thai

Noodles play an important part in Thai cuisine, especially for lunch and snacks. *Pad Thai*, made with rice noodles, comes in many versions, using pork, chicken, eggs, and even tofu. If rice noodles are not available, you may substitute Italian linguine.

Sauce

    2 tablespoons Thai fish sauce (*nam pla*)
    1-2 teaspoons tomato ketchup
    2 tablespoons fresh lime juice or rice
        vinegar
    2 teaspoons sugar

• • •

    6 oz (75 g) dried flat rice noodles
    1-2 tablespoons vegetable oil
    3 large cloves garlic, chopped
    1-3 fresh chiles, seeded and chopped, or
    dried red pepper flakes, chili powder or
        ground red pepper, to taste
    6 oz (200 g) medium shrimp, shelled and
        deveined, keeping tails intact
    2 whole eggs or 1 whole egg and 2 egg
        whites, lightly beaten (optional)
    2 green onions (scallions), cut into 1-in
        (2½-cm) lengths
    4 oz (50 g) fresh bean sprouts, trimmed

Garnishes

    2 tablespoons roasted peanuts, chopped
    1-2 fresh red chiles, sliced, or dried red
        pepper flakes, to taste
    Fresh bean sprouts
    Fresh coriander leaves (cilantro)
    1 lime, quartered

1. Combine the sauce ingredients in a small bowl and stir until the sugar dissolves. Set aside. Prepare the remaining ingredients and place them within easy reach of the stove.
2. Soak the rice noodles in a large bowl of hot water for 15 minutes. If substituting linguine, cook it in an ample amount of boiling water, until tender but firm. Drain. Or follow instructions on the noodle wrapper.
3. Heat a nonstick wok (or skillet) over high heat. Add the oil and stir-fry the garlic and chiles for 3–4 seconds. Add the shrimp and stir-fry about one minute or until they begin to turn pink. They

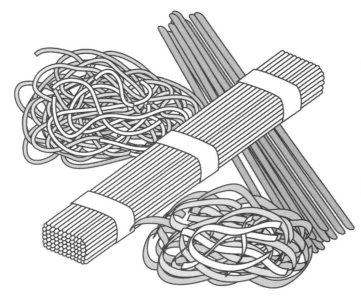

should be only partially cooked at this point. Remove from the wok and keep warm.

4. If you are using the beaten eggs, add a few drops of the oil to the wok and when hot, add the eggs. Let them sit in the wok for 20–30 seconds to begin to firm up. Then scramble them gently, breaking them into small pieces.

5. Return the shrimp to the wok with the eggs and mix well. Stir in the sauce and bring to a gentle boil.

6. Drain the noodles and gently toss them into the shrimp mixture. Cook until the noodles have heated through and absorbed the sauce, stirring constantly. Add the green onions and bean sprouts, reserving a few to garnish the finished dish. Stir until heated through.

7. Transfer to a platter and serve sprinkled with garnishes.

VARIATION: *Pork or chicken, cut into bite-size pieces, may be substituted for the shrimp, or you may wish to use a combination of these ingredients.*

Makes 2–3 servings

■ Chicken ■

Stir-Fried Chicken with Cilantro

Kai Phat Pak Chi

Fresh coriander leaves (cilantro) have a pungent flavor, which some people love and others find too strong. Adjust the quantity to suit your own taste.

1 tablespoon vegetable oil

3 large cloves garlic, finely chopped

1–3 fresh red chile peppers, seeded and chopped, or dried red pepper flakes, to taste

8–12 oz (200–300 g) boneless, skinless, chicken breast or leg meat cut into thin bite-size slices

½ to 1 cup (25 g) chopped fresh coriander leaves (cilantro), coarse stems removed

½ to 1 teaspoon freshly ground black pepper, or to taste

1–2 tablespoons Thai fish sauce (*nam pla*)

1 tablespoon fresh lime juice, or substitute lemon juice or rice vinegar

½ teaspoon sugar

2 green onions (scallions) cut into 2-in (5-cm) lengths, for garnish

1. Start rice. Prepare the ingredients and place them within easy reach of the stove.

2. Heat a nonstick wok (or skillet) over high heat. Add the oil and stir-fry the garlic and chiles for 3–4 seconds. Add the chicken and stir-fry 1–2 minutes or until it is no longer pink.

3. Add the coriander leaves and stir-fry 10 seconds, or until wilted.

4. Stir in the remaining ingredients, except the garnish, and cook for a minute or two to blend the flavors. If the mixture seems dry, add a tablespoon or two of water to prevent scorching. Garnish with the green onions and serve with rice.

Makes 2 servings

Stir-Fried Basil Chicken with Eggplant

Kai Phat Bai Kaprao

Several varieties of basil are used in Thai cooking, and some are more mintlike than others. Western sweet basil is close enough to make a good substitute, or use fresh mint.

> 2 tablespoons vegetable oil
> 1 small onion, quartered and finely chopped
> 1-3 fresh green chiles, chopped, or dried red pepper flakes, to taste
> 2 large cloves garlic, chopped
> 8-12 oz (200–300) boneless chicken breast or leg meat, cut into thin bite-size slices
> 1 Thai (or Chinese or Japanese) eggplant (about 6 oz/175 g), unpeeled, cut in half lengthwise and thinly sliced
> 1 tablespoon Thai fish sauce (*nam pla*)
> 1 tablespoon reduced-sodium soy sauce
> ½ teaspoon sugar
> 1 tablespoon rice vinegar
> About ¾ cup (40 g) fresh basil leaves

1. Start rice. Prepare the ingredients and place them within easy reach of the stove.

2. Heat a nonstick wok (or skillet) over high heat. Add half of the oil and stir-fry the onion and chiles until the onion softens, 1–2 minutes. Add the garlic and stir-fry 3–4 seconds.

3. Add the chicken and stir-fry 1–2 minutes or until it is no longer pink. Remove from the wok and keep warm.

4. Heat the wok again over high heat and add the remaining oil. Stir-fry the eggplant slices for 4–5 minutes, or until they soften and begin to brown.

5. Return the chicken to the wok. Add the fish sauce, soy sauce, sugar and vinegar. Stir well to dissolve the sugar. If the mixture seems dry, add a tablespoon or two of water to keep it from scorching. Cook until the chicken is heated through.

6. Turn off the heat. Add the basil leaves and stir for another minute, or until the leaves begin to wilt. Serve immediately with rice.

Makes 2–3 servings

Chicken with Chiles and Cashews

Kai Phat

Originally a Chinese dish, Thai cooks have changed the seasoning to make this their own. As with other dishes, there are many variations. This one is simple and mild. Leaving the chiles whole adds more visual and aromatic impact than heat.

Sauce

> 1 tablespoon Thai fish sauce (*nam pla*)
> 1 tablespoon oyster sauce
> 1-3 teaspoons Thai red curry paste or Thai chili sauce, preferably Sriracha brand
> 1 teaspoon sugar
> 2-3 tablespoons unsalted chicken stock or water
> 1 teaspoon cornstarch (optional)

• • •

2 tablespoons vegetable oil

4 small fresh red chiles, preferably Thai or bird chiles

2 large cloves garlic, crushed

8-12 oz (200-300 g) boned chicken breast or leg meat, cut into thin bite-size slices

12 snow peas, tips and strings removed

3 tablespoons whole roasted cashews

Fresh coriander leaves (cilantro), for garnish

1. Start rice. Prepare the ingredients and place them within easy reach of the stove.
2. Combine the sauce ingredients in a small bowl and set aside. If you prefer a thicker sauce, mix the cornstarch with 2 tablespoons of water and stir in with the sauce.
3. Heat a nonstick wok (or skillet) over high heat. Add the oil and stir-fry the chiles (left whole) until they begin to darken. Place them on a paper towel to drain and set aside.
4. Stir in the garlic and cook for 3–4 seconds, until fragrant. Add the chicken and stir-fry briskly 1–2 minutes, or until it is no longer pink. Add the snow peas and stir-fry another minute.
5. Stir in the sauce, reduce the heat and simmer for 1 minute. Add more water if the mixture seems dry. Mix in the cashews. Turn onto a heated platter and garnish with the reserved chiles and coriander leaves. Serve with rice.

Makes 2 servings

Thai-Style Barbecued Chicken

Kai Yang

Barbecued chicken may be found from morning till night in outdoor stalls all over Thailand. Each region of the country has its own marinade, but the look of the bird is the same—tiny butterflied chickens, grilled over charcoal fires, brown and crisp, served with a spicy sauce.

Curry marinade

2 large cloves garlic, minced

2 tablespoons grated fresh ginger

1-2 tablespoon Thai yellow curry paste or

2 tablespoons curry powder mixed with ½ teaspoon turmeric and ground red pepper

1-2 tablespoons Thai fish sauce (*nam pla*)

2 teaspoons brown sugar

1 tablespoon mild vinegar

1 tablespoon vegetable oil

• • •

About 1 lb (425 g) bone-in chicken pieces, cut into small pieces for faster cooking

Chopped fresh coriander leaves (cilantro) or green onions (scallions), for garnish

1. Start rice.
2. Combine the marinade ingredients in a large bowl and coat the chicken pieces thoroughly. If there is time, marinate them in the refrigerator for 15 minutes to 2 hours or overnight.
3. The chicken may be broiled or baked. *To Broil*: Preheat broiler to low. Broil the chicken on both sides until done. *To Bake*: Place the chicken in a lightly oiled baking dish and bake at 375°F (190°C) for about 20 minutes, turning to brown both sides. (Larger pieces may take 30 minutes, or a little longer.)
4. Garnish with the coriander leaves and serve with rice, Thai Cucumber Salad (page 127) and Red Chili Dipping Sauce (*Nam Prik*, page 132) or Sweet-and-Sour Chili Sauce (page 192).

Makes 2 servings

Seafood

Garlic-Ginger Shrimp with Vegetables

Phat Kung kap Khing

Some markets sell shrimp already peeled and deveined, and others sell them pre-cooked, which reduces preparation and cooking time considerably.

Sauce

2 tablespoons Thai fish sauce (*nam pla*)

1 teaspoon sugar

Freshly ground black pepper and ground red pepper, to taste

2 tablespoons unsalted chicken stock or water

• • •

1½ tablespoons vegetable oil

2 tablespoons grated fresh ginger

2 large cloves garlic, crushed

1–3 fresh red chiles, seeded and thinly sliced, or dried red pepper flakes, to taste

8–12 oz (300–450 g) medium shrimp, shelled and deveined, leaving tails intact

1 green bell pepper, cut into thin strips, or 1 cup (175 g) broccoli florets or another quick-cooking green vegetable

6 fresh mushrooms, sliced, or canned straw mushrooms

6 ears baby corn, frozen or canned

Chopped fresh coriander leaves (cilantro), for garnish

1. Start rice. Prepare the ingredients and place them within easy reach of the stove.
2. Combine the sauce ingredients in a small bowl and set aside.
3. Heat a nonstick wok (or skillet) over high heat. Add half of the oil and stir-fry the ginger, garlic and chiles for a few seconds to flavor the oil.
4. Add the shrimp and stir-fry until they begin to change color, 1–2 minutes depending on their size. If you're using cooked shrimp, stir-fry them a few seconds to coat them with the flavored oil. Remove from the pan and keep warm.
5. Add the remaining oil and heat over high heat. Add the bell pepper, mushrooms and baby corn, and stir-fry until tender but still crunchy, 2–3 minutes.
6. Return the shrimp to the wok. Mix in the sauce and stir until the sugar dissolves and the shrimp heats through. If the mixture seems dry, add another tablespoon or two of water to prevent scorching. Do not overcook or the shrimp will toughen. Garnish with the coriander leaves (cilantro) and serve with rice.

Makes 2–3 servings

Pan-Fried Fish with Mushrooms and Ginger Sauce

Pla Tod kap Khing

Any fish fillet or fish steak may be prepared this way. The secret to success is to use the freshest fish and to not overcook it.

Sauce

> 1 tablespoon Thai fish sauce (*nam pla*)
> 1 teaspoon reduced-sodium soy sauce
> 3 tablespoons fresh lime or lemon juice or rice vinegar
> 2 teaspoons sugar
> 2 tablespoons water
>
> • • •
>
> 8-12 oz (225-350 g) fish steaks or fillets
> Cornstarch or flour, for dredging
> 1 tablespoon vegetable oil
> 6 fresh mushrooms, sliced
> 4 tablespoons grated fresh ginger
> Chopped fresh coriander leaves (cilantro) or green onions (scallions), for garnish

1. Start rice. Prepare the ingredients and place them within easy reach of the stove.
2. Combine the sauce ingredients in a small bowl and set aside.
3. Dredge the fish lightly in the cornstarch or flour. Heat a nonstick wok (or skillet) over medium-high heat. Add 1 tablespoon of the oil and brown both sides of the fish. Depending on thickness, this should take barely 1–2 minutes on each side. Test for donenesss with a fork. Remove to a heated platter and keep warm.
4. In the same wok, add a few drops more of the oil if necessary, and stir-fry the mushrooms until they soften.
5. Add the ginger and stir-fry another few seconds. Add the sauce and stir until the mixture comes to a boil. Reduce the heat and simmer for

about 1 minute. Pour over the fish and garnish with the coriander leaves or green onions. Serve with rice.

Makes 2 servings

Cod Fillets with Snow Peas and Lemongrass

In addition to cod, other firm white fish will be equally delicious in this recipe.

Sauce

> 1-2 tablespoons Thai fish sauce (*nam pla*)
> Juice of 1 lime
> ½-1 teaspoon freshly ground black pepper
> 1 teaspoon sugar
>
> • • •
>
> 1-2 tablespoons vegetable oil
> 2 large cloves garlic, chopped
> 2 stalks fresh lemongrass, ends trimmed, tough outer leaves removed, thinly sliced, or substitute grated zest of 1 lemon
> 1-3 fresh or dried chiles, seeded and chopped, or dried red pepper flakes, to taste
> 8-12 oz (225-350 g) cod or other firm fish fillets, cut into 4 serving pieces
> 4 fresh mushrooms, sliced (optional)
> 6 oz (100 g) snow peas, tips and strings removed
> Fresh coriander leaves (cilantro), for garnish

1. Start rice. Prepare the ingredients and place them within easy reach of the stove.
2. Combine the sauce ingredients in a small bowl and set aside.
3. Heat a nonstick wok (or skillet) over medium heat. Add half of the oil and stir-fry the garlic, lemongrass and chiles for 3–4 seconds
4. Add the fish fillets and brown on both sides. Depending on thickness, this should take 1–2 minutes

on each side. Test for doneness with a fork. Remove from the wok and keep warm.

5. Heat the wok over high heat and add the remaining oil. Stir-fry the mushrooms and snow peas for 1–2 minutes, until tender-crisp. Stir in the sauce and bring to a boil. Reduce the heat and simmer for 30 seconds.

6. Return the fish to the wok and cook for a few seconds until it is heated through. Garnish with the coriander leaves and serve with rice.

Makes 2 servings

Fillet of Snapper with Lime-Chile Sauce

This is the simplest of fish recipes. The sauce ingredients can be adjusted to suit your own taste.

Sauce
    1-3 fresh red chiles, seeded and chopped,
        or dried red pepper flakes or Thai chile
        sauce, preferably Sriracha brand, to taste
    1 tablespoon Thai fish sauce (*nam pla*)
    4 tablespoons fresh lime juice
    1 tablespoon sugar
    2-3 tablespoons water

         •   •   •

    1 tablespoon vegetable oil
    8-12 oz (225–350 g) snapper fillets (or
        substitute salmon, cod or tilapia)
    2 large cloves garlic, chopped
    Chopped fresh coriander leaves (cilantro)
        and lime wedges, for garnish

1. Start rice. Prepare the ingredients and place them within easy reach of the stove.

2. Combine the sauce ingredients in a small bowl and set aside.

3. Heat a nonstick wok (or skillet) over medium heat. Add the oil.

Lightly brown the fish, depending on thickness, about 1–2 minutes on each side. Remove to a serving platter and keep warm.

4. Add a few more drops of the oil, if necessary, and stir-fry the garlic and chiles for 3–4 seconds until fragrant. Add the sauce and stir until the mixture comes to a boil. Reduce the heat and simmer for about 1 minute. Pour over the fish and garnish with the coriander leaves.

Makes 2 servings

Fish Steamed with Ginger
Pla Nung Khing

This is a basic recipe for steamed fish. Almost any whole fish, fillet or steak may be used. If you don't own a steamer, improvise one in your wok or skillet. Use an empty tuna can (top and bottom removed) as a stand under a heatproof dish.

    8-12 oz (225–350 g) fish fillets or steaks
        (snapper, halibut, sole or salmon) or
        1 small whole fish for (2 servings),
        cleaned, scaled and scored
    1-2 tablespoons Thai fish sauce (*nam pla*)
    1 tablespoon or more fresh lemon juice
    One 2-in (5-cm) piece fresh ginger, peeled
        and cut into thin matchsticks
    2 large cloves garlic, chopped
    2 stalks fresh lemongrass, ends trimmed,
        tough outer leaves removed, thinly sliced,
        or substitute grated zest of 1 lemon
    1-2 fresh red chiles, seeded and thinly
        sliced, or dried red pepper flakes or
        Thai chile sauce, preferably Sriracha
        brand, to taste
    2 green onions (scallions), sliced
    Freshly ground black pepper, to taste
    Chopped fresh coriander leavers (cilantro),
        for garnish

1. Start rice.
2. Rub the fish on both sides with the fish sauce and lemon juice and place in a shallow, heatproof serving dish that will fit in your steamer.
3. Sprinkle the remaining ingredients, except the garnish, on top. If you're cooking a whole fish, place some of the ingredients inside the cavity.
4. Bring water in the steamer to a rolling boil. Put the dish over the water inside the steamer. Do not allow water to get onto the platter with the fish. Turn the heat down, cover and steam 8–10 minutes to the inch, or until it flakes when prodded with a fork and is cooked through to the middle. Do not overcook. Remove the dish from steamer and garnish with the coriander leaves. Serve with rice.

Makes 2–3 servings

Pork

Stir-Fried Pork with Green Beans

Phat Mu

This is a very colorful dish with lots of red and green. Do not overcook the vegetables or they will lose their bright color. Though Thai cooks prefer pork, beef or chicken may be substituted.

> 1 tablespoon vegetable oil
> 2 large cloves garlic, finely chopped
> 1-2 red chiles, seeded and thinly sliced
> One 1-in (2½-cm) piece fresh ginger, peeled and sliced (optional)
> 8-12 oz (200-300 g) lean, boneless pork, cut into thin bite-size pieces
> 8-12 oz (175-250 g) Chinese long beans or regular green beans, trimmed and cut diagonally into 1-in (2½-cm) lengths
> 1-2 tablespoons Thai fish sauce (*nam pla*)
> Freshly ground black pepper, to taste

1. Start rice. Prepare the ingredients and place them within easy reach of the stove.
2. Heat a nonstick wok (or skillet) over high heat. Add the oil and stir-fry the garlic, chiles and ginger for 3–4 seconds. Add the pork and stir-fry about 2 minutes, or until it is no longer pink.
3. Add the green beans and stir-fry briskly about 2 minutes.
4. Reduce the heat. Stir in the fish sauce, black pepper and 2 tablespoons of water to further cook beans. Simmer until the water is absorbed. The beans should be tender but crisp and green. Serve with rice.

Makes 2 servings

Sweet-and-Sour Pork

Phat Mu Prio Wan

This dish derives from south China (Canton), where the meat of choice is pork. Some cooks add a little tomato sauce or even ketchup to the sauce.

Sauce

> 2 tablespoons white vinegar
> 2 tablespoons sugar
> 1 tablespoon Thai fish sauce (*nam pla*)

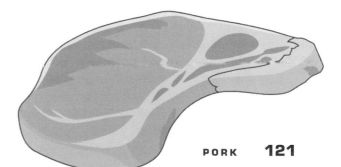

1 tablespoon tomato sauce or ketchup

2 tablespoons juice from pineapple or
    unsalted chicken stock or water

1 teaspoon cornstarch (optional)

• • •

1½–2 tablespoons vegetable oil

1 small onion, chopped

2 large cloves garlic, chopped

1-3 fresh chiles, seeded and thinly sliced,
    or dried red pepper flakes or ground
    red pepper, to taste

8-12 oz (200–300 g) lean, boneless pork or
    beef, cut into thin bite-size pieces

2 tomatoes, chopped (optional)

1 small cucumber or half of a large one,
    peeled, leaving strips of green for
    color, cut in half lengthwise and sliced

4 fresh mushrooms, sliced, or use canned
    straw mushrooms

2 slices fresh or canned pineapple (reserve
    juice for sauce), cut into bite-size pieces

3 green onions (scallions), cut into 1-in
    (2½-cm) lengths

Fresh coriander leaves (cilantro), for garnish

1. Start rice. Prepare the ingredients and place them within easy reach of the stove.

2. Combine the sauce ingredients in a small bowl and stir until the sugar dissolves. Set aside.

3. Heat a nonstick wok (or skillet over) high heat. Add half of the oil and stir-fry the onion for 1–2 minutes, or until soft. Add the garlic and chiles and stir-fry 3–4 seconds.

4. Add the pork or beef and stir-fry over high heat about 2 minutes, or until the pork, if using, is no longer pink. Remove to a platter and keep warm.

5. Heat the remaining oil and add, one at a time, the tomatoes, cucumber, mushrooms, pineapple and green onions, stir-frying after each addition.

6. Return the meat to the wok and stir-fry for a few seconds. Blend in the sauce and bring to a boil. If you prefer a thicker sauce, add the cornstarch mixed with 1 tablespoon of water. Reduce the heat and simmer for 1 minute. Garnish with the coriander leaves and serve with rice.

VARIATION: *Fresh shrimp may be substituted for the pork. Stir-fry about 1 minute or until the shrimp turns pink. Do not overcook or it will toughen.*

Makes 2 servings

■ Soups ■

Hot-and-Sour Shrimp Soup

Dom Yam Kung

Hot-and-sour shrimp soup is enjoyed by both Thais and Vietnamese, and is known by the latter as *Can Chua Tom*. In an effort to make it a full-meal soup, this is an adaptation of both versions. The base is chicken stock to which sour and spicy seasonings are added. Whole chiles add color, flavor and a little heat. For a spicier dish, bruise the chiles slightly or slice them.

Stock

3 cups (700 ml) unsalted chicken stock

2 fresh whole red chiles

2 fresh or dried kaffir lime leaves (*bai makrut*) or strips of peel from 1 lime

2 slices fresh or frozen galangal (*kha*) or substitute 2 slices peeled fresh ginger

2 stalks fresh lemongrass, ends trimmed, tough outer leaves removed, sliced and then chopped, or substitute strips of peel from 1 lemon

2 cloves garlic, chopped

½–1 teaspoon sugar

• • •

4 fresh mushrooms, sliced, or canned straw mushrooms

2 tomatoes, quartered

6–8 oz (225–300 g) medium shrimp, shelled and deveined, leaving tails intact

1 handful fresh bean sprouts, trimmed

1 slice fresh or canned pineapple, cut into small pieces

2 tablespoons fresh lime juice

2 tablespoons Thai fish sauce (*nam pla*)

Freshly ground black pepper and ground red pepper, to taste

Chopped fresh coriander leaves (cilantro) and lime wedges, for garnish

1. Start rice. Prepare the ingredients and place them within easy reach of the stove.

2. In a large soup pot, bring the stock ingredients to a boil, reduce the heat and simmer for about 5 minutes.

3. Add the mushrooms and tomatoes and simmer for another 2 minutes.

4. Add the shrimp and cook for 1 minute or until the shrimp turn pink. Do not overcook or they will become rubbery.

5. Add the bean sprouts, pineapple, lime juice, fish sauce and pepper, and simmer for another minute. Sprinkle with the coriander leaves and serve with rice. The soup should have a sour taste. Add more lime juice, fish sauce and chili sauce at the table for stronger taste, if desired.

Note: For a more flavorful broth, some cooks do not discard the shrimp shells, but instead boil them with the chicken stock and then strain the stock before adding the remaining ingredients.

VARIATION 1: *Boneless and skinless chicken cut into bite-size pieces may be substituted for the shrimp. This variation is known as* Dom Yam Kai.

VARIATION 2: *For a vegetarian soup, substitute tofu cut into ½-inch cubes for the shrimp and substitute vegetable stock for the chicken stock.*

Makes 2–3 servings

Noodle Soup with Chicken and Shrimp

This wholesome and quick soup gets its delicious and unmistakably Thai flavor signature from *nam pla*, or Thai fish sauce, and the bright pungency of fresh coriander leaves (cilantro).

4 oz (50 g) cellophane noodles

1 tablespoon vegetable oil

2 cloves garlic, minced

⅓ cup finely chopped onions

6 oz (150 g) boneless dark meat chicken, cut into small pieces

6 mushrooms, sliced

6 shrimp, shelled and deveined, keeping tails intact

2–3 cups (475–700 ml) unsalted chicken broth

2 teaspoons Thai fish sauce (*nam pla*), or to taste

1 teaspoon ground coriander

Salt, freshly ground black pepper and chili pepper, to taste

Chopped fresh coriander leaves (cilantro), for garnish

1. Soak the noodles in warm water for 15 minutes. Rinse, drain and cut into short lengths.
2. Heat the oil in a large saucepan over high heat. Stir-fry the garlic and onions for 2 minutes until translucent. Add the chicken and mushrooms and stir-fry 2 minutes. Add the chicken stock, fish sauce, noodles and seasonings. Add the shrimp and cook until done, about 2 minutes
3. Garnish with the coriander leaves.

Makes 2–3 servings

Chicken Soup with Coconut Milk
Dom Kha Kai

One of the most popular Thai dishes, this creamy soup is suitable for a light meal. Though galangal (*kha*), is a member of the ginger family, it has a different taste and aroma from ginger root. It is available in Asian shops and some supermarkets. When left whole, chiles add color, flavor and a little heat. For a spicier dish, bruise the chiles slightly or slice them.

> 1½ cups (375 ml) unsalted chicken stock
> 1 can (14 oz/415 ml) unsweetened coconut milk (shake can before using)
> 4 thin slices fresh or frozen galangal (*kha*) or fresh ginger
> 1 stalk fresh lemongrass, end trimmed, tough outer leaves removed, sliced into 2-in (5-cm) pieces, or substitute strips of peel from ½ lemon
> 4 kaffir lime leaves (*bai makrut*) or substitute strips of peel from ½ lime
> 2 fresh whole chiles
> 8-12 oz (200-300) boned chicken breast meat or leg meat, cut into thin bite-size slices (pre-cooked chicken may also be used)

> 4 large fresh mushrooms, sliced, or canned straw mushrooms
> 1 tablespoon or more Thai fish sauce (*nam pla*)
> 1 tablespoon or more fresh lime juice
> Freshly ground black pepper and ground red pepper, to taste
> Fresh coriander leaves (cilantro), for garnish

1. Start rice. Prepare the ingredients and place them within easy reach of the stove.
2. Over medium heat, bring the chicken stock, coconut milk, galangal, lemongrass, lime leaves and chiles to a very gentle simmer, stirring constantly. Do not boil.
3. Add the chicken and simmer it until it is cooked, about 2–3 minutes, depending on size of pieces. Breast meat will toughen if overcooked.
4. Add the mushrooms and simmer another minute or two.
5. Stir in the fish sauce, lime juice and pepper, and remove from the heat. Sprinkle with the coriander leaves and serve with rice. Add more fish sauce or lime juice at the table for stronger taste, if desired.

Makes 2–3 servings

Thai Noodle Soup
Gwaytio Nam

A popular lunch, this soup can be purchased from street vendors all over Thailand. *Gwaytio* is a wide, fresh rice noodle served in stock. Pork is the meat of choice for this dish, but slices of chicken, seafood or tofu may be added. The diner then selects the seasonings and condiments he or she prefers and sprinkles them on top of the soup. For this recipe, almost any kind of noodle—rice, egg or wheat—will do.

6 oz (75 g) fresh or dried noodles, cooked,
or soaked and drained

3 cups (700 ml) unsalted chicken stock plus
1 tablespoon Thai fish sauce (*nam pla*)

1 cup (about 225 g) chicken, beef, pork,
shrimp, or tofu, or a mixture, cut into
bite-size pieces (pre-cooked chicken,
meat or shrimp may also be used)

2 green onions (scallions), cut into 1-in
(2½-cm) pieces

Chopped fresh coriander leaves (cilantro),
for garnish

Seasonings and condiments

4 large cloves garlic, sliced and crisply
browned in 1 teaspoon oil

Onions, sliced and crisply browned (may be
purchased already cooked in jars or packets)

Dried red pepper flakes

Thai fish sauce (*nam pla*) and soy sauce

Thai chili sauce, preferably Sriracha brand

Roasted peanuts

1 lime, cut into wedges

1. Prepare the ingredients, seasonings and condiments.
2. Cook the noodles in an ample amount of boiling water until tender but firm, or follow instructions on the noodle wrapper. Drain. Divide the hot noodles into large, deep soup bowls. Keep warm.
3. In the meantime, bring the chicken stock to a boil. Add the chicken meat and tofu, return to a boil and cook for about 2 minutes, or until done. Add the green onions and cook for another 30 seconds.
4. Pour the boiling soup over the noodles. Garnish with the coriander leaves.
5. Serve with the condiments, seasonings and rice.

Makes 2–3 servings

Salads & Vegetables

Thai Beef Salad

Yam Nya

This is best when the steak is broiled over coals, but oven broiling will produce very good results too. For a fine meal without doing any cooking at all, buy pre-cooked beef from a good delicatessen and assemble it with the other ingredients. Adjust the amount of hot pepper to suit your own taste.

Dressing

6 tablespoons fresh lime juice

2 tablespoons Thai fish sauce (*nam pla*)

2 tablespoons each coarsely chopped fresh
mint leaves and fresh coriander leaves
(cilantro)

1 large clove garlic, crushed

1 teaspoon sugar

1–2 fresh chiles, seeded and chopped, or
dried red pepper flakes or ground red
pepper, to taste

• • •

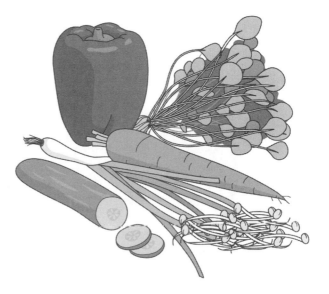

1 small cucumber, scored and thinly sliced

2 tomatoes, sliced

1-2 shallots or 1 small red onion, thinly sliced

Lettuce leaves

8-12 oz (225–350 g) flank steak or other lean, tender beef

1 green onion (scallion), sliced, and 1 lime cut into wedges, for garnish

1. Combine the dressing ingredients in a bowl and set aside.
2. Slice the vegetables and arrange on a platter lined with lettuce leaves.
3. Grill or broil the steak until medium rare, about 3–5 minutes on each side. Let stand 5 minutes. Slice the meat across the grain into thin slices and arrange on the platter with the vegetables.
4. Pour the dressing over the meat and vegetables and garnish with green onions and lime wedges. Serve with rice or crusty bread.

VARIATION: *Cooked chicken may be substituted for the beef.*

Makes 2 servings

Sweet-and-Sour Fruit Salad with Shrimp
Yam Polamai kap Kung

In recent years, Thai chefs in Bangkok have extended traditional recipes to include unusual combinations like this one, which is made with local fruits, both sour and sweet. Sour green mangoes and green papayas are served with sweet roseapples, mangosteens and pomelo. However, unless you live in the tropics or your grocer stocks exotic fruits, the above combination is out of the question. Why not use whatever fruits are in season where you live? This makes a light, refreshing meal and, if you buy the shrimp pre-

cooked at your local fish market, the recipe will require no cooking at all.

14 pre-cooked or raw medium shrimp

A selection of fruit, cut into bite-size pieces, such as:

    Green tart apple and 1 grapefruit or 2 oranges, peeled and sectioned

    Pear, peach, plum or melon, and a few grapes

    Strawberries

    Mangoes or papayas

1 teaspoon fresh lime juice

1 handful chopped roasted peanuts and mint leaves, for garnish

2 cloves garlic and 1 shallot or half of a small red onion, thinly sliced, for garnish (optional)

Dressing

6 tablespoons fresh lime juice

2 tablespoons Thai fish sauce (*nam pla*), or to taste

1-2 teaspoons sugar

1 fresh chile, seeded and chopped, or dried red pepper flakes, to taste

1. Arrange the sliced fruit on a platter. Sprinkle with the lime juice to keep from oxidizing.
2. Optional Step: If you are using uncooked shrimp, boil them in about a quart of water with 2 bay leaves and 2 garlic cloves. Simmer the shrimp for 2–4 minutes, depending on size, or until pink but not tightly curled. Drain immediately and chill.
3. Combine the dressing ingredients in a bowl and dip the cooked shrimps in the sauce briefly to season them. Remove the shrimp from the dressing and arrange them alongside the fruit. Pour the remaining dressing over the fruit.
4. Sprinkle with the peanuts and garnish with the mint leaves.
5. Optional Step: If you're using the optional garnish, lightly brown

Thailand

the sliced garlic and shallot (or red onion) in a teaspoon of oil, then sprinkle over the salad and serve.

VARIATION: *Cooked chicken may be substituted for shrimp, or use a combination of both.*

Makes 2 servings

Cucumber Salad
Yam Daengwa

Highly-seasoned foods need mild-flavored accompaniments for balance and contrast. What could be better than the cool, crisp texture of the cucumber? It is served frequently in Southeast Asian cooking alongside curries, satays and other highly seasoned dishes. The thin Japanese or English cucumber is preferable and does not need peeling. The thick-skinned Western variety does. Note that no oil is used in Asian salads, making them lower in calories. However, the ubiquitous fish sauce and other seasonings are high in sodium so should be used sparingly.

> 2 small cucumbers or 1 large one, cut in
> half lengthwise and thinly sliced

Dressing
> ¼ cup fresh lime or lemon juice or rice
> vinegar
> 2 teaspoons sugar
> 2 small shallots or ¼ small red onion,
> finely chopped
> 1-2 fresh chiles, seeded and finely
> chopped, or dried red pepper flakes or
> ground red pepper, to taste
> 1 tablespoon Thai fish sauce (*nam pla*)
> 1-2 tablespoons chopped fresh coriander
> leaves (cilantro) or mint leaves

1. Slice the cucumbers and place them in a serving bowl.

2. Combine the dressing ingredients and stir until the sugar dissolves. Pour over the cucumbers and mix well.

Makes 2–3 servings

Pomelo Salad
Yam Som-O

Pomelo, a tropical citrus fruit, looks and tastes like a grapefruit, but has a different texture. It has become available in some markets, but if you cannot find it, substitute grapefruit.

> 1 pomelo or 2 grapefruits, peeled, skinned
> and sectioned

Dressing
> 1 large clove garlic, chopped
> ½-1 tablespoon Thai fish sauce (*nam pla*)
> 3-4 tablespoons fresh lime juice
> 2 teaspoons palm or brown sugar

Garnish
> 2 small shallots or ½ small red onion,
> finely chopped
> 2 large cloves garlic, thinly sliced
> 1 tablespoon vegetable oil

1. Arrange the pomelo or grapefruit on a serving platter. Mix the dressing and pour over the fruit.
2. Brown the shallots and garlic in a little oil. Drain on a paper towel and sprinkle on top of the dressed fruit.

Makes 3–4 servings

Stir-Fried Greens

Thai stir-fries are similar to Chinese ones, but instead of soy sauce, the seasoning of choice is fish sauce (*nam pla*). *Pak bung*, the most common green vegetable in Thailand, grows in water and looks like spinach. It is delicious stir-fried, and almost all greens may be cooked this way. You may substitute spinach, dandelion greens, mustard greens, bok choy, Chinese cabbage or Swiss chard. Tender young greens cook quickly within a minute or two. Only 2 garlic cloves are used in this recipe, but Thai and Vietnamese cooks use as many as 8 cloves.

1 tablespoon vegetable oil
1 bunch fresh spinach, about 1 lb (450 g), stemmed and washed
2 cloves garlic, finely chopped
1 tablespoon Thai fish sauce (*nam pla*)
Lime or lemon wedges

Heat a nonstick wok (or skillet) over high heat. Add the oil and stir-fry the garlic for 3–4 seconds. Add the spinach and stir-fry briskly until it begins to wilt, about 1 minute. Stir in the fish sauce and cook for another 30 seconds to 1 minute. Serve with lime or lemon wedges.

Makes 2–3 servings

■ Curry ■

Most of the curries in Southeast Asia are based on coconut milk mixed with a highly seasoned paste, while many of those in India, especially the north, use yogurt. Some Thai curries contain none of the pungent spices associated with Indian curry, but only herbs, aromatic leaves and chiles—a combination that may have been the original native Thai curry. Spices were added later through the influence of India. Thai curries are referred to by color, with yellow curry paste, colored with turmeric, being generally the mildest, and red and green curries, made with dried and fresh chiles, the hottest. Burmese, Malay and Indonesian curries generally rely more on ground spices rather than on the intense heat of chiles.

Of course, the best curry pastes are made from scratch pounded in a mortar and pestle, but it is a time-consuming process that could not possibly be included in a book that purports to get a meal on the table in 30 minutes. An easy way to make curries is with commercially prepared curry pastes made in Thailand and India, which are available in Asian food stores and most supermarkets. But you must be careful. Some of these ready-made pastes are extremely hot. Start with a small amount, taste the dish, and add more if necessary. The Indian curries I have used come in two strengths, hot and mild. You can produce a quick, delicious curry with these pastes that will be ready in the time it takes to cook rice. If you're having guests, you can easily increase the quantity without much effort.

Note: Many of the curry recipes call for coconut milk, which is easy to find canned or frozen. If you wish to cut back on fat, substitute nonfat yogurt.

Massaman Curry

Kaeng Massaman

This is a mild curry that contains more of the aromatic spices, such as cloves, cinnamon and nutmeg, that link it to its Indian origins. This curry paste is available in cans or packets.

> One 14-oz (400-ml) can unsweetened coconut milk (do not shake can)
> 2 tablespoons Massaman curry paste
> 8-12 oz (225-350 g) lean, tender beef cut into ½-in (1¼-cm) cubes
> 2 tablespoons tamarind water (see page 245) or fresh lime juice
> 1 teaspoon palm or brown sugar
> 1 tablespoon Thai fish sauce (*nam pla*)
> 1 cinnamon stick, about 2 in (5 cm) long
> 12 whole basil leaves and some roasted peanuts, for garnish

1. Start rice. Prepare the ingredients and place them within easy reach of the stove.
2. Skim the cream off the top of the canned coconut milk and put it into a large saucepan. Heat the coconut cream over very low heat and stir in the curry paste. Cook the mixture until it is fragrant and the oil begins to separate, stirring constantly.
3. Add the beef and mix well to coat with the paste.
4. Stir in the remaining coconut milk, the tamarind water or lime juice, sugar, fish sauce and cinnamon stick. Bring to a slow simmer. Continue to cook over low heat until the meat is done and the sauce begins to thicken slightly. Do not boil.
5. Stir in the basil leaves and sprinkle the peanuts on top. Serve with rice and two or more accompaniments to curry, listed below.

Makes 2–3 servings

Shrimp in Green Curry

Kaeng Kheeo Wan Kung

This is a very easy and elegant dish. Be careful, though, some green curry pastes are very hot.

> One 14-oz (400-ml) can unsweetened coconut milk (do not shake can)
> 1-2 tablespoons Thai green curry paste
> 1 tomato, chopped
> 8-12 oz (300-450 g) medium shrimp, shelled and deveined, leaving tails intact
> 1 tablespoon Thai fish sauce (*nam pla*)
> 1 teaspoon sugar
> About ⅓ cup chopped fresh coriander leaves (cilantro) or basil leaves

Accompaniments to Curry

Serve curry with plenty of rice and two or more of the following accompaniments:

Chutney ■ Roasted peanuts ■ Sliced bananas ■ Fresh pineapple ■ Crisply fried chopped shallots, onions or garlic ■ Sliced green onions (scallions) ■ Fresh coriander leaves (cilantro) ■ Cucumber Salad (see page 127) ■ Cucumber Raita (see page 174)

Thailand

1. Start rice. Prepare the ingredients and place them within easy reach of the stove.
2. Skim the cream off the top of the canned coconut milk and put it into a large saucepan. Heat the coconut cream over very low heat and stir in the curry paste. Cook it until fragrant and the oil begins to separate.
3. Add the remaining coconut milk and bring to a gentle simmer, stirring constantly. Continue to cook over very low heat until the sauce begins to thicken slightly, about 2 minutes. Do not boil. Add the tomato and stir a few seconds.
4. Drop in the shrimp and cook until they become pink, 1–2 minutes, depending on size. Do not overcook or they will toughen.
5. Season with the fish sauce and sugar. Add the chopped coriander leaves. Cook for one minute. Serve with rice and two or more accompaniments to curry from the list on page 129.

VARIATION: *Substitute boneless, skinless chicken meat cut into thin bite-size pieces, or use cooked chicken for shorter cooking time. Chicken thigh meat is more moist and thus superior to breast meat for this dish, but breast meat is fine if you don't overcook it.*

Makes 2–3 servings

Chicken in Yellow Curry Paste

Kaeng Kari Kai

Before the invention of commercial curry powders and curry pastes, individual spices were ground on a grinding stone and added to dishes in a

variety of combinations and amounts. Modern home cooks now have the luxury of being able to make delicious curries, such as this one, that are very easy and quick to prepare.

> One 14-oz (400 ml) can unsweetened coconut milk (do not shake can)
> 1–2 tablespoons Thai yellow curry paste
> 8–12 oz (200–300 g) skinless, boneless chicken (raw or cooked), preferably leg meat, cut into thin bite-size pieces
> 1 potato, peeled and cut into tiny cubes for faster cooking
> 1 cinnamon stick, about 2 in (5 cm) long
> 1 tablespoon Thai fish sauce (*nam pla*)
> 1 teaspoon sugar
> 1 green onion (scallion), cut into 1-in (2½- cm) pieces

1. Start rice. Prepare the ingredients and place them within easy reach of the stove.
2. Skim the cream off the top of the coconut milk and put it into a saucepan. Heat the coconut cream over very low heat and stir in the curry paste. Cook it until fragrant and the oil begins to separate, stirring constantly.
3. Add the chicken and turn it with a spoon until it is evenly coated with the spice mixture. Add the potato, cinnamon stick and remaining coconut milk, and bring to a gentle simmer. Cook over low heat 3–4 minutes, or until the potatoes are tender and the sauce begins to thicken. Do not boil.
4. Season with the fish sauce and sugar to taste. Cook for another minute to blend the flavors. Add the green onion pieces. Serve with rice and at least two accompaniments to curry from the list on page 129.

Makes 2 servings

Eggs

Thai-Style Omelet
Kai Yat Sai

Again, the Thai meat of choice for a filling is pork, but for this omelet ground chicken or beef or chopped shrimp are equally delicious. The eggs are cooked more like a crepe than an omelet, then filled and wrapped securely, like a package. Feel free to vary the vegetables, but do include something red for color. For the best results, use a 9-inch skillet.

> 1½ tablespoons vegetable oil
>
> ½ small onion, finely chopped
>
> 2 large cloves garlic, finely chopped
>
> 2 oz (75 g) very lean ground or finely cut pork, chicken, beef or shrimp (leftover, pre-cooked meat may also be used)
>
> ¼ cup (50 g) tiny green peas or finely chopped snow peas or diced bell pepper
>
> 1 tomato, finely chopped
>
> 1 tablespoon Thai fish sauce (nam pla)
>
> ½ teaspoon sugar
>
> Freshly ground black pepper and a dash of ground red pepper
>
> 4 eggs and 1 tablespoon water, lightly beaten
>
> Chopped fresh coriander leaves (cilantro) or basil leaves, for garnish

1. Start rice. Prepare the ingredients and place them within easy reach of the stove.
2. Heat a nonstick skillet over medium heat. Add ½ tablespoon of the oil and stir-fry the onion until it softens. Add the garlic and cook a few seconds more. Add the pork and stir-fry about 2 minutes or until it loses its pink color, separating the morsels of meat if they stick together.
3. Add the peas and tomato and stir-fry about 1 minute. Mix in the fish sauce, sugar and pepper, and stir-fry another minute. The meat should be done by now. Remove the mixture from the skillet and keep warm.
4. Wipe the skillet with a paper towel. Coat it with a little oil and heat it over medium heat. To make two omelets, pour in half of the beaten eggs and tilt the skillet to cover the surface evenly with the eggs. When the eggs are set and hold their shape, place half of the reserved filling in the center. Fold both sides of the omelet over the filling. Repeat the processs to make a second omelet. To make a traditional Thai-style omelet, fold four sides up over the filling to form a square package. Slide the omelet onto a warmed plate. Garnish with the coriander leaves (cilantro) and serve with rice and chili sauce.

Makes 2 servings

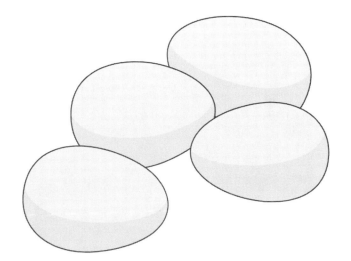

Sauces

Red Chili Dipping Sauce

Nam Prik

This dipping sauce appears on every table with vegetables, salads and other meat and seafood dishes. The word *nam* means water and *prik* means chile; the result is hot, indeed. There are many versions of this sauce, so adjust the heat to suit your own taste.

> 2 large cloves garlic, crushed or finely chopped
> 1-2 fresh red chiles, seeded and minced, or ½-1 teaspoon ground red chile or ground red pepper, to taste
> ¼ cup (50 ml) fresh lime juice or rice vinegar
> 1-2 tablespoons Thai fish sauce (*nam pla*), or to taste
> 1-2 tablespoons sugar
> 2 tablespoons water

Combine the sauce ingredients in a blender or food processor. Alternately, you may find it easier to combine the ingredients in a small saucepan and cook them until well blended and the sugar is dissolved. Use more water to dilute the sauce if it is too strong for your taste.

Makes about ⅔ cup

Vietnam

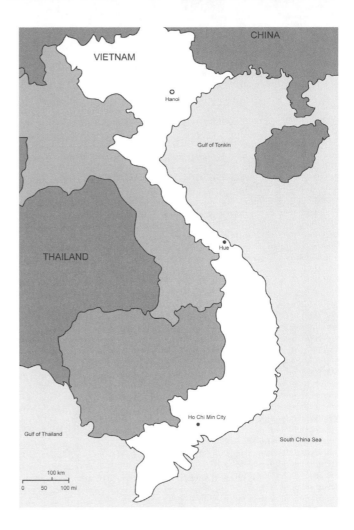

S haped like a giant letter *S*, extending some 1,000 miles from the Chinese border in the north, Vietnam is smaller than Japan and about three-fourths the size of California. It is divided by natural geographic formations into three distinct regions: the north, the center and the south. Much of the country is rugged and densely forested, and a chain of mountains forms most of its western border with Laos and Cambodia. Its eastern border is the South China Sea. Vietnam faces the Philippines to the east and Malaysia and Indonesia to the southeast.

The Vietnamese have had a turbulent history. They emerged as a distinct agrarian civilization along the southern coast of China and as far south as the Yuan Delta during the first millennium BC. This small state, calling itself Van Lang, was overrun by Chinese forces from the north and was gradually absorbed by the expanding Chinese empire. Despite intensive Chinese cultural and political influence, the Vietnamese sense of cultural uniqueness did not disappear, and in the

tenth century, after a thousand years of Chinese rule, rebel groups drove out the Chinese. A continuous struggle to maintain their independence has been the recurrent story of the Vietnamese ever since.

In the seventeenth century, two rivaling aristocratic ruling families squabbled to dominate the monarchy, and European adventurers with commercial and missionary designs on Southeast Asia exacerbated this internal strife. Finally, in the nineteenth century, the Nguyen dynasty prevailed with the help of the French, establishing a capital at Hue. For their help, the French expected commercial and economic privileges. When these were not granted, the French emperor Napoleon III ordered an attack on Vietnam in 1857. This resulted in a Vietnamese defeat and the concession of several provinces in the south, which the French transformed into the new colony, Cochin China. Twenty years later, the French completed the conquest of Vietnam and, by 1893, all of Vietnam was conquered. Along with Cambodia and Laos, Vietnam was absorbed into what became known as French Indochina, which the French ruled from 1883 to 1954.

As food often reflects the history of a nation, China and France have had a strong influence on Vietnamese cuisine. The most obvious is in the manner of eating. The Vietnamese are the only people in Southeast Asia who eat with chopsticks. Like the Chinese, they tend to eat their rice plain or after other dishes, unlike the people of Thailand and Indonesia who mix rice with other foods. The Chinese also brought the use of the wok, stir-frying, deep-frying, tofu, noodles and soy sauce. Europeans brought vegetables not previously grown in Vietnam, such as corn, tomatoes, potatoes and peanuts. Peas from the Dutch are called Holland peas, and asparagus from France is known as Western bamboo. Also from the French, the

The Vietnamese pride themselves on their healthy cuisine. They use an absolute minimum of oil in their cooking, and prefer thin light sauces free of any thickening agents.

Vietnamese learned to love café au lait, French bread, milk, butter and pastries. But it is actually surprising that the French, who ruled French Indochina for 71 years, have had practically no influence on the cooking of Vietnam.

Still other culinary influences have become part of Vietnamese cuisine. From India and from its neighbors to the west—Thailand, Laos and Cambodia, as well as Malaysia and Indonesia to the south—the Vietnamese were introduced to spices and curried dishes. A legacy from the Mongolian invasions in the thirteenth century was beef. *Pho*, a northern specialty, has become almost a national dish. Served in various forms throughout Vietnam, it is a sort of soup-salad. A rich beef broth is ladled over noodles and paper-thin slices of beef, then garnished with bean sprouts, green onions (scallions) and fresh coriander leaves (cilantro), and seasoned with *nuoc mam* (fish sauce). Pho is served for breakfast or any time of the day in the busy outdoor market food stalls, where steaming cauldrons of soup simmer from dawn to sunset, ready to serve to workers and shoppers walking through the market. The noodles and "salad" ingredients are added to the broth just before serving. Because the stock is supposed to cook for hours—the longer the better because a very rich broth is the essence of the dish—I've not included a recipe for it in this cookbook of 30-minute meals.

No matter what the dish or what region it comes from, central to Vietnamese cuisine is nuoc mam, a sauce made from fermented anchovies. It is as important to Vietnamese cuisine as soy sauce is to Chinese and fish sauce (*nam pla*) is to Thai. Like olive oil, there are varying qualities of this sauce, the first pressing being the best. It is present in almost every dish and on almost every table. It is used as a marinade and as the basis of other sauces.

Another touch that is distinctly Vietnamese is the platter of raw vegetables—lettuce, watercress, cucumbers, fresh coriander leaves (cilantro) and mint for example—that is served as part of nearly every Vietnamese meal. Lettuce, fresh coriander leaves (cilantro), and mint leaves are also served with an appetizer called *goi cun*. Cooked shrimp or chicken is wrapped at the table in a lettuce leaf with a sprig of mint or fresh coriander leaves (cilantro) and dipped in *nuoc cham* sauce. Although each region has its own style, the differences are not strong. In general, the cooking of the center and south tends to be spicier and sweeter, and cooked with a wider variety of fruits and vegetables. Southerners like raw vegetables, and northerners, like their Chinese neighbors, prefer their vegetables cooked. Also, as is true all over Southeast Asia where coastlines are long and the seas teem with life, fish and seafood are enjoyed by all.

Since the country's leaders have embarked on an economic reform program, and more entrepreneurs and tourists are in evidence, the availability of good food has increased dramatically. In Ho Chi Minh City, baguettes poke out of baskets on every street corner, pastry shops abound, and food overflows the stalls in the bustling markets found in every city. To meet the needs of this influx of new visitors, a recent development has been the emergence of more and more restaurants, some of them quite elegant. In northern cities like Hanoi and Hue, these restaurants feature the regional cuisines of the country and well-known traditional dishes. A few, for the first time,

even spotlight the simple food of the countryside.

The Vietnamese pride themselves on their healthy cuisine. They use an absolute minimum of oil in their cooking, and prefer thin light sauces free of any thickening agents. Though the cuisine has assimilated many influences, it has retained a character that is uniquely Vietnamese. While many flavoring ingredients, such as chiles and spices, have been borrowed from their neighbors, they have succeeded in combining them in a style that is light and subtle. For example, a spicy Vietnamese dish using the same ingredients as a Thai dish (curry, fish sauce, lemongrass and chiles) will always be less intense than the Thai equivalent.

Vietnamese Pantry

To keep shopping to a minimum, and to speed preparation and cooking time, it is helpful to keep these Vietnamese staples on hand in your kitchen.

Ingredients with a Long Shelf Life

black pepper

chiles, dried and whole, or red
   pepper flakes

cinnamon, ground

coriander, ground

curry powder

fish sauce (*nuoc mam*)

red pepper, ground

rice vinegar

rice wine

soy sauce

Fresh Ingredients

basil leaves

chiles, red and green

coriander leaves
   (cilantro)

garlic

ginger

green onion (scallions)

lemongrass

limes

mint leaves

onions

■ Rice ■

Plain Rice

Follow the recipe for Boiled Rice, Chinese Style (page 26) using a long-grain rice.

■ Chicken ■

Chicken Stir-Fry with Lemongrass
Ga Xao Sa Ot

This is a classic Vietnamese combination, and the aroma of fresh lemongrass is essential. Substituting grated lemon zest makes it a different dish, but it is still delicious.

Marinade
  3 large cloves garlic, crushed
  2 stalks fresh lemongrass, ends trimmed, tough outer leaves discarded or trimmed, tender inner core sliced, then chopped, or substitute grated zest of 1 lemon

2 tablespoons Vietnamese fish sauce (*nuoc mam*)
Generous grinding of black pepper

• • •

1 tablespoon vegetable oil
8–12 oz (200–300 g) boneless, skinless chicken meat, preferably from the leg, cut into bite-size pieces
1 teaspoon sugar
2 green onions (scallions), cut into 1-in (2½-cm) pieces
1–2 fresh red chiles, seeded and cut into thin strips, or red bell pepper strips (for color) and ground red pepper, to taste
2 tablespoons fresh lemon juice
10 fresh basil or mint leaves, for garnish

1. Start rice. Prepare the ingredients and place them within easy reach of the stove.
2. Combine the marinade ingredients in a bowl and coat the chicken pieces thoroughly. If there is time, let them marinate for a few minutes.
3. Heat a nonstick wok (or skillet) over high heat. Add the oil and rotate the wok to coat the sides. Stir-fry the chicken with the marinade until the chicken is no longer pink, or about 1–2 minutes.
4. Add the sugar, green onions and chiles and stir-fry 1–2 minutes longer. Add the lemon juice and cook

a few more seconds. If the mixture seems dry, add a tablespoon or two of water to keep it from scorching.

5. Remove from the heat and stir in the basil or mint leaves. Serve with rice.

VARIATION: *Thin, bite-size pieces of tender beef may be substituted for the chicken.*

Makes 2 servings

Ginger Chicken
Ga Xao Gung

This is a toothsome, gingery dish that is very easy to prepare. The amount of liquid you add at the end will depend on how much moisture your vegetables contain.

Sauce

>   1 tablespoon Vietnamese fish sauce (*nuoc mam*)
>   1 tablespoon reduced-sodium soy sauce
>   2 teaspoons brown sugar
>   1 tablespoon fresh lime juice or rice vinegar
>   1 tablespoon vegetable oil
>   1 small onion, thinly sliced
>   3 large cloves garlic, finely chopped
>   4 tablespoons grated fresh ginger
>   8–12 oz (200–300) boneless, skinless chicken meat, preferably from the leg, cut into thin, bite-size slices
>   4 fresh mushrooms, thinly sliced (optional)
>   Freshly ground black pepper
>   2 green onions (scallions) cut into 1-in (2½-cm) pieces
>   Fresh coriander leaves (cilantro), for garnish

1. Start rice. Prepare the ingredients and place them within easy reach of the stove.
2. Combine the sauce ingredients in a small bowl and set aside.

3. Heat a nonstick wok (or skillet) over high heat. Add the oil and rotate the wok to coat the sides. Stir-fry the onion until it softens and becomes translucent, 1–2 minutes. Stir in the garlic and ginger and stir-fry 3–4 seconds until fragrant.
4. Add the chicken and stir-fry briskly about 2 minutes or until it begins to brown. Add the mushrooms and stir-fry one more minute.
5. Stir in the sauce and cook until the sugar dissolves. Add a tablespoon or two of water to avoid scorching if the mixture seems dry. Stir in the green onions. Remove from the stove and garnish with the coriander leaves. Serve with rice.

Makes 2 servings

Sweet Chicken with Onions and Peppers

In Southeast Asia, chicken legs are preferred over white breast meat because leg meat does not dry out from long cooking. Be careful not to overcook white meat if you use it. Pork can also be used for this recipe.

>   1 tablespoon vegetable oil
>   8–12 oz (200–300 g) boned chicken leg or breast meat or tender pork loin, cut into bite-size cubes
>   2 tablespoons sugar
>   2 tablespoons Vietnamese fish sauce (*nuoc mam*)
>   1 tablespoon reduced-sodium soy sauce
>   1 onion, cut into eighths, then separated into pieces
>   2 large cloves garlic, chopped
>   1 red bell pepper, seeded and cut into 1-in (2½-cm) squares
>   2 green onions (scallions), cut into 1-in (2½-cm) lengths

Freshly ground black pepper and fresh
coriander leaves (cilantro) or mint
leaves, for garnish

1. Start rice. Prepare the ingredients and place them within easy reach of the stove.
2. Heat a nonstick wok (or skillet) over high heat. Add the chicken and stir-fry until it changes color, 1–2 minutes.
3. Add the sugar and fish sauce and stir-fry briskly for ½ minute.
4. Add the onion, garlic, bell pepper and green onions, and stir-fry until onions and pepper are tender, 3–4 minutes. Sprinkle with a generous grinding of black pepper and garnish with the coriander or mint leaves. Serve with rice and Raw Vegetable Platter, page 150.

Makes 2 servings

Spicy Grilled Chicken

Ga Nuong Sa

Chicken is grilled this way all over Southeast Asia, with minor variations in the marinade. This is a Vietnamese version. If it is more convenient, the chicken may also be oven broiled or baked.

Marinade

2 large cloves garlic, crushed
1 tablespoon grated fresh ginger
2 chiles, finely chopped, or dried pepper flakes or ground red pepper, to taste
1 tablespoon Vietnamese fish sauce (*nuoc mam*)
1 tablespoon reduced-sodium soy sauce
1 teaspoon brown sugar
1 stalk fresh lemongrass, end trimmed, tough outer leaves discarded or trimmed, tender inner core sliced, then chopped, or substitute grated zest of ½ lemon

1 tablespoon vegetable oil
¼ teaspoon each ground cinnamon and ground coriander
½ teaspoon freshly ground black pepper

• • •

2 whole chicken legs, cut in half for faster cooking, or substitute any other chicken parts cut into small pieces

1. Start rice, and heat the oven broiler to medium.
2. Combine the marinade ingredients in a large bowl and stir well to dissolve the sugar.
3. Score the chicken pieces in several places to allow the marinade to penetrate. Add the chicken pieces to the sauce bowl and coat them thoroughly. Marinate for at least 20 minutes, or as long as overnight, in the refrigerator. The flavor will be stronger the longer they marinate. If there is no time to marinate the chicken, baste frequently during cooking.
4. Grill the chicken pieces for 10–20 minutes over coals or under an oven broiler, turning and brushing with the marinade during cooking. Alternately, bake on a baking sheet in an oven preheated to 400°F (200°C) oven until the pieces are brown on the outside and there is no trace of pink on the inside. The thickness of the chicken will determine cooking time.

Makes 2 servings

Serving Suggestion

Serve with Vietnamese Dipping Sauce (page 150), Raw Vegetable Platter (page 150) and rice.

Vietnam

Quick Chicken Stir-Fry

It will take very little preparation and cooking time to produce this dish. Add a quick-cooking vegetable of your choice. I used snow peas because they are so easy. Asparagus would be a good choice, too.

 1 tablespoon vegetable oil
 2 large cloves garlic, finely chopped or
  crushed
 1 tablespoon grated fresh ginger
 8–12 oz (200–300 g) boneless, skinless
  chicken meat, preferably from the leg,
  cut into bite-size pieces
 2 teaspoons reduced-sodium soy sauce
 1 tablespoon Vietnamese fish sauce (*nuoc
  mam*)
 3–4 tablespoons Chinese rice wine or pale
  dry sherry
 Dried red pepper flakes or ground red
  pepper, to taste
 8 oz (150 g) snow peas, tips and strings
  removed, or frozen green peas or
  green asparagus
 Freshly ground black pepper, to taste

1. Start rice. Prepare the ingredients and place them within easy reach of the stove.
2. Heat a nonstick wok (or skillet) over high heat, add the oil and stir-fry the garlic and ginger for 3–4 seconds. Add the chicken and stir-fry briskly for 1–2 minutes or until it begins to brown.
3. Stir in the soy sauce, fish sauce, wine and red pepper flakes or ground red pepper. Cook for another minute, stirring constantly.
4. Add the snow peas and black pepper and cook for another minute. The peas should remain green and crisp. Serve with rice and Raw Vegetable Platter (page 150).

Makes 2–3 servings

Chicken and Cabbage Salad with Sweet-and-Sour Dressing
Ga Xe Phai

Here is a salad that is prepared using roast chicken from the supermarket rotisserie. Vegetables can even be bought pre-washed and pre-cut from the salad section of some markets.

 8–12 oz (200–300 g) boned, cooked chicken
  cut into bite-size pieces
 2 cups (200 g) finely shredded cabbage
 1 carrot, cut into matchsticks
 ½ red bell pepper, cut into matchsticks
 1 green onion (scallion), cut into 1-in (2½-
  cm) pieces
 ½ small red onion, thinly sliced
 Freshly ground black pepper, lime wedges,
  and fresh mint leaves, for garnish

Dressing
 1 tablespoon rice vinegar
 2 tablespoons fresh lime juice
 1 tablespoon Vietnamese fish sauce (*nuoc
  mam*)
 1½ teaspoons sugar
 1–2 fresh chiles, seeded and minced, or
  dried red pepper flakes or ground red
  pepper, to taste
 1 large clove garlic, finely chopped
 ¼ cup chopped fresh mint and coriander
  leaves (cilantro)

1. Prepare the salad ingredients and place them in a large bowl.
2. Combine the dressing ingredients and stir until the sugar dissolves. Pour the dressing over the salad and toss well. Top with a generous grinding of the black pepper and garnish with the limes and mint. Serve with French bread.

Makes 2 servings

■ Beef ■

Steak with Ginger Sauce

This steak can be cooked over coals or broiled in the oven; do whichever is more convenient.

Ginger sauce

    2 tablespoons grated fresh ginger

    1 large clove garlic, crushed

    1 fresh red chile, seeded and minced, or
        dried red pepper flakes or ground red
        pepper, to taste

    2 teaspoons sugar

    1 tablespoon Vietnamese fish sauce (*nuoc mam*)

    2 tablespoons fresh lime or lemon juice

    1 tablespoon reduced-sodium soy sauce

    2-3 tablespoons unsalted beef stock or water

    • • •

    8-12 oz (225-350 g) beef fillet or flank steak

    Chopped fresh coriander leaves (cilantro)
        or mint, for garnish

    1 handful fresh beansprouts (optional)

    3 oz (35 g) dried Vietnamese rice noodles,
        "vermicelli" width (optional)

    Lettuce (optional)

1. Start rice and prepare Raw Vegetable Platter (page 150).

2. Mix the sauce ingredients until well blended and the sugar is dissolved. Divide into small individual bowls to be used as a dipping sauce.

3. Broil the steak to desired doneness—rare, medium or well done—about 2–5 minutes on each side, depending on thickness. Cut across the grain into very thin slices and arrange on a warmed plate. Sprinkle with the chopped coriander leaves and serve with rice.

VARIATION: *To eat the steak in the Vietnamese style, each diner takes a leaf of lettuce and places a slice of steak on it. Then he or she selects a vegetable, such as fresh bean sprouts, a leaf or two of the coriander or mint, some cooked Vietnamese rice noodles (see note), and wraps the lettuce securely around the foods. The bundle is then dipped into the ginger sauce and eaten out of the hand.*

Makes 2 servings

Note: To cook dried Vietnamese rice noodles, first pre-soak them in hot water for 15 minutes. Place the presoaked noodles in a large pot of boiling water and cook for a minute or two. Drain and serve.

Vietnamese Beef Curry
Cari

This is a mild and simple curry to prepare. Chicken meat, preferably from the leg, may be substituted for the beef.

    1 tablespoon vegetable oil

    2 large cloves garlic, crushed

    1 stalk fresh lemongrass, end trimmed, tough
        outer leaves discarded or trimmed,
        tender inner core cut into thin slices, or
        substitute grated zest of ½ lemon

    8-12 oz (225-350 g) tender beef fillet or flank
        steak cut into thin bite-size pieces

    1 onion, quartered and thinly sliced

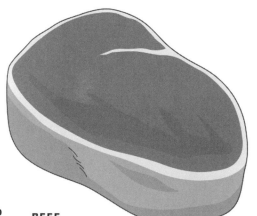

1 fresh red chile, seeded and thinly sliced, or
½ red bell pepper (for color), seeded and
thinly sliced, and dried red pepper flakes
or ground red pepper, to taste
1 tablespoon Vietnamese fish sauce (*nuoc mam*)
1 tablespoon curry powder
¾ cup (150 ml) canned, unsweetened
coconut milk (shake can well before
measuring)
Roasted peanuts and chopped fresh
coriander leaves (cilantro) or mint
leaves, for garnish

1. Start rice. Prepare the ingredients and place them within easy reach of the stove.
2. Heat a nonstick wok (or skillet) over high heat and add the oil. Stir-fry the garlic and lemongrass (or lemon zest) for 3–4 seconds, then add the beef and stir-fry 1–2 minutes until it begins to brown.
3. Add the onion and pepper and stir-fry until the onion softens but does not brown, about 2 minutes.
4. Stir in the fish sauce, curry powder and coconut milk. Bring to a gentle simmer, stirring constantly. Do not allow the coconut milk to boil or it may curdle. Reduce the heat and simmer gently for 4–5 minutes, to blend flavors. Top with the peanuts and the coriander leaves. Serve with rice and Raw Vegetable Platter (page 150).

Makes 2 servings

Stir-Fried Beef on Watercress

Bo Luc Lac

Bo luc lac translates into "shaking beef," which describes the action of the meat as it cooks. This refreshing watercress salad is lightly dressed with a vinegar and oil dressing, and

the seasoned beef is stir-fried and served hot on top of it.

Marinade

2 large cloves garlic, crushed
1 tablespoon Vietnamese fish sauce (*nuoc mam*)
1 tablespoon reduced-sodium soy sauce
1 teaspoon sugar

• • •

8–12 oz (225–350 g) beef fillet or flank steak,
cut into thin bite-size pieces
1 tablespoon vegetable oil
2 large cloves garlic, crushed

Salad with dressing

1 mild onion, preferably red, quartered and
thinly sliced
½ red bell pepper, seeded, quartered and
cut into narrow strips
1 bunch watercress, trimmed and cut into
small sprigs
2 tablespoons rice vinegar
1 tablespoon vegetable oil
Salt and freshly ground black pepper, to taste

1. In a large bowl, combine the marinade ingredients, mixing until the sugar dissolves. Add the beef pieces to the bowl, coating them well with the marinade. The flavor will be stronger the longer they are allowed to stand.
2. To prepare the salad, place the onion, bell pepper, and watercress in a shallow serving bowl. Combine the vinegar, oil, salt and pepper and toss with the salad. Set aside.
3. Heat a nonstick wok (or skillet) over high heat. Add 1 tablespoon of oil and stir-fry the 2 garlic cloves for 3–4 seconds. Add the meat and stir-fry briskly, until the pieces are nicely browned, 3–5 minutes. Arrange the meat attractively over the salad and serve with French bread.

Makes 2 servings

Sweet-and-Sour Fish

Ca Ran Chua Ngot

There are many versions from all over Asia of this classic fish recipe. However, it is always an elaborate presentation of a deep-fried, glazed whole fish with a rich vegetable sauce, and is usually served on special occasions. This recipe is very much simplified, and is not deep-fried.

Sauce

1 tablespoon Vietnamese fish sauce (*nuoc mam*)
1 tablespoon reduced-sodium soy sauce
1 tablespoon sugar
1 tablespoon white vinegar
1 teaspoon cornstarch
¼ cup (50 ml) pineapple juice or 2–3 tablespoons water

• • •

8–12 oz (225–350 g) firm fish fillets or steaks
Cornstarch or flour, for dredging fish
1½ tablespoons vegetable oil

1 small onion, thinly sliced
2 large cloves garlic, chopped
1 tomato, cut into 8 wedges
2 green onions (scallions), cut into 2-in (5-cm) lengths
1 slice fresh or canned pineapple, cut into 4 pieces
1-2 chiles, seeded and sliced, or dried red pepper flakes or ground red pepper, to taste
Fresh coriander leaves (cilantro) or mint leaves, for garnish

1. Start rice. Prepare the ingredients and place them within easy reach of the stove.
2. Combine the sauce ingredients in a bowl and stir until the sugar and cornstarch dissolve. Set aside.
3. Dredge the fish lightly in cornstarch. Heat a nonstick wok (or skillet) over medium-high heat. Add half of the oil and brown the fish on both sides, 1–2 minutes, depending on thickness. Do not overcook. Test for doneness with a fork. Remove to a serving platter and keep warm.
4. In the same wok, heat the remaining oil and stir-fry the onion until it softens, about 1–2 minutes. Add the garlic and stir-fry 3–4 seconds. Drop in the remaining ingredients and stir-fry about 2 minutes.
5. Stir in the reserved sauce mixture and bring to a boil. Reduce the heat, and simmer for about 2 minutes to blend the flavors. Pour over the fish. Garnish with the coriander or mint leaves. Serve with rice and Raw Vegetable Platter (page 150).

Makes 2 servings

Vietnam

Stir-Fried Noodles with Crabmeat

This substantial dish is a meal in itself. As with fried rice dishes, the proportion of meat to starch is variable and can be increased or decreased according to your taste.

6 oz (75 g) wide Chinese dried wheat
    noodles or other flat wheat noodle,
    such as linguini
1-2 tablespoons vegetable oil
1 small onion, thinly sliced
2 large cloves garlic, thinly sliced
4-6 oz (75-100 g) cooked crabmeat, fresh
    or canned, flaked into small pieces, or
    cooked shrimp
1½ tablespoons Vietnamese fish sauce
    (*nuoc mam*)
Freshly ground black pepper
1-2 handfuls of fresh bean sprouts,
    trimmed, or ¾ cup (100 g) fresh or
    frozen green peas
1 green onion (scallion), cut into 1-in (2½-
    cm) lengths
¼ cup (10 g) chopped fresh coriander
    leaves (cilantro) leaves

1. Prepare the ingredients and set them within easy reach of the stove.
2. Boil a large quantity of water and cook the noodles according to instructions on the package. Do not overcook. The noodles should be firm to the bite. Drain immediately and keep warm.
3. Heat a nonstick wok (or skillet) over high heat. Add the oil and stir-fry the onion until it softens, 1-2 minutes. Add the garlic and cook for 3-4 seconds.
4. Stir in the crab and cook for about 30 seconds to heat through. Stir in the fish sauce and cook for another 30 seconds. If the mixture seems dry, add 1-2

tablespoons of water to prevent scorching.
5. Add the noodles and stir gently until heated through, mixing well with the other ingredients. Sprinkle with the pepper.
6. Add the bean sprouts and stir-fry about 30 seconds, or until they begin to wilt. Stir in the green onions and coriander leaves and remove from the heat.

Makes 2–3 servings

Caramelized Garlic Shrimp
Tom Rim

Caramelized syrup is prepared and added to a number of Vietnamese recipes, including this one. In this simplified version, brown sugar is substituted. A very minimum of cooking is required—just stir-fry the shrimp and serve them with a spicy dipping sauce.

1 tablespoon vegetable oil
5 large cloves garlic, crushed
1 lb (450 g) medium shrimp, peeled and
    deveined, leaving tails intact
1 tablespoon Vietnamese fish sauce (*nuoc
    mam*)
Freshly ground black pepper and ground
    red pepper, to taste
2-3 tablespoons brown sugar
2-3 tablespoons water
2 green onions (scallions), thinly sliced,
    for garnish

1. Start rice.
2. Make Vietnamese Dipping Sauce (page 150) and let stand while you prepare and cook the shrimp. Prepare the Raw Vegetable Platter (page 150) or another salad of your choice.

3. Heat a nonstick wok (or skillet) over high heat. Add the oil and stir-fry the garlic for 3–4 seconds.

4. Add the shrimp and stir-fry until they turn pink, about 1–2 minutes, depending on their size. Be careful not to overcook them or they will toughen.

5. Add the fish sauce, pepper, sugar and water to keep the mixture from scorching. Stir-fry another minute or until the sugar has dissolved. Remove to a warmed serving plate and garnish with the green onions. Serve with Vietnamese Dipping Sauce, a salad of your choice and rice.

Makes 2–3 servings

Pan-Fried Fish Fillets with Tomato Sauce
Ca Chien Sot Ca Chua

The fish is pan-fried and served with a light tomato sauce. This seemingly French-Italian sauce becomes authentically Vietnamese with the addition of *nuac mam*, or Vietnamese fish sauce.

1 tablespoon vegetable oil
8-12 oz (225–350 g) firm fish steaks or fillets, such as snapper, sea bass or halibut, or 1 small whole fish, cleaned and scored

2 large cloves garlic, chopped
2 green onions (scallions), cut into 1-in (2½-cm) pieces
2 tomatoes, coarsely chopped
1 tablespoon Vietnamese fish sauce (*nuoc mam*)
2 teaspoons sugar
Generous grinding of black pepper
Lime or lemon wedges and fresh coriander leaves (cilantro), for garnish

1. Start rice. Prepare the ingredients and place them within easy reach of the stove.

2. Heat a nonstick skillet over high heat. Add the oil and brown the fish lightly on both sides, about 1–2 minutes, depending on thickness. Test for doneness with a fork. Remove to a heated platter and keep warm.

3. In the same skillet, stir-fry the garlic and green onions for 3–4 seconds. Add the tomatoes and cook for another minute or two.

4. Stir in the fish sauce, sugar and pepper and cook for 2–3 minutes. Pour the sauce over the fish, garnish with the lime or lemon wedges and coriander leaves. Serve with rice and Raw Vegetable Platter (page 150).

Makes 2 servings

■ Tofu ■

Stir-Fried Tofu with Garden Vegetables

Dau Phu Sot Ca Chua

The French influence is evident in the use of tomatoes in this delicious, low-calorie, low-fat, one-dish vegetarian meal. Vary the vegetables as you wish.

> 1 block, about 14 oz (400 g) firm tofu, cut into 1-in (2½-cm) cubes
> 1-2 tablespoons vegetable oil
> 1 leek, white part, thinly sliced, with some of the tender green cut into strips, or substitute a small onion, thinly sliced
> 2 large cloves garlic, thinly sliced
> 1 small zucchini, thinly sliced
> 1 small green bell pepper, seeded and cut into narrow strips
> 2-3 tomatoes, coarsely chopped
> 1 tablespoon Vietnamese fish sauce (*nuoc mam*)
> 1 teaspoon reduced-sodium soy sauce, or more to taste
> ½ teaspoon sugar
> 2 tablespoons water
> 1 green onion (scallion), cut into 1-in (2½-cm) pieces
> About ¼ cup (10 g) chopped fresh coriander leaves (cilantro) leaves
> Freshly ground black pepper and ground red pepper, to taste

1. Start rice. Prepare the ingredients and place them within easy reach of the stove.
2. Heat a nonstick wok (or skillet) over medium-high heat. Add half of the oil and lightly brown the tofu cubes, about 5 minutes. Remove and drain on paper towels.
3. Heat the wok again and add more oil if necessary. Stir-fry the leek until it softens slightly, about 1 minute, then add the garlic and stir-fry 3–4 seconds. Add the zucchini and green pepper and stir-fry 1–2 minutes.
4. Add the tomatoes, fish sauce, soy sauce, sugar and water and simmer about 5 minutes. Add more water, if necessary, to keep the mixture from scorching.
5. Return the tofu to the wok, coating gently with the sauce and cooking only long enough to heat through. Stir in the green onions and coriander leaves and sprinkle with the pepper. Remove from heat and serve with rice.

Makes 2–3 servings

Tofu with Asian Eggplant

This tasty, whole-meal vegetarian dish is flavored with the classic Vietnamese sauce *nuoc mam*. Use the long, thin Chinese or Japanese eggplants, which do not need to be peeled.

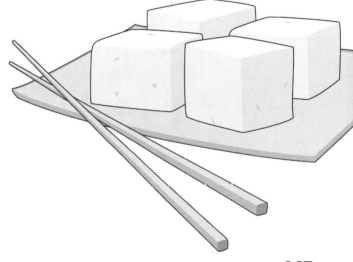

Sauce

- 1 tablespoon Vietnamese fish sauce (*nuoc mam*)
- 1 teaspoon reduced-sodium soy sauce
- 1 tablespoon fresh lime or lemon juice
- 1 teaspoon sugar
- 2 tablespoons water

• • •

- 2 tablespoons vegetable oil
- 2 large cloves garlic, crushed
- 2 long, thin eggplants (about 8 oz/250 g), cut on the diagonal into thin slices
- 1 block, about 14 oz (400 g), firm tofu, cut into 1-in (2½-cm) cubes
- 1–2 fresh red chiles, seeded and sliced, or dried red pepper flakes or ground red pepper, to taste
- 1 tomato, coarsely chopped (optional)
- ¼ cup (10 g) fresh basil or mint leaves

1. Start rice. Prepare the ingredients and place them within easy reach of the stove.

2. Combine the sauce ingredients in a small bowl and set aside.

3. Heat a nonstick wok (or skillet) over medium-high heat. Add the oil and stir-fry the garlic for 3–4 seconds. Add the eggplant slices and stir-fry them until they are lightly browned, 3–4 minutes.

4. Add the tofu cubes and stir gently to keep them intact. Cook for 4–5 minutes, or until they are golden.

5. Stir in the chiles, tomato, if using, and sauce and cook for another minute or so. Stir in the basil or mint leaves and remove the wok from the stove when they begin to wilt. Serve with rice.

Makes 2–3 servings

■ Soups ■

Asparagus and Crab Soup

Mang Tay Cua

Brought to Vietnam by the French, canned white asparagus is usually

used in this recipe, as well as pork stock. Chicken stock is substituted here. Fresh green asparagus may also be substituted if the white variety is not available. Served with rice or French bread and a salad, this makes a pleasant, light meal.

- 1 tablespoon vegetable oil
- 3 shallots or the white part of 3 green onions (scallions) or 1 small onion, coarsely chopped
- 1 large clove garlic, chopped
- 6 oz (100 g) cooked crabmeat, fresh or canned
- 1½ tablespoons Vietnamese fish sauce (*nuoc mam*)
- 2½–3 cups unsalted chicken stock
- 12 fresh white or green asparagus spears, ends trimmed where they break off naturally, spears cut into 1-in (2½ cm) pieces

1 teaspoon cornstarch dissolved in 1
    tablespoon water (optional)
1 egg white, lightly beaten
Freshly ground black pepper
6 whole fresh mint leaves, for garnish

1. Start rice. Prepare the ingredients and set them within easy reach of the stove.
2. Heat a heavy soup pot over medium-high heat and add the oil. Stir-fry the shallots and garlic until the shallots soften, about 30 seconds. Add the crabmeat and 1 teaspoon of the fish sauce. Stir-fry about 1 minute. Remove from the pot and set aside.
3. Add the stock to the pot and bring to a boil. Add the asparagus and the remaining fish sauce. Cook less than a minute. If you prefer a thicker sauce, add the cornstarch mixture and cook until the broth thickens and clears.
4. Return the crabmeat mixture to the pot, reduce the heat and cook gently until heated through.
5. Pour the beaten egg white slowly into the boiling soup, stirring constantly. Sprinkle with the pepper, add the mint leaves and serve immediately.

Makes 2–3 servings

Beef, Pineapple and Tomato Soup

Canh Ca Chua Thom Bit Bo

Fruits are plentiful in the tropics, and pineapple makes an appearance in this dish. An unusual combination, this soup makes a good, light meal.

1½ tablespoons vegetable oil
2 shallots, finely chopped, or the white
    part of 2 green onions (scallions) or ½
    small mild onion
2 large cloves garlic, chopped
6 oz (175 g) lean, tender beef, cut into thin
    1-in (2½-cm) pieces
Freshly ground black pepper
2 slices fresh or canned pineapple, cut into
    bite-size pieces
2 tomatoes, cut into thin wedges
2½-3 cups (600–700 ml) unsalted chicken
    stock
1 stalk fresh lemongrass, end trimmed,
    tough outer leaves discarded or
    trimmed, tender inner core sliced, then
    chopped, or substitute grated zest of
    ½ lemon
2 tablespoons Vietnamese fish sauce (*nuoc
    mam*)
1 green onion (scallion), thinly sliced
6 whole fresh mint or basil leaves

1. Start rice. Prepare the ingredients and place them within easy reach of the stove.
2. Heat a heavy soup pot over high heat and add half of the oil. Stir-fry the shallots and garlic until the shallots soften, about 1 minute.
3. Add the beef and stir-fry briskly for 1 minute or until the meat begins to brown. Add a generous grinding of the pepper.
4. Drop in the pineapple and tomatoes and stir-fry 30 seconds. Add the stock, lemongrass and fish sauce and bring to a boil. Reduce the heat and simmer for 3–4 minutes.
5. Add the green onions and mint or basil leaves. Serve with rice.

Makes 2–3 servings

Salads

Raw Vegetable Platter with Nuoc Cham

Dia Rau Song

No Vietnamese table would be complete without a salad platter of fresh green leaves and aromatic herbs (generically known as *rau*), and the sweet-sour-spicy dipping sauce called *nuoc cham*. These are usually served as an accompaniment to a Vietnamese meal. Select from the following list, or substitute according to availability and personal taste.

> Soft lettuce leaves
> Fresh mint, basil and coriander leaves (cilantro)
> 1 cucumber, peeled in stripes, leaving some green for color, and thinly sliced
> 3–4 green onions (scallions), cut into 2-in (5-cm) lengths

> 1–2 handfuls fresh bean sprouts, ends trimmed
> Lime or lemon wedges
> Sliced fruits (optional)

Arrange the raw vegetables of your choice attractively on a platter. Serve with the lime or lemon wedges and Vietnamese Dipping Sauce (below).

Sauces

Vietnamese Dipping Sauce

Nuoc Cham

There are as many versions of nuoc cham as there are cooks. Adjust it to your own taste—hotter, sweeter or more sour—and add more water to dilute it if it seems too strong.

> 1 large clove garlic, crushed
> ½ small fresh chile, seeded and minced, or dried red pepper flakes or ground red pepper, to taste
> ½ cup (125 ml) Vietnamese fish sauce (*nuoc mam*)
> 2 tablespoons sugar
> ¼ cup (50 ml) fresh lime or lemon juice or a mild vinegar
> ¼ cup (50 ml) water
> 1 tablespoon finely chopped fresh coriander leaves (cilantro)

Combine the sauce ingredients and stir until the sugar dissolves. Let stand while you prepare the rest of your meal. Divide the sauce into small dipping bowls.

Makes about 1 cup

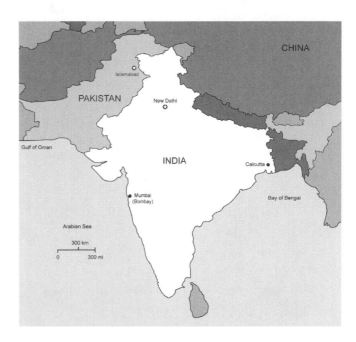

India

To understand and appreciate the extraordinary diversity of the cuisines of India, it is necessary to learn a little about the history of the country and some of the dominant influences that have shaped and refined it. The roots of Indian culture are of great antiquity. One of the world's oldest and greatest civilizations, similar to the cultures of Mesopotamia, took shape around the Indus Valley in present-day Pakistan, as well as other locations in India between 3000 and 2500 BC. Excavations have uncovered towns with two- and three-storied buildings, drainage systems, copper and bronze tools, sophisticated cooking and serving utensils, and a written language, not yet deciphered.

It was not until 500 BC that the Hindu scriptures show prohibition against meat. The reasons for this prohibition can only be conjectured. It was around this time that the reverence for life (*Ahimsa*), the prime virtue in Buddhist teachings, began to gain acceptance among Indians. It was also about this time that a religious cult began, centering around Lord Krishna, who was cared for by a milkmaid and whose companions were cowherds. Great value was placed on milk and milk products in the Indian diet. Also, there came the rise of Jainism, with its very strict emphasis on the sanctity of all life, including insects. Furthermore, there was the question of the hated foreign rulers—the Muslims and the British—who ate beef. Because the idea of protecting cattle had already been a part of Hindu ethics and religion, the next step was to incorporate the Hindu reverence for cows into Indian nationalism.

In about the eighth century, the country was subject to Muslim conquests by Arabs, Turks, Afghans, Persians and Mongols, who converted many Buddhists and Hindus to Islam as they swept across India.

The first Muslim empire based in India was established in Delhi in 1206, and continued under the Mogul Empire, which was established in 1526 under Babur, a descendant of Genghis Khan. The Mogul courts adopted Persian customs, language, art and architecture, and its cuisine, which is one of the most lavish and refined cuisines in the world, but based on meat. Elaborate lamb dishes are richly prepared with almond, cashew and pistachio nuts, raisins, and a myriad of spices, as well as onions, garlic and yogurt.

It is these three great civilizations and religions—Hindu, Buddhist and Muslim—that are the main influences on Indian culture and have dictated the style and form of Indian cooking. There are minorities of other cultural and religious traditions that have also had a notable influence. These include Christians, Sikhs, Jains and Zoroastrians, or Parsis, who fled religious persecution in Persia more than 1200 years ago. In more recent times, there were also European incursions—Portuguese, Dutch, French and, after 1750, the British began absorbing parts of India bit by bit. After India gained independence in 1947, the two predominantly Muslim regions in the northwest and northeast became the separate states of Pakistan and Bangladesh.

The majority of Indians (81 percent) follow the Hindu religion. They regard the cow as a sacred animal and do not eat beef. It was among Brahmins, traditionally the caste of priests and scholars,

that the stricture against eating meat came to be most rigorously enforced. The truth is that most Indians do not eat meat because it is an expensive luxury that they cannot afford except on very special festive occasions. Only upperclass Muslims and Hindus can afford to eat meat more frequently.

But like everything else in India, vegetarianism is a complex matter subject to qualifications and exceptions. For example, Kashmiri Brahmins will eat lamb and fish but not chicken or eggs, while many non-Brahmin families all over India remain strict vegetarians. Another feature of Kashmiri Brahmin cooking is the absence of onions and garlic, which are said to inflame the baser passions. Some Brahmins in Bengal eat fish but call it "fruit of the sea," and Jains will not eat roots or tubers for fear that in uprooting them they will accidentally kill worms or insects. They also refuse to eat tomatoes or beets because they are red, the color of blood.

Thirteen percent of Indians are followers of Islam, making India one of the four largest Muslim nations in the world. Muslims follow dietary laws set down in the Koran. They may eat beef and lamb, but not pork or shellfish. Christians from Goa, once colonized by the Portuguese, in addition to their many seafood specialties, use pork in many dishes.

Besides religion, climate also determines differences between the cuisines of the north and the south. Wheat grows in the north and rice in the south, and the difference between bread eaters and rice eaters determines the thickness of sauces. In northern India, where wheat grows well and flat breads (*chapatis*) are freshly made and eaten with most meals, the food is drier and the sauces thicker, and *chapatis* and *parathas* are used to mop up sauce.

In the south, where there is no wheat but many varieties of rice, the sauces are thinner and are meant to be absorbed by the rice. Although vegetarians are to be found in every part of the country, it is the south, with its overwhelming variety of vegetables and fruit, that has created one of the most varied and imaginative vegetarian cuisines in the world. But to merely divide the country between north and south is still not enough to describe the diversity and complexity of Indian culinary traditions, or to speak of a national cuisine in India. Perhaps it would help to compare it to Europe, with each state, like each European nation, having its own language, culture and foods.

However, there is one main unifying factor in Indian cooking—spices. Whatever the cooking style in the various states on this vast continent, it is spices that are at the heart of Indian cooking. The function of spices as preservative, medicine and seasoning, has been recognized from ancient times and chronicled in Sanskrit writings. Spices were prescribed to treat a whole array of ailments from digestive problems, insomnia, headaches and fevers to rheumatism, and heart and kidney disorders. Today, emphasis is placed on seasoning. Complex mixtures of ground or whole spices called masalas, so mild as to be almost imperceptible, or sharp enough to scald your palate, are ground on a flat stone with a pestle in the right combinations for whatever dishes are to be cooked that day. But Indian cookery differs so widely from region to region, and from one cook to the next, that even the best-known traditional dishes have many variations.

Although there are no hard-and-fast rules for the use of spices, there are a few principles that I believe most cooks would agree upon. Certain spices—turmeric, coriander, cumin and pepper—are too strong, too sharp or too bitter to be used in sweets. However, those that *are* used in sweets—cardamom, saffron and cinnamon—are frequently used in savory dishes as well. Also, turmeric is not usually used in dry dishes that have very short cooking time because it needs a sauce to counteract its acrid taste.

Besides these generalizations, there are one or two other points to be made that characterize Indian cooking. The wheat-producing north usually uses more dry spices than the south, and pounds them to make a powder rather than grinding them with a liquid to make a paste. These dry spices are used to produce dishes that have a minimum of sauce or no sauce at all, and bread is used as a utensil to pick up foods that are easier to manage if they are dry. But in mixing these spices, first they must be lightly toasted in a dry pan to bring out their maximum aroma and flavor.

In contrast to the north, the rice-eaters of the south grind their spices—usually fresh or green spices that cannot be stored—with lime juice, coconut milk or vinegar to make wet masalas (pastes) in order to produce sauces that will counteract the dryness of plain boiled rice. Coconuts and chiles, both prolifically grown in the south, come into their own in south Indian cooking. It is interesting to note that wet masalas, not dry spices, are used in many parts of Southeast Asia where rice, not wheat, is the main staple. Indian cooking styles, especially south Indian, as well as other Indian cultures and religions, found their way to the rice eating countries of Indonesia, Malaysia and Thailand as a consequence of the spice trade and of immigration.

Having read this far, you must be wondering whether there is such a thing as a quick and easy Indian recipe. With such a reliance on long lists of spices that have to be ground, Indian cooking is obviously labor intensive. I have two answers to that question. If spices are stored together in a drawer or on a shelf, it would take seconds to remove a little from each jar. They can also be ground together ahead of time in a pepper or coffee grinder and stored, or they can be used whole (and discarded later) for a milder, fragrant sauce. But if you really don't want to expend the effort to grind your own spices, there is help. Asian food shops and some supermarkets carry commercially prepared masalas, both wet and dry, as well as prepared curry powders and tandoori mixes.

As for chutney, Indian cooks generally prepare their own from fresh ingredients. There are also commercial brands of many of these condiments and seasonings. Times have changed, and urban Indians buy many ready-made preparations, including chutneys and masalas, tandoori mixes and curry pastes. Try them. They can be very good substitutes for mixtures prepared at home.

Indian cooks have their favorite spice combinations and there is no reason why a Western cook cannot experiment with these combinations. There are no hard-and-fast rules for the use of spices.

Above all, keep it simple. Plain rice can be started in your rice cooker while you prepare the main dish, which should take 30 minutes or less. If you are missing an ingredient, leave it out. Don't be afraid to make changes. Choose one of the simple Indian vegetable dishes or a salad to serve with it, and you ought to be sitting down to eat in not much more time than it takes to cook the rice.

On Curry

The origin of the English word *curry* is probably *kari*, which is a Tamil word meaning sauce. Critics have said that this word is a British oversimplification for the richly varied cuisine of India. The same is said of curry powder, which is a standard mixture of several spices. Americans, Europeans and the Japanese tend to think of a curry as a dish made with this Indian-style curry powder. Actually it is not an ingredient, but a cooking method, and in all its regional forms, from India to Indonesia, it refers to any dish that combines meat, seafood or vegetables in a seasoned liquid and that is eaten mixed with rice. Many of the stewed and simmered dishes of Southeast Asia fall under this general heading. Still, like it or not, the word *curry* persists.

Indian Pantry

To keep shopping to a minimum, and to speed preparation and cooking time, it is helpful to keep these Indian staples on hand in your kitchen.

Ingredients with a Long Shelf Life

black mustard seeds

black peppercorns, whole and ground

cardamom, whole pods and ground

chiles, dried and whole

cinnamon, sticks and ground

cloves, whole and ground

coconut milk, unsweetened, canned

coriander seeds, whole and ground

cumin seeds, whole and ground

curry powder

fennel seeds, whole and ground

fenugreek seeds, whole or ground

garam masala (You can find this spice mixture at specialty stores or, to make it yourself, see the recipe on page 182.)

lentils, red (*masur dal*)

nutmeg, whole and ground

onion seeds (*kalonji*)

palm sugar (*jaggery*)

Bengali five-spice mixture (*Panch phoran*; you can find this spice mixture at specialty stores or, to make it yourself, see the recipe on page 182.)

red chile, ground

red pepper flakes

red pepper, ground

saffron

tandoori spice mixture

turmeric, ground

Fresh Ingredients

chiles, red and green

coriander leaves (cilantro)

garlic

ginger

mint leaves

onions

yogurt, plain

■ Rice ■

Plain Rice, Indian Style
Namkin Chaval

Although rice is eaten all over India, it is the staple food in the southern, central and eastern parts. Like a Middle Eastern pilaf, it is sautéed for a few minutes before it is boiled. Traditional Indian rice is sautéed in ghee (clarified butter), but for convenience and healthier, less caloric meals, I suggest using vegetable oil for this and the other recipes in this chapter. Basmati rice is the rice of choice, but any long-grain rice will yield good results. As is common everywhere in Asia, the rice is washed thoroughly before it is cooked. Most American brands of rice do not require washing, which saves a lot of time. If you do wash rice, it must be drained thoroughly and dried. For the best results, use a heavy pan with a close-fitting cover.

> 1 tablespoon vegetable oil
> 1 cup (225 g) long-grain rice
> 2 cups (475 ml) boiling water (more water will produce softer rice)
> Pinch of salt (optional)

1. Put a kettle of water on the stove to boil.
2. Heat a medium saucepan over medium heat and add the oil. When hot, add the rice and cook for 3–4 minutes, sautéing almost constantly until the grains turn white and lose their translucent character.
3. Add the boiling water (and salt for seasoning, if you wish) and stir well. Reduce the heat to low, cover and cook, without removing the lid, for 15 minutes. Taste for doneness, cover and leave to steam for a minute or two. Lightly fluff the rice with a fork and serve.

Makes 2–3 servings

Rice Pilaf with Green Peas
Mattar Pulao

This is mildly spiced rice *pulao* (pilaf) that will go well with any main dish. Adjust the seasonings to suit your own taste. As is common all over Asia, the rice is washed thoroughly before it is cooked. Most American

brands do not require the rice to be washed and that saves a lot of time. If you do wash it, it must be drained thoroughly and dried.

> 1 tablespoon vegetable oil
> 1 short cinnamon stick
> 3 cardamom pods
> ½–1 teaspoon cumin seeds
> 4 cloves
> 1 cup (225 g) long-grain rice
> 2 cups (475 ml) boiling water (more water will produce softer rice)
> Pinch of salt for seasoning (optional)
> About ⅔ cup (100 g) fresh or frozen green peas

1. Put a kettle of water on the stove to boil.
2. Heat a heavy pan with a close-fitting cover over medium heat. Add the oil and toast the spices, shaking the pan constantly, for a few seconds or until they sputter and pop. Do not burn. Keep a lid handy to keep them from popping out of the pan.
3. Add the rice and cook for 3–4 minutes, stirring almost constantly until the grains turn white and lose their translucent character. Add the boiling water and salt, if using, and stir well. Reduce the heat to low, cover and cook, without removing lid, for 15 minutes.
4. Gently stir in the peas. Cover and steam another minute or so, or until the peas are done. Taste for doneness. Lightly fluff the rice with a fork, removing the cinnamon stick. You may remove or leave the other whole spices as you wish. Serve with other dishes.

Makes 2–3 servings

■ **Seafood** ■

Shrimp in Yogurt Masala Sauce

Jhinga Kabab

These shrimp (or prawns) are marinated in a mildly spiced yogurt combination. They may be skewered and barbecued over coals or under an oven broiler. If it is more convenient, they can also be quickly sautéed. While they marinate, start rice and prepare a salad or raita (pages 174–176).

Yogurt marinade

> 1 small onion, chopped
> 2 large cloves garlic, chopped
> 1 tablespoon grated fresh ginger
> 1–2 fresh chiles, seeded and chopped, or dried red pepper flakes or ground red pepper, to taste

2 tablespoons fresh lemon juice

1 tablespoon garam masala, commercially
    prepared or homemade (see page 182)

Salt and freshly ground black pepper, to
    taste

3-4 tablespoons plain yogurt

• • •

8-12 oz (300-450 g) medium shrimp or
    large prawns, peeled and deveined,
    leaving tails intact

1 tablespoon vegetable oil

¼ teaspoon garam masala, to sprinkle
    over finished dish

Fresh parsley or coriander leaves
    (cilantro), for garnish

1. Combine the marinade ingredients
in a food processor or blender and
blend until smooth. Add more
yogurt, if necessary, to facilitate
the blending process. If you don't
have a blender, finely chop and
combine the ingredients in a bowl.
Add the shrimp, and marinate for
at least 20 minutes. If there is no
time to marinate the shrimp, coat
them well before cooking and
baste frequently. I guarantee they
will be just as delicious.

2. Grill the shrimp quickly over hot
coals, or under a preheated oven
broiler, a minute or two on each
side, depending on size, or until
they turn pink. Baste with the
marinade.

3. To sauté, heat a nonstick skillet over medium heat and add
the oil. Sauté the shrimp on both
sides until they change color, 2–4
minutes, depending on size. Keep
them coated with the marinade.
Do not overcook or they will
toughen. Remove to a warmed
platter, sprinkle with the garam
masala and garnish with the coriander leavevs or parsley. Serve
with rice.

Makes 2 servings

Pan-Fried Shrimp in Whole Spices

The whole spices are toasted in the
skillet before the shrimp are added.
Spices are more flavorful and aromatic if they are bruised slightly
before they are fried. Measure them
out on a cloth, cover them, and
pound them lightly with a rolling
pin or press them with the back of
a heavy spoon. This is an optional
step. Cooking time is very short and
the aroma of the spices is wonderful.
Prepare a salad or other accompaniment before you begin cooking the
shrimp.

Spices

    Seeds of 8 cardamom pods (about ½
        teaspoon)

    6 whole cloves

    6 whole black peppercorns

    One 2-in (5-cm) piece of stick cinnamon

• • •

1 tablespoon vegetable oil

2 cloves garlic, thinly sliced

2 thin slices peeled fresh ginger

8-12 oz (300-450 g) medium shrimp,
    peeled and deveined, leaving tails
    intact

¼ teaspoon garam masala, commercially
    prepared or homemade (see page 182)

Fresh parsley or coriander leaves
    (cilantro), for garnish

1. Start rice. Prepare the ingredients
and place them within easy reach
of the stove.

2. Bruise the spices with the back of
a wooden spoon.

3. Heat a nonstick skillet over
medium heat and add the oil.
Drop in the spices and toast them
about 1 minute, while constantly
shaking the pan, until their fragrance is released and they begin
to sizzle. Be careful not to burn

them. Add the garlic and ginger and stir another half a minute.

4. Add the shrimp and lightly brown on both sides until they change color, 2–4 minutes, depending on size. Do not overcook or they will toughen. Remove to a warmed platter, sprinkle with the garam masala and garnish with the coriander or parsley leaves. Serve with rice.

Makes 2 servings

Shrimp in Coconut Milk
Jhinga Molee

This method of cooking is popular in southern India, Sri Lanka and Malaysia, where the long, tropical coastlines provide a myriad of seafood. The main ingredient is gently simmered in a previously prepared and mildly seasoned coconut milk sauce. The shrimp are often cooked in their shells to enhance the sauce, and then peeled at the table.

1 tablespoon vegetable oil
1 onion, thinly sliced
2 large cloves garlic, finely chopped
1 teaspoon grated fresh ginger
1–2 fresh chiles, seeded and sliced, or dried red pepper flakes or ground red pepper, to taste
2 teaspoons curry powder
¼ teaspoon ground turmeric
1 cup (250 ml) canned, unsweetened coconut milk (shake can well before measuring)
Salt and freshly ground black pepper, to taste
8–12 oz (300–450 g) medium shrimp or large prawns, preferably unpeeled
2 tablespoons fresh lemon juice, or to taste
Lemon wedges and chopped fresh parsley or coriander leaves (cilantro), for garnish

1. Start rice. Prepare the ingredients and place them within easy reach of the stove.

2. Heat a nonstick skillet over medium heat. Add the oil and sauté the onion, garlic, ginger and chiles, about 2 minutes, or until the onion softens.

3. Stir in the curry powder and turmeric and cook for another minute.

4. Add the coconut milk, salt and pepper and stir constantly over low heat until the mixture comes to a boil. Cook for about 5 minutes, stirring frequently to prevent the coconut milk from curdling.

5. Add the shrimp (or prawns) and cook for 2–4 minutes, depending on size, or until they begin to turn pink. Do not overcook or they will toughen. Add the lemon juice. Garnish with the lemon wedges and the coriander or parsley leaves. Serve with rice.

VARIATION: *Fish fillets, cut into small pieces, may be substituted for the shrimp.*

Makes 2–3 servings

Steamed Fish Packets
Patrani Machli

Wrapping foods in a banana leaf and steaming them over a charcoal fire is a common cooking method in many South Asian countries. Seasonings are pounded to a paste and included in the package. Since banana leaves are not easy to come by, aluminum foil is substituted here. The paste in this recipe is green because it consists of a large quantity of fresh coriander leaves (cilantro).

India

Seasoning paste

1 onion, coarsely chopped

2 large cloves garlic, finely chopped or
    crushed

1 small fresh hot green chile, seeded and
    minced, or ground red pepper, to taste

½ cup (25 g) firmly packed, fresh
    coriander leaves (cilantro), trimmed
    and chopped

½ teaspoon ground cumin

½ teaspoon ground coriander

½ teaspoon garam masala, commercially
    prepared or homemade (see page 182)
    (optional)

2 tablespoons fresh lemon juice

Salt and freshly ground black pepper, to
    taste

¼ cup (25 g) grated, fresh, unsweetened
    coconut (optional)

• • •

8-12 oz (225-350 g) fish fillets of choice
    or 2 small whole trout, scaled and
    washed

Lemon wedges, for garnish

1. Start rice.
2. Preheat the oven to 450°F (230°C).
3. Combine the paste ingredients in a small food processor and blend until smooth. You may need to add a tablespoon of water to facilitate blending. If you don't have a food processor, finely chop everything and mix well.
4. Coat the fish fillets with the mixture. If using a whole fish, place some of the mixture inside the cavity.
5. Lay out 2 large sheets of heavy-duty aluminum foil. (If using thin aluminum foil, use double sheets to prevent leakage.) Place each serving of fish in the center of the foil. Fold the foil around the fish into a package and wrap it securely so it will not leak, keeping the seam side up. Place it in a baking dish in the center of the hot oven and bake for 15–20 minutes. Open to see if the fish is done. Serve the package on a plate garnished with the lemon wedges.

VARIATION: *A combination of fish and shrimp may be used.*

Makes 2 servings

Fish Curry

Using commercially prepared curry powder makes this a quick and easy way to prepare any fish. Fenugreek is a powerful, aromatic and bittersweet spice, not unlike burnt sugar. It adds another level of complexity to curries that some like and some don't. Try for yourself to decide.

8-12 oz (225-350 g) fish fillets or steaks
    of choice

Fresh lemon juice from ½ lemon

1 tablespoon vegetable oil

2 onions, thinly sliced

2 large cloves garlic, finely chopped or
    crushed

1 teaspoon curry powder

½ teaspoon garam masala, commercially
    prepared or homemade (see page 182)

¼ teaspoon ground fenugreek (optional)

Salt, freshly ground black pepper and
    ground red pepper, to taste

½ cup (125 g) plain yogurt

Lemon wedges and chopped fresh
    coriander leaves (cilantro), for garnish

1. Start rice. Prepare the ingredients and place them within easy reach of the stove.
2. Sprinkle the fish with the lemon juice and set aside.
3. Heat a nonstick skillet over medium-high heat and add the

oil. Add the onion and sauté for 1–2 minutes, or until the onion softens. Add the garlic and stir for 3–4 seconds.

4. Reduce the heat. Mix in the curry powder, garam masala, fenugreek, salt and pepper and cook for 1–2 minutes.

5. Add the yogurt and stir constantly until it just begins to simmer. Do not let the yogurt boil. Cook gently over low heat for 2–3 minutes.

6. Place the fish in the skillet, arranging the onion mixture around it. Cover and simmer over low heat until cooked through, 2–5 minutes depending on thickness. Test for doneness with a fork—do not overcook. Add more of the lemon juice, to taste. Garnish with the lemon wedges and chopped coriander leaves. Serve with rice.

Makes 2 servings

Fish and Tomatoes in a Spicy Sweet-and-Sour Sauce

Machli aur Tamatar

The combination of vinegar and sugar give this dish its distinctive sweet-and-sour flavor. *Jaggery* (palm sugar) is the usual sweetener, but brown cane sugar can be substituted.

1 tablespoon vegetable oil

1 onion, thinly sliced

2 large cloves garlic, finely chopped or crushed

2 teaspoons grated fresh ginger

1 small fresh red or green chile, seeded and chopped, or dried red pepper flakes or ground red pepper, to taste

1 tablespoon ground coriander

1 teaspoon ground cumin

2 tomatoes, coarsely chopped

2 tablespoons palm sugar (*jaggery*) or dark brown sugar

2 tablespoons white vinegar

Salt and freshly ground black pepper, to taste

8-12 oz (225-350 g) fish fillets of choice

Lemon wedges and chopped fresh coriander leaves (cilantro), for garnish

1. Start rice. Prepare the ingredients and place them within easy reach of the stove.

2. Heat a nonstick skillet over medium-high heat and add the oil. Sauté the onions until they begin to soften, about 2 minutes. Add the garlic and ginger and sauté for a few seconds. Add the chile, ground coriander and cumin and stir for a few more seconds.

3. Add the tomatoes and sauté about 2 minutes.

4. Stir in the sugar, vinegar, salt and pepper and bring to a boil. Add 2–3 tablespoons of water to prevent scorching. Cover and simmer about 5 minutes.

5. Gently add the fish fillets and spoon the sauce over them. Cover and simmer over low heat for 3–4 minutes, depending on the thickness of the fillets, or until the fish is done. Transfer the fish and sauce to a serving bowl. Garnish with the lemon wedges and coriander leaves. Serve with rice.

Makes 2 servings

Chicken

Cardamom Chicken
Murg Ilayachi

The spice blend in this chicken dish emphasizes cardamom. The flavor and aroma is dramatically more intense if you grind the seeds of the cardamom and fennel in the pepper grinder yourself, just before cooking, rather than using ready-ground spices. Boneless chicken cubes will cook in half the time.

> 1 lb (450 g) bone-in chicken parts, cut into very small pieces, or boneless, skinless chicken breast, cut into bite-size cubes
> 1½ tablespoons vegetable oil
> 1 onion, thinly sliced
> 2 large cloves garlic, finely chopped or crushed
> 1 tablespoon grated fresh ginger
> 1 teaspoon ground cardamom
> ½ teaspoon ground fennel seed
> One 2-in (5-cm) piece of stick cinnamon
> 4 whole cloves
> ¼ teaspoon dried hot pepper flakes or ground red pepper, or to taste
> ½ cup (125 g) plain yogurt
> Salt and freshly ground black pepper, to taste
> Chopped fresh parsley or coriander leaves (cilantro), for garnish

1. Start rice. Prepare the ingredients and place them within easy reach of the stove.
2. Heat a nonstick skillet over medium-high heat and add half of the oil. Brown the chicken pieces lightly on both sides, 3–5 minutes. Remove the chicken from the skillet and keep warm.
3. Add the remaining oil and sauté the onion, garlic and ginger for 2–3 minutes, or until the onion softens. Add the spices and cook over medium heat for 1–2 minutes, stirring constantly.
4. Reduce the heat to low. Add the yogurt and slowly bring to a simmer, stirring all the time. Do not boil.
5. Return the chicken to the skillet, and coat well with the spice mixture. Add the salt and pepper, cover and cook over medium heat for about 10 minutes, or until the chicken is tender. If you're using cubes of chicken, simmer for 3–5 minutes. Garnish with the coriander leaves or parsley. Serve with rice and your choice of raita (pages 174–175).

VARIATION: *Tender lamb, cut from the leg into thin bite-size pieces, may be substituted for the chicken.*

Makes 2–3 servings

Chicken Tikka Patties
Murg Tikka

Breaded chops and "cutlets" (Americans say "patties") are believed to have been brought to India by the British. However, these cutlets bear no resemblance to bland British food when they contain the wonderful spices that Indian cooks have added to

India

them. This delicious chicken patty is simple and quick to put together. Feel free to vary the spices.

8-12 oz (225-350 g) ground lean chicken
1 onion, finely chopped
1 large clove garlic, finely chopped or crushed
1 tablespoon grated fresh ginger
¼ cup (10 g) fresh mint or coriander leaves
    (cilantro), finely chopped
1 teaspoon garam masala, commercially
    prepared or homemade (see page 182)
½ teaspoon ground coriander
½ teaspoon ground cumin
Salt, freshly ground black pepper and
    ground red chile, to taste
2-3 tablespoons plain yogurt or 1 egg,
    lightly beaten
1 tablespoon vegetable oil
Bread crumbs for dipping the cutlets
    before frying (optional)
Green onions (scallions), sliced into 2-in
    (5-cm) pieces, for garnish

1. Start rice. Make a salad or a raita (pages 174–176).
2. Combine all the ingredients except the oil in a deep bowl. Knead them vigorously until they are well blended and smooth. To intensify the flavor, let the mixture sit in the refrigerator for a while. Divide the chicken mixture into 8 equal portions and shape them into thin, flat patties. If using the breadcrumbs, dip patties on both sides.
3. Heat a nonstick skillet over medium heat. Add the oil and fry the cutlets about 5 minutes on each side until they are crisp and brown, with no sign of pink in the center. Garnish with the sliced green onions and serve with rice or crusty bread, or inside pita bread pockets.

VARIATION: *Ground lamb or beef may be substituted for chicken.*

Makes 2 servings

Tandoori Chicken
Tandoori Murg

Tandoori chicken originated along the northwest border of India and has become a universal favorite. The clay tandoor oven, shaped like the jar in which the famous Ali Baba hid, is either sunk neck-deep in the ground or, if it is built above ground, is heavily insulated on the outside with a thick layer of plaster. A charcoal fire is at the bottom, and heats the sides to almost scorching temperatures. Small, whole chickens are marinated in a *masala* (colored red from saffron, food dye and red chiles), and pierced on long thin iron spikes. The spikes are taken out every few minutes so that the chickens may be basted with the marinade and, in traditional Indian cookery, with ghee (clarified butter). The heated clay releases a fragrance and smoke that influences the final taste of the chicken in a way that cannot be duplicated either over a charcoal barbecue or in a kitchen oven. Still, I think it is a very good dish for the busy home cook since it can be marinated up to 24 hours before cooking. By dinner time, when the hurried cook comes home from work, it is ready to be barbecued, broiled or baked in just 20 minutes with no work at all but a little basting to keep it moist. It also makes an easy summer meal when barbecued outdoors. Instead of cooking chickens whole, this recipe uses chickens cut up into small serving pieces.

To make preparation easier, use commercially prepared tandoori spice mix or tandoori marinade, which are sold alongside garam masala and curry powder in supermarkets or specialty shops. Or use the mix suggested in this recipe.

½ teaspoon saffron threads (optional)

2 tablespoons boiling water

1 lb (450 g) bone-in chicken parts, cut into small pieces for faster cooking

Tandoori marinade

1 small onion, coarsely chopped

2 large cloves garlic, chopped

One 1-in (2½-cm) piece of fresh ginger, peeled and coarsely chopped or grated

¼ cup (50 ml) fresh lemon juice

½ cup (125 g) plain yogurt

Green onions (scallions), lime or lemon wedges and radishes, for garnish

1 tablespoon commercially prepared tandoori mix, or use the following combination of spices:

    ¼ teaspoon ground red chile, or to taste

    1½ teaspoons garam masala, commercially prepared or homemade (see page 182)

    ½ teaspoon curry powder

    ½ teaspoon paprika (for color)

Note: Leaving the skin on will produce moister chicken, needing little if any basting. Removing the skin is more authentic, and it lowers the fat and allows the chicken to cook more quickly. The choice is yours. To ensure that the marinade will permeate the chicken, make 3 or 4 diagonal slits halfway down to the bone of each piece.

1. If using the saffron threads, soak them in the boiling water for 5 minutes while you prepare the chicken.

2. Place the saffron and water in a small food processor. Add the onion, garlic, ginger and lemon juice and blend to a smooth paste. If necessary, add a little yogurt to the mixture to facilitate blending. (If you don't have a food processor,

just chop ingredients very fine and mix well.) Transfer the onion mixture to a large bowl and add the remaining ingredients. Mix well.

3. Dry the chicken with paper towels and rub the spice mixture all over the chicken pieces, especially into the slits. Cover the bowl and refrigerate until you are ready to cook.

4. You may grill the chicken over hot coals, broil it under a preheated oven broiler, or bake it in an oiled baking dish in a preheated oven. For easier cleanup, place aluminum foil in the pan under the broiler to catch drips or, if baking, under the chicken in the baking dish. Cook for 5–10 minutes on each side, depending on the size of the chicken pieces. Baste as needed with marinade juices or a little oil. The chicken should be a golden-red color, crisp and without gravy.

Makes 2 servings

Serving Suggestion

Traditionally tandoori chicken and other tandoori meats, such as Lamb Kebabs (page 166) and Ground Lamb Kebabs (page 167), are served on a platter of salad greens. The vegetables should be raw and crisp, served only with salt and a squeeze of lime. You might try the Mixed Vegetable Salad (page 175) or Tomato-Ginger Salad (page 176), both of which go well with tandoori. Cucumber-Tomato Raita (page 174) and a chutney also work well. Commercially prepared mango chutney would be ideal. These wonderful tandoori dishes are also served with bread—*naan or roti*—freshly baked in the tandoor, and that is the rub. Only a magician could do all that in 30 minutes. So, I recommend pita bread or whatever else your preference may be.

India

Chili-Garlic Chicken

This South Indian dish is said to have originated in the Chettiar community. It is as quick as a Chinese stir-fry if you use boneless chicken cut into small cubes. Bruise the whole spices with the back of a heavy spoon for more flavor and aroma.

1 tablespoon vegetable oil
¼ teaspoon mustard seeds, preferably black
¼ teaspoon fennel seeds
¼ teaspoon black peppercorns
1-2 dried red chiles, or dried red pepper flakes or ground red pepper, to taste
1 small onion, finely chopped
2 large cloves garlic, chopped or crushed
8-12 oz (200–300 g) boneless chicken, cut into bite-size pieces
Salt, to taste
1 tomato, coarsely chopped (optional)

1. Start rice. Prepare the ingredients and place them within easy each of the stove.
2. Heat a nonstick skillet over medium-high heat and add the oil. When hot, add the mustard seeds, fennel seeds, peppercorns and dried chiles. Stir a few seconds until they darken, sputter and pop.
3. Add the onion and sauté 1–2 minutes, or until softened. Add the garlic and sauté a few seconds.
4. Add the chicken pieces and salt, sautéing vigorously until the chicken begins to brown, about 5 minutes. The chicken should be well done. Add the tomato, if using, and keep sautéing until the mixture is almost dry. Serve with rice and a salad or vegetable.

Makes 2 servings

■ Lamb ■

Lamb Kebabs

This is the lamb version of Tandoori Chicken (page 164), easy to prepare with moderate seasoning and no hot pepper. Marinate the meat for as little or as long as you wish. The longer you wait, the more intense the taste.

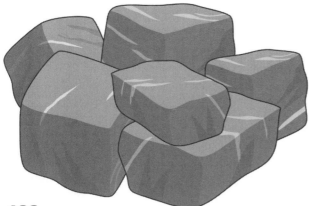

8-12 oz (225–350 g) boneless, tender lamb preferably from the leg, cut into bite-size cubes
1 teaspoon ground cumin
¼ teaspoon ground turmeric
Salt and freshly ground black pepper, to taste
2-4 tablespoons plain yogurt
1 tablespoon fresh lemon juice
½ small onion, finely chopped
2 large cloves garlic, finely chopped
1 tablespoon grated fresh ginger (optional)
2 tablespoons fresh coriander leaves (cilantro), finely chopped
½ teaspoon garam masala, commercially prepared or homemade (see page 182)

1. Place the lamb cubes in a large bowl and sprinkle them with the cumin, turmeric, salt and pepper. Turn the cubes to coat evenly. Add the remaining ingredients,

India

except the garam masala, and mix thoroughly. Cover and marinate up to 30 minutes at room temperature. Place in the refrigerator if marinating longer.

2. String the cubes on 4 long metal skewers and grill over a hot charcoal fire. If you wish to broil them, preheat the broiler to high and suspend the skewers side by side across the length of a baking dish. Broil the kabobs about 3 inches from the heat, turning over occasionally to brown all sides. High-quality lamb may be cooked rare, medium or well done, according to individual taste.

3. When cooked, remove from the heat and serve with Mixed Vegetable Salad (page 175). Arrange the salad on a large platter, place the kebabs directly on top of it, and sprinkle with the garam masala. Tomato-Ginger Salad (page 176) may also be served with the lamb, as well as some pita bread.

Makes 2 servings

Ground Lamb Kebabs

Kheema Kabab

This lamb mixture may be broiled on skewers or formed into patties and pan-fried. Leave out the chiles if you prefer a milder dish.

8-12 oz (225–350 g) lean ground lamb
1 small onion, finely chopped
2-3 tablespoons fresh coriander leaves (cilantro), finely chopped
1 teaspoon ground cumin
1 teaspoon ground coriander
1 teaspoon garam masala, commercially prepared or homemade (see page 182)
1 tablespoon grated fresh ginger (optional)

1-2 fresh chiles, seeded and minced, or ground red chile or ground red pepper, to taste (optional)
1 tablespoon fresh lemon juice
1 tablespoon plain yogurt
Salt, freshly ground black pepper and ground red pepper, to taste
1 egg, lightly beaten

1. Combine all the ingredients, except the egg, in a bowl. Knead the mixture vigorously while adding the beaten egg. Form into sausage-shaped kebabs 2 inches (5 cm) long and 1-inch (2½-cm) thick and mold them around long skewers, keeping them in the shape of a sausage.

2. Broil the skewered lamb over a hot charcoal fire or under a broiler that has been preheated to high. Place them about 3 inches from the heat. Turn frequently to brown all sides. Alternately, shape the mixture into thin patties and pan-fry them with a little oil in a nonstick skillet. They should be cooked until they are well done, with no pinkness left in the meat.

VARIATION: *Ground beef or chicken may be substituted for the lamb.*

Makes 2 servings

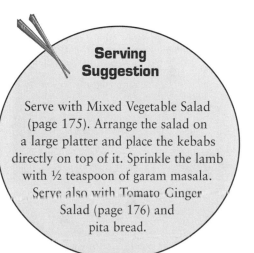

Serving Suggestion

Serve with Mixed Vegetable Salad (page 175). Arrange the salad on a large platter and place the kebabs directly on top of it. Sprinkle the lamb with ½ teaspoon of garam masala. Serve also with Tomato-Ginger Salad (page 176) and pita bread.

India

Kashmir Spiced Meatballs

Kashmiri Kofta

Garlic and onion are never used by Kashmiri Brahmin cooks, who believe that both ingredients heat the blood and encourage unbridled passion.

Meatball mixture

8-12 oz (225-350 g) ground lean lamb

1 tablespoon grated fresh ginger

1-2 fresh chiles, seeded and finely chopped, or ground red chile or ground red pepper, to taste

½ teaspoon ground coriander

½ teaspoon ground cumin

1 teaspoon garam masala, commercially prepared or homemade (see page 182)

Salt, to taste

½ cup (125 g) plain yogurt

• • •

1 tablespoon vegetable oil

2-3 tablespoons water

¼ teaspoon freshly ground black pepper, or to taste

¼ teaspoon ground cardamom or grated nutmeg

Chopped fresh coriander leaves (cilantro) or mint leaves, for garnish

1. Start rice.
2. In a large bowl, combine the lamb, ginger, chiles, ground coriander, cumin, garam masala, salt and a tablespoon of the yogurt. Knead vigorously until the mixture is smooth and the spices are evenly distributed. Form into small oval-shaped balls about the size of a golf ball.
3. Heat a nonstick skillet over medium heat and add the oil. Add the meatballs and fry them until they begin to brown, gently turning to cook on all sides.
4. Add the water, bring to a boil, cover and cook for 4–5 minutes, or until the liquid evaporates and the meatballs are cooked through.
5. Add the remaining yogurt and black pepper and simmer over very low heat for another minute or so. Do not boil. Sprinkle with the cardamom or nutmeg and garnish with the coriander leaves or mint. Serve with rice.

VARIATION: *Ground beef may be substituted for the lamb, though the dish will no longer be authentically kashmiri since Brahmins don't eat beef.*

Makes 2–3 servings

■ Vegetables ■

Mixed Vegetable Curry

This is a one-dish vegetarian meal. There is no fixed combination so the choice of vegetables is up to the cook. Add longer-cooking vegetables first, and when they are half done, add the shorter cooking ones. To add tofu, see the variation at the end of this recipe.

1 tablespoon vegetable oil

¼-½ teaspoon mustard seeds, preferably black

1 small onion, cut in quarters and thinly sliced

2 large cloves garlic, sliced

1 teaspoon grated fresh ginger

1 tablespoon ground coriander

¼–½ teaspoon ground turmeric

Salt, freshly ground black pepper and
ground red pepper, to taste

2 small red potatoes, scrubbed, left
unpeeled, and cut into very small cubes
for faster cooking (optional)

2 small carrots, scraped and cut into thin
rounds

¼ cup water

1 green bell pepper, seeded and cored, and
cut into narrow strips

1 zucchini, cut into thin rounds

8–12 small cauliflower or broccoli florets

1–3 fresh chiles, seeded and chopped
(optional)

⅔–1 cup (150–225 g) plain yogurt

1 handful fresh coriander leaves (cilantro),
chopped

1. Start rice. Prepare the ingredients and place them within easy reach of the stove.

2. Heat a nonstick skillet or large, heavy saucepan over medium heat and add the oil. Add the mustard seeds and toast for about 1 minute, or until they begin to sizzle and pop, while shaking the pan constantly to prevent burning. Add the onions and sauté for 1–2 minutes or until they soften and begin to brown. Add the garlic and ginger and sauté 3–4 seconds. Stir in the ground coriander, turmeric, salt and pepper.

3. Add the potatoes and carrots, stirring to coat them evenly with the spice mixture. Add the water and bring to a boil over high heat. Reduce the heat to low, cover and simmer for 3–4 minutes, or until potatoes are barely tender.

4. Stir in the remaining vegetables and cook them until they are nearly tender but still crisp and crunchy. You may need to add a tablespoon or

two more water if it has completely evaporated.

5. Add the yogurt and cook at a slow simmer until it is heated through, and the vegetables are cooked to desired tenderness. Add more yogurt if more sauce is desired. Stir in the chopped coriander leaves and serve with rice.

VARIATION: *Though it is not authentic to Indian cooking, cubes of tofu would add protein to make this a nutritionally balanced meal. Add 6–7 oz (175–200 g) of firm tofu, cut into ½-inch (1¼-cm) cubes, at the end of Step 3, and stir a minute or two or until they heat through. Some cooks prefer to pan-fry the cubes in a little oil before adding them. If you add tofu, increase the quantity of mustard seeds, ground coriander and black pepper.*

Makes 2–3 servings

Coconut Vegetable Curry

Coconut milk is used instead of yogurt in most South Indian and Sri Lankan dishes. This is a simple, basic recipe, in which a single vegetable, or any combination, may be cooked. Longer-cooking vegetables, such as potatoes, should be cooked first, and the shorter-cooking ones added later. In this recipe only squashes are used.

One 14-oz (400 ml) can coconut milk (do
not shake can)

1 onion, thinly sliced

1 teaspoon grated fresh ginger

1 or 2 fresh chiles, seeded and cut in half,
or, if you don't want a spicy dish, ½ red
bell pepper, chopped

2 cloves garlic, chopped or sliced

One 2-in (5-cm) cinnamon stick

1 teaspoon ground coriander

½ teaspoon ground cumin

Salt, freshly ground black pepper and
    ground red chile or ground red pepper,
    to taste

2 zucchini and 2 yellow squash, cut into
    ¼-in (½-cm) rounds, or 3 cups (225 g)
    butternut squash, cubed

Coconut cream, from the canned coconut
    milk

1. Start rice. Prepare the ingredients and place them within easy reach of the stove.
2. Open the can of coconut milk. Skim the cream off the top and set aside.
3. In a large saucepan, combine all of the ingredients except the zucchini, yellow squash and coconut cream. Bring to a slow simmer and cook gently over low heat for about 5 minutes. Do not boil.
4. Add the zucchini and yellow squash and simmer over low heat until they are just tender. Add the reserved coconut cream and simmer for 1–2 minutes longer, stirring constantly. Serve as a side dish or with rice as part of a vegetarian meal.

Makes 2–3 servings

Spiced Potatoes with Peas

Alu Bhaji

This may be prepared either with potatoes that have been previously boiled or uncooked ones. This dish goes well with Lamb Kebabs (page 166).

1 large boiling potato or 4 small potatoes

1 tablespoon vegetable oil

¼ teaspoon mustard seeds

¼ teaspoon cumin seeds

¼ teaspoon coriander seeds

½ small onion, finely chopped

1 clove garlic, finely chopped (optional)

1-2 fresh chiles, seeded and chopped
    (optional)

¼ teaspoon ground turmeric

½ cup (75 g) fresh or frozen green peas

Salt, freshly ground black pepper and ground
    red chile or ground red pepper, to taste

Chopped fresh coriander leaves (cilantro),
    for garnish

1. Parboil the potato(es) for 4–5 minutes, cool slightly, then peel and cube.
2. Heat a nonstick skillet over medium-high heat and add the oil. Add the mustard, cumin and coriander seeds and toast for about 1 minute, shaking the pan to prevent burning.
3. Add the onion, garlic and chiles and sauté 2–3 minutes, or until the onion becomes soft and transparent. Stir in the turmeric.
4. Add the potatoes and sauté them gently for 4–5 minutes or until they begin to brown.
5. Stir in the peas, salt and pepper, reduce the heat to low and cook for 1–2 minutes. Garnish with the coriander leaves. Serve as a side dish or as one of multiple dishes in a vegetarian meal.

Makes 2–3 servings

Sautéed Eggplant and Tomatoes

Baingan Bhaji

Eggplant is one of my favorite vegetables, and it pairs so well with tomatoes. But it has one fault, and that is its blotterlike tendency to soak up oil. That fact is legendary, as is told in an old Turkish folktale. One version explains why a Turkish eggplant concoction got the name of *Imam Bayildi* (literally, "the Imam fainted"). It seems that the Imam was so fond of this dish that he had his cook prepare it for his dinner every day. One day it did not appear, and when he learned that his favorite dish had exhausted his entire supply of olive oil, he fell into a faint.

Happily, there is help for this problem. Dieticians tell us that eggplant contains numerous air cells, which soak up oil like a sponge. As a result, fried eggplant can easily absorb several times its weight in oil. Flattening the eggplant with a heavy weight squeezes the air out of the cells and reduces the amount of oil it can absorb. Also, cooking in a nonstick pan makes a big difference because much less oil is required to keep the eggplant from scorching.

1½–2 tablespoons vegetable oil

¼ teaspoon mustard seeds, preferably black

¼ teaspoon cumin seeds

½ teaspoon coriander seeds

1 small onion, finely chopped

2 large cloves garlic, finely chopped

1-2 small fresh red or green hot chiles, seeded and minced, or ¼ teaspoon ground red chile or ground red pepper, or to taste

1 lb (450 g) eggplant, peeled and cut into 1-in (2½-cm) cubes

6 cherry tomatoes, halved, or 2 small tomatoes, quartered

1 teaspoon garam masala, commercially prepared or homemade (see page 182)

Salt and freshly ground black pepper, to taste

1 handful chopped fresh coriander leaves (cilantro)

1. Heat a nonstick skillet over high heat and add 1 teaspoon of the oil. Drop in the mustard, cumin and coriander seeds and toast, shaking the pan, for about 1 minute or until the seeds begin to sizzle and pop.

2. Add the onion, garlic and chiles and sauté until the onion becomes soft and transparent, but not brown, 1–2 minutes.

3. Add the remaining oil. When hot add the eggplant cubes and sauté until they begin to brown, about 10 minutes, tossing well in the spice mixture.

4. Add the tomatoes and sauté until they soften, mixing well with the eggplant. Add a tablespoon or two of water to prevent scorching if the mixture seems dry. Stir and toss until the vegetables are cooked.

5. Stir in the garam masala, salt and pepper, and half of the chopped coriander leaves. Cook 2 more minutes. Garnish with the remaining coriander leaves and serve as a side dish or part of a vegetarian meal.

VARIATION: *To make Spiced Bell Peppers with Tomato, substitute 1 large green and 1 large red bell pepper for the eggplant in Step 3, use only 1 tablespoon oil, and sauté about 5 minutes.*

Makes 2–3 servings

Bengali Five-Spice Zucchini

The spices in this mixture are left whole and have a wonderful aroma when they are toasted. Buy the mixture in a jar ready-made, or make your own very easily from the recipe on page 182.

1 tablespoon vegetable oil

1 teaspoon Bengali five-spice mixture (*panch phoran*, see page 182)

2 zucchini, sliced into thin rounds

½ cup (115 g) plain yogurt

Freshly ground black pepper

1. Heat a nonstick skillet over medium heat. Add the five-spice mixture and toast for a few seconds until the spices sizzle and pop. Shake the pan to keep the spice mixture from burning.
2. Add the zucchini rounds and sauté them until they soften and begin to brown, about 5 minutes.
3. Stir in the yogurt and cook until it heats through. Do not let it boil. Sprinkle with the pepper and serve.

Makes 2 servings

Cauliflower and Red Pepper Sauté

Gobi ki Sabzi

The red bell pepper adds a note of color to the bland appearance of cauliflower, making this dish beautiful to behold and delicious.

1 tablespoon vegetable oil

½ teaspoon mustard seeds, preferably black

½ teaspoon cumin seeds

1 small onion, finely chopped

1 large clove garlic, finely chopped

1-2 small fresh red or green chiles, seeded and minced, or ¼ teaspoon ground red chile or ground red pepper

Salt and freshly ground black pepper, to taste

¼ teaspoon ground turmeric

1 small cauliflower, divided into small florets

1 small red bell pepper, seeded and cut into narrow strips

1 tablespoon fresh lemon juice

½ teaspoon garam masala, commercially prepared or homemade (see page 182)

1 handful fresh coriander leaves (cilantro), chopped

1. Heat a nonstick skillet over high heat and add the oil. Add the mustard and cumin seeds and toast for a few seconds to 1 minute, or until they begin to sizzle and pop. Shake the pan to prevent burning.
2. Add the onion, garlic and chile and sauté about 1 minute. Add the salt, black pepper and turmeric. Continue stirring for another minute or until the onion becomes soft and transparent, but not brown.
3. Add the cauliflower and red bell pepper and stir until they are well coated with the spice mixture. Sauté until the edges of the cauliflower begin to brown. If necessary, add a tablespoon or two of water to prevent scorching. Cook until the vegetables are tender but still very crisp.
4. Sprinkle with the lemon juice, garam masala and half of the chopped coriander leaves. Stir well. Transfer to a serving dish and garnish with the remaining coriander leaves. Serve as a side dish or as part of a vegetarian meal.

VARIATION: *Green or wax beans may be substituted for the cauliflower.*

Makes 2–3 servings

Mushroom Sauté with Peas

Khumbi Bhaji

This is an excellent and especially quick vegetable sauté. Any variety of fresh mushrooms will do.

1 tablespoon vegetable oil

¼ teaspoon mustard seeds, preferably black

¼ teaspoon cumin seeds

2 fresh or dried red chiles, cut in half and seeded

½ small onion, finely chopped

¼ teaspoon ground turmeric

8 oz (125 g) fresh mushrooms, trimmed and sliced

8 oz (150 g) green peas or snow peas, tips and strings removed, fresh or frozen

½ teaspoon garam masala, commercially prepared or homemade (see page 182)

Chopped fresh coriander leaves (cilantro), for garnish

1. Heat a nonstick skillet over medium heat and add the oil. Drop in the mustard and cumin seeds and toast for a few seconds to 1 minute, or until the seeds begin to sputter and pop. Shake the pan to prevent burning. Add the chiles and onion and sauté them until the onion softens and begins to brown, about 2 minutes. Stir in the turmeric.

2. Add the mushrooms and sauté 1–2 minutes or until they soften. Add the green peas or snow peas and sauté another 2 minutes, or until the mushrooms are done and the peas are just tender. If the mixture seems dry, add a tablespoon or two of water to prevent scorching. The dish may be served at this point as a dry sauté. Sprinkle with the garam masala and garnish with the chopped coriander leaves. Serve as a side dish or as part of a vegetarian meal.

VARIATION: *Some cooks add yogurt at the end to produce a dish with a sauce. Add ½ cup (125 g) plain yogurt and stir over low heat until yogurt is heated through.*

Makes 2–3 servings

Spicy Okra
Bhendi Bhaji

Okra is only good when it is young and fresh. If the tip of the pod snaps off when you bend it, it is tender and young. If the tip merely bends and does not break off, it will be tough and stringy. This is a very quick recipe to prepare and may even make you an okra devotee.

1-2 tablespoons vegetable oil

1 onion, thinly sliced

12 oz (300 g) okra, ends trimmed and pods sliced in bite-size pieces

1 teaspoon ground coriander

1 tablespoon ground cumin

½ teaspoon ground fennel seeds

Salt, freshly ground black pepper and ground red pepper, to taste

Chopped fresh coriander leaves (cilantro), for garnish

1. Heat a nonstick skillet over medium heat and add the oil. Add the onions and sauté until they soften and turn golden brown.

2. Add the okra, ground coriander, cumin, fennel, salt and pepper. Continue to sauté, turning the okra pieces to brown on all sides, about 4–5 minutes. Cook until the okra is tender-crisp. Transfer to a warmed platter and garnish with the chopped coriander leaves. Serve as a side dish or as a part of a vegetarian meal.

Makes 2–3 servings

Tomatoes Stewed with Toasted Spices

Canned tomatoes may be substituted for fresh ones. Bengali five-spice mixture is available ready-mixed in a jar, or make your own from the recipe on page 182).

½ teaspoon vegetable oil
1 teaspoon Bengali five-spice mixture
(*panch phoron*, see page 182)
1-2 dried red chiles, seeded and chopped,
or dried red pepper flakes, to taste
4 tomatoes, cut in half, then into thin
slices
1 teaspoon palm sugar or brown sugar
Freshly ground black pepper

1. Heat a saucepan over medium heat and add the oil. Add the Bengali five-spice mixture and toast a few seconds until the spices sizzle and pop. Shake the pan to keep the spice mixture from burning. Add the chiles and stir for a few seconds.

2. Add the tomato slices, sugar and black pepper. Mix well. To keep the mixture from scorching, you may need to add a tablespoon or two of water. Cover the pan and simmer for 3–5 minutes on low heat, or until the tomatoes are cooked through.

Makes 2 servings

■ **Raitas & Salads** ■

Raitas are refreshing, saladlike combinations that use yogurt as a base, to which vegetables or fruits are mixed and seasoned with spices. Some are even made with dumplings. Like a salad, a raita provides a cool contrast to highly seasoned main dishes. The following are common combinations, which require little or no cooking. You may adjust ingredients and seasonings according to availability and taste. Serve one or more of these as an accompaniment to a main dish, or as part of a vegetarian meal.

Cucumber Raita
Kheera ka Raita

1 cup (225 g) plain (full- or low-fat) yogurt
1 cucumber, peeled, cut in half lengthwise,
seeded and cut into thin slices
1 large clove garlic, finely chopped or crushed
1 teaspoon ground or whole cumin seeds,
toasted in a small skillet over low heat
for 30 seconds or less (do not burn)
1 tablespoon chopped fresh coriander
leaves (cilantro) or mint leaves or 1½
teaspoons crumbled dried mint leaves
Salt and freshly ground black pepper, to
taste

Place all the ingredients in a bowl and mix well.

VARIATION: *Cucumber-Tomato Raita. Dice a small, firm, tomato and add to the mix.*

Makes 2–3 servings

Potato Raita

Alu ka Raita

4 small or 2 medium potatoes, boiled,
    cooled, peeled and cut into ½-in
    (1½-cm) cubes
1½ tablespoon vegetable oil
¼ teaspoon fenugreek seeds (optional)
½ teaspoon whole or ground cumin seeds
½ teaspoon whole or ground mustard seeds
1 small onion, finely chopped
Salt, freshly ground black pepper and
    ground red pepper, to taste
½ to 1 cup (115–225 g) plain (full- or low-
    fat) yogurt
About 2 tablespoons chopped fresh
    coriander leaves (cilantro)

1. Prepare the potatoes and set aside.
2. Heat a nonstick skillet over
   medium-high heat and add the
   oil. Add the fenugreek, if using,
   the cumin and mustard seeds and,
   while shaking the pan, toast the
   seeds for about 1 minute or until
   they sputter and crackle.
3. Add the onion and sauté until it
   softens and begins to brown. Add
   the potatoes, salt and the black
   and red pepper, and stir to coat
   the potatoes with the spices.
4. Transfer to a serving bowl. Add
   the yogurt and coriander leaves
   and gently stir the mixture.

Makes 2–3 servings

Spinach Raita

Palak ka Raita

½ tablespoon vegetable oil
½ teaspoon mustard seeds, preferably black
½ teaspoon cumin seeds
¼ teaspoon fenugreek seeds
1 small onion, cut in half and thinly sliced
1 bunch fresh spinach, about 1 lb (450 g),
    stemmed and washed, but not dried

Salt, freshly ground black pepper and
    ground red pepper, to taste
½ cup (125 g) plain yogurt

1. Heat a nonstick skillet over
   medium-high heat and add the
   oil. Add the spices and toast a
   few seconds until they sputter
   and crackle. Add the onion and
   sauté until it softens and begins to
   brown.
2. Add the spinach, salt and the black
   and red pepper, and stir until the
   spinach wilts. Cover for a few seconds to steam the spinach.
3. Remove from the heat and stir in
   the yogurt. Transfer to a serving
   bowl.

Makes 2–3 servings

Mixed Vegetable Salad

Salad is a traditional accompaniment
to tandoori and kebab dishes. The
meat is cooked and placed on top of
the salad, and usually sprinkled with
a little ground red chile or garam
masala. This, and the next two salads, can all be served this way. The
salad ingredients may be varied to
include vegetables and fruits in season. Lettuce is not usually included
but, if you wish, you may start with a
bed of fresh lettuce leaves.

Lettuce leaves (optional)
1 large onion, preferably a mild red one,
    cut in half and thinly sliced
2 tomatoes, sliced
Red radishes or Japanese daikon, trimmed
    and sliced
Fresh coriander leaves (cilantro) and/or
    green onions (scallions)
Salt and freshly ground black pepper
Fresh lemon juice
A pinch of garam masala, commercially

prepared or homemade (see page 182),
or ground red chile

1 lemon, cut into wedges

Arrange a bed of lettuce leaves, if using, on a platter. Spread the onion slices on top and decoratively place the radishes, coriander leaves and green onions around the plate. Add the salt and pepper and sprinkle generously with the lemon juice. Place tandoori (page 164) or kebabs (page 166) on top, sprinkle with the garam masala or ground red chile and garnish with the lemon wedges.

Makes 2–3 servings

Tomato-Ginger Salad

Kachumbar

1 onion, preferably a mild red one, cut into
quarters and thinly sliced

2 tomatoes, diced

1 generous tablespoon peeled and finely
shredded fresh ginger

1 or 2 fresh hot chiles, seeded and cut
into thin rings, or, for a milder dish,
Anaheim or bell peppers, thinly sliced

1-2 tablespoons chopped fresh coriander
leaves (cilantro)

3-4 tablespoons fresh lemon juice

Salt and freshly ground black pepper, to
taste

Combine the salad ingredients in a serving bowl. Sprinkle with the lemon juice, salt and pepper. Mix well.

Makes 2–3 servings

Tomato, Green Onion and Mint Salad

Tamatar Salad

2 tomatoes, sliced

3 green onions (scallions), thinly sliced

10 or 12 fresh mint leaves, finely chopped

Dressing

3-4 tablespoons fresh lemon juice

1-2 tablespoons vegetable oil

Salt, freshly ground black pepper and
ground red chile, to taste

Place the salad ingredients in a serving bowl. Combine the dressing ingredients in a small bowl, mix well and pour over the salad. Toss and serve.

Makes 2–3 serving

◼ Chutneys ◼

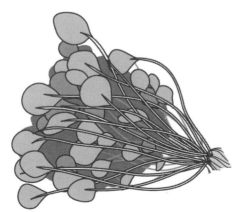

Chutneys

Fresh chutneys are the genuine chutneys of India, whereas the preserved ones, like Major Grey's, are most popular with Westerners. Fresh chutneys are a simple mixture of raw foods, ground or finely cut, and blended with seasonings. A dab or two of this spicy condiment always accompanies an Indian curry.

The following two chutneys were chosen because they are easy to make in a food processor.

Mint Chutney
Podina Chatni

> 1 cup firmly packed fresh mint leaves
> ½ small onion or 3 green onions (scallions), chopped
> 1 teaspoon grated fresh ginger
> 1 teaspoon minced fresh green chile
> ½ teaspoon sugar
> 2–3 tablespoons fresh lemon juice
> Salt and freshly ground black pepper, to taste

Combine the ingredients in a small food processor and blend to a smooth paste. Add a little water to facilitate the process. It may be necessary to process half a cup at a time if the machine labors. The chutney will keep in the refrigerator for about a week in a jar with a tight lid.

Makes about 1 cup

Cilantro Chutney
Dhania Chatni

Substitute fresh coriander leaves (cilantro) for the mint leaves in the recipe above.

Makes about 1 cup

■ Eggs ■

Sautéed Omelet, Parsi-Style
Bhurji Anda

Parsis, who fled Persia more than a thousand years ago to escape religious persecution, settled in Bombay, where Zoroastrianism is still widely practiced. The Persians also brought their culinary traditions, which have since merged with those of India. Adding vegetables to this egg dish is optional.

> 4 whole eggs or 2 whole eggs and 4 egg whites, lightly beaten
> 1–2 tablespoons water
> Pinch of salt and freshly ground black pepper
> 1 tablespoon vegetable oil
> 2 green onions (scallions) or ½ small onion, finely chopped
> 1 teaspoon grated fresh ginger
> 1 teaspoon minced fresh green chile, or to taste
> 1 small tomato, coarsely chopped (optional)
> ¼–½ small zucchini, coarsely grated (optional)
> ¼–½ teaspoon ground cumin
> 1 tablespoon chopped fresh coriander leaves (cilantro)

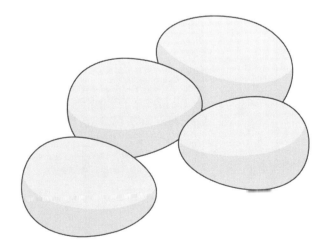

Garnishes

> Garam masala or ground cumin
>
> 1 tomato, cut into quarters
>
> Sprigs of fresh coriander leaves (cilantro)

1. Combine the eggs, water, salt and pepper and beat lightly until just mixed but not frothy. Set aside.
2. Heat a nonstick skillet over medium heat and add the oil. Sauté the onions, ginger and chiles until the onions are soft but not brown, about 2 minutes.
3. Add the tomato and/or zucchini (if including vegetables), and sauté them for a minute or two until softened. Add the cumin and coriander leaves and stir a few seconds to mix thoroughly.
4. Pour in the beaten egg mixture and reduce the heat to low. Stir and lift the eggs as they begin to set and form creamy curds. The omelet should not be cooked dry. Serve on a warmed platter and sprinkle with a pinch of the garam masala or cumin. Garnish with the tomato wedges and coriander sprigs.

Makes 2 servings

Eggs Fried with Eggplant and Tomato

Eggs cooked with eggplant is an unusual, but delicious, combination. For some facts and lore about eggplant, see the recipe Sautéed Eggplant and Tomatoes on page 170.

> 4 whole eggs or 2 whole eggs and 4 egg whites, lightly beaten

> 1–2 tablespoons water
>
> Pinch of salt and freshly ground black pepper
>
> 1½ tablespoons vegetable oil
>
> ½ small onion finely chopped
>
> 1 teaspoon minced fresh green chile, or to taste
>
> 1 small slender Chinese or Japanese eggplant, cut into very small pieces
>
> ¼–½ teaspoon ground cardamom
>
> 2 whole cloves
>
> 1 small tomato, coarsely chopped
>
> Garam masala, commercially prepared or homemade (see page 182), or ground cumin, to sprinkle over finished dish
>
> Lemon wedges and fresh coriander leaves (cilantro), for garnish

1. Combine the eggs, water, salt and pepper and beat lightly until mixed but not frothy. Set aside.
2. Heat a nonstick skillet over medium heat and add the oil. Add the onions, chiles and eggplant and sauté until the onions and eggplant become soft but not brown, 3–5 minutes. Stir in the spices and cook for another minute or so.
3. Add the tomato and continue to sauté another 2–3 minutes, or until the mixture is blended and well done.
4. Pour in the beaten egg mixture and reduce the heat to low. Stir and lift the eggs as they begin to set and form creamy curds. Serve on a warmed platter and sprinkle with a pinch of the garam masala or cumin. Garnish with the lemon wedges and coriander leaves.

Makes 2 servings

Legumes ■ Dal

Dal is the Hindi name for all members of the legume family, encompassing lentils, beans and peas that come in a variety of colors, sizes and tastes. In some form or other, they are eaten daily in almost every Indian home, providing an important source of protein. Dal is always eaten with rice or Indian breads, which makes a lot of sense from a dietary point of view. The amino-acid balance of legumes is improved when eaten with rice, corn, or any grain or cereal food.

The simplest cooking method is to fry the spices, onions, garlic, ginger or tomato and add to this mixture (*tarka*), the lentils, beans or peas and water, which are simmered together until done. Another common method is to fry the seasonings separately while the legumes are simmering, pouring them over the dal once it is cooked. Each region in India cooks its dals in different ways and with different seasonings. They may be very spicy or very mild, sweet and sour, or cooked with vegetables. The consistency varies, but in general it should be thick. Indians from the North prefer their dals thicker because they eat them with bread; Indians from the South prefer them thinner, because they eat them with rice.

Aromatic Red Lentils
Masur Dal

Any type of lentils may be used in this recipe, but the quickest cooking variety is the orange-red colored lentil known as *masur dal*, which cooks in about 15 minutes. Longer-cooking green or brown lentils may also be prepared this way, but they will take about 20 to 25 minutes to cook.

> 1 cup (about 7 oz/200 g) red lentils
>   (*masur dal*)
> 1 tablespoon vegetable oil
> 1 onion, coarsely chopped
> 1-2 large cloves garlic, chopped
> 1 tablespoon grated fresh ginger
> ¼-½ teaspoon ground turmeric
> Salt and freshly ground black pepper, to taste
> 2 dried chiles or hot red pepper flakes, to
>   taste (optional)
> ½-1 teaspoon garam masala, commercially
>   prepared or homemade (see page 182)
> Chopped fresh coriander leaves (cilantro)
>   or mint leaves, for garnish

1. Wash the lentils, discarding those that float to the surface as well as any foreign matter. Drain well.
2. Heat a large saucepan over medium heat. Add the oil and sauté the onions, garlic and ginger until the onions soften and begin to brown. Stir in the turmeric and mix well.
3. Add the lentils, about 3 cups (750 ml) hot water, the salt, black pepper and chiles. Mix well and bring to a boil over high heat.

Turn the heat down to low, and cook until the lentils are half done, about 7 minutes. Stir in the garam masala and continue to cook until the lentils are tender but still intact, about 7 more minutes. Taste for doneness. Add more water if necessary, or if there is too much liquid, leave the lid off the pan for a few minutes. When done, the lentils should have a thick consistency. Garnish with the coriander or mint leaves. Serve with rice and a vegetable as a vegetarian meal, or with a simple meat dish and a salad or raita for a non-vegetarian meal.

Makes 2–3 servings

Kitchery

The name of this dish, spelled in many ways—khichuri, kitcherie, kitchri and kedgeree—is an Anglo-Indian word that, as described in the Oxford English Dictionary, is "a mess of rice cooked with butter and dal and flavored with a little spice, shredded onion and the like; a common dish all over India." Because it is also common all over the Middle East, I would guess that it is probably an ancient food combination. It is very nutritious and may be served as the main course in a vegetarian meal. However, even if you use the quick-cooking red lentil, *masur dal*, it will take about 30–35 minutes to cook from start to finish. Prepared with more liquid, it will have the consistency of a thick soup, or with just enough liquid, it will produce a dry, fluffy result.

½ cup (4 oz/100 g) red lentils
½ cup (4 oz/100 g) long-grain rice

2 tablespoons vegetable oil
1 large onion, coarsely chopped
1 teaspoon garam masala, commercially prepared or homemade (see page 182), or 1 short cinnamon stick, 3 cardamom pods, 4 whole cloves and 6 peppercorns
1¾ cups (425 ml) boiling water or, for a soupier consistency, use 2½ cups (625 ml) water
Salt, to taste
Chopped fresh mint or coriander leaves (cilantro), for garnish

1. Put a kettle of water on the stove to boil. Wash the lentils, discarding those that float to the surface as well as any foreign matter. If you wish, you may also wash the rice as Indian and other Asian cooks typically do. Drain well.
2. Heat a nonstick soup pot over medium-high heat, add the oil and sauté the onions until soft and golden brown, 2–3 minutes. Remove half of the onions from the pot and set aside for garnish.
3. If using whole spices, add them now. Toast them for about 1 minute, or until they are fragrant and begin to sputter and pop. Be careful not to burn them. If using garam masala, stir it into the onions for a few seconds. (For a spicier dish, use both garam masala and whole spices.) Add thte lentils and rice and cook with the onions and spices for 2–3 minutes, stirring constantly.
4. Add the hot water and bring to a boil. Cover and simmer over low heat for about 20 minutes. Do not let the mixture stick to the pot. After about 15 minutes, check to see if the rice and lentils are tender.
5. Garnish with the reserved browned onions and mint or coriander leaves. Serve with a salad

(pages 175–176) and plain yogurt or a raita (pages 174–175).

VARIATION: *Brown lentils may be substituted for the red ones, but the dish may take longer to cook.*

Makes 2–3 servings

Chickpea Salad
Channa Salad

This recipe will not require cooking because chickpeas, as well as other beans, are conveniently available canned. Some are overly salted and should be rinsed well in a colander under cold running water before adding the seasoning. Reduced-salt varieties are also available.

One 15-oz (425-g) can chickpeas, rinsed
and drained well

Dressing
1 tablespoon olive oil
2 tablespoons fresh lemon juice
1 large clove garlic, crushed
2 green onions (scallions), finely chopped
1 fresh red chile, seeded and finely
chopped, or dried red chile or ground
red pepper, to taste
¼ teaspoon ground cumin
Freshly ground black pepper, to taste
Generous quantity chopped fresh coriander
leaves (cilantro) or mint leaves

Place the drained chickpeas in a serving bowl. Combine the dressing ingredients in a small bowl, mix well and pour over the chickpeas. Toss well and serve.

VARIATION: *Canned red kidney beans or black-eyed peas may be substituted for the chickpeas.*

Makes 2–3 servings

Spiced Three-Bean Salad
Rajma-Chana Masala

Using 3 cans of beans will produce more than 2–3 servings, but the salad keeps well and may be even more flavorful the next day.

One 15-oz (425-g) can chickpeas, rinsed
and drained
One 15-oz (425-g) can red kidney beans,
rinsed and drained
One 15-oz (425-g) can black-eyed peas,
rinsed and drained

Dressing
2 tablespoons olive oil
4 tablespoons fresh lemon juice
2 large cloves garlic, crushed
1 teaspoon garam masala, commercially
prepared or homemade (see page 182)
Salt, freshly ground black pepper and
ground red pepper, to taste
Generous quantity of chopped fresh
coriander leaves (cilantro) or mint
leaves

Place the rinsed and drained beans in a serving bowl. Combine the dressing ingredients in a small bowl and pour over beans. Toss well.

Makes about 6 servings

India

Spices

Garam Masala

There are many versions of the spice blend called garam masala, which literally means hot (*garam*) spice (*masala*). They not only vary from region to region, but also from cook to cook. Some contain only hot spices, others only fragrant ones. The following combination contains a little of both. Garam masala is available ready-mixed in jars at Asian food stores and many supermarkets.

    4 tablespoons coriander seeds
    2 tablespoons cumin seeds
    1–2 tablespoons black peppercorns
    2 teaspoons cardamom seeds
    2 cinnamon sticks or 2 tablespoons ground
        cinnamon
    1 teaspoon cloves
    1 whole nutmeg

1. Heat a small frying pan over medium-low heat and toast all the spices, except the nutmeg. Shake the pan to keep the spices from burning. The process will take 1 or more minutes, depending on the intensity of the heat. Do not brown or burn the spices or they will need to be discarded. Keep a lid handy to keep them from jumping out of the pan. As soon as they start to release their aroma and begin to sputter and pop, remove them to a plate and cool.
2. Finely grind the toasted spices in a pepper grinder or a clean coffee grinder. Grate the nutmeg and add it to the mixture.
3. Store in an airtight jar in a cool, dark place. Garam masala will keep for several months.

Bengali Five-Spice Mixture
Panch Phoron

This five-spice mixture (*panch* means five) is not to be confused with the Chinese five-spice mixture. *Panch phoron* is known as the salt and pepper of Bengal. Proportions vary from cook to cook; some use an equal quantity of each spice, as I have done. Less fenugreek is used in this mixture because it can have a bitter edge to it.

    1 tablespoon cumin seeds
    1 tablespoon fennel seeds
    1 tablespoon mustard seeds
    1 tablespoon onion seeds (*kalonji*)
    1 teaspoon fenugreek seeds

Combine the spices and store in an airtight jar in a cool dry place. Before using, measure out the quantity you need. Toast the seeds in a dry (or slightly oiled) frying pan over medium heat for a few seconds, or until they crackle and pop. Shake the pan to avoid browning or burning them. Keep a lid handy to keep the seeds from jumping out of the pan.

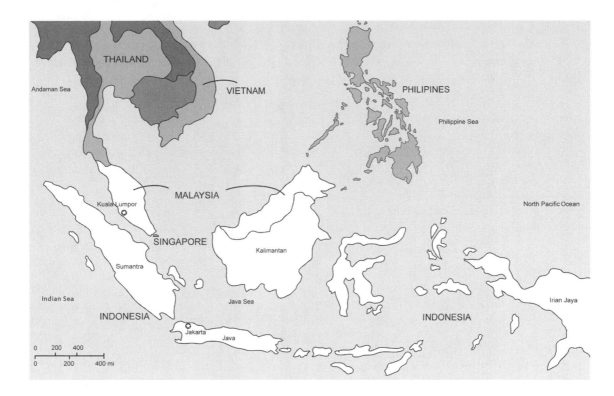

Indonesia & Malaysia

Straddling the equator between Australia and the Asian mainland are 13,500 islands, of which about 6,000 are inhabited, stretching for more than 3,000 miles. Within this span lie thousands of tiny coral atolls, dense jungle and, in some remote areas, tribes living a subsistence lifestyle virtually untouched by the modern world. The distances are immense and the contrasts startling. In the steamy, tropical coastal areas there are thriving cosmopolitan cities, bustling seaports and lush, green terraced rice fields. A spine of chilly mountain ranges extends throughout the main islands, including more than 400 volcanoes.

Blessed with abundant rainfall, rich soil and seas teeming with edible life, this tropical paradise is home to the world's fourth most populous nation, Indonesia, in which more than 200 million people live in an area only three times that of Texas.

Indonesia is thought to have been settled by peoples from Malaya and Oceania. The first foreign visitors came for trade and commerce from India and China. From the third to the thirteenth century, Indonesia was dominated by Indian civilizations through an influx of Indian traders and Hindu and Buddhist monks, and by the ninth century, the spectacular Buddhist temples of Borobudur were built. Hindus and Chinese settled on the larger islands, bringing their cultures, traditions and cuisines. These three cultures co-existed peacefully, learning from each other until the arrival of the Arabs in the thirteenth century, who came not only for trade but also as evangelists for Islam. Their mission succeeded. Islam replaced other religions in most areas except Bali, and today 85 percent of Indonesia's population is Muslim.

But some Hindus refused to accept Allah and under the leadership of a prince of the last Hindu-Javanese Empire, a group of priests, artists, dancers, musicians and probably chefs, fled east to Bali, the only Hindu island in Muslim Indonesia. Protected from invaders by seas and mountains, and left more or less alone, even by the Dutch, the Javanese Hindus managed to preserve their culture and integrate it with their pre-Hindu worship of nature gods. Religion is a vital force in Bali, and entire villages participate.

No history of Indonesia would be complete without some mention of the spice trade. Located at the crossroads of the great trade route between the Middle East and Asia, "the Indies," as they were called, have, through the centuries, lured traders, pirates and immigrants, all eager to share in the riches of the Moluccas—the Spice Islands. They traveled through the sultry waterway known as the Malacca Strait,

Indonesian and Malaysian cuisines have been influenced by a variety of external cultures, giving them a distinct and multi-textured culinary stamp.

which today is an international boundary for Sumatra, Singapore and the Malay Peninsula. As early as 2000 BC, spices such as cinnamon (from Sri Lanka) and cassia (from China) found their way along this spice route to the Middle East. Spices were what Columbus was looking for when he sailed from Spain heading west. But long before Columbus, cloves, nutmeg and other spices from the Moluccas made their way through India and Arabia to the Mediterranean Sea and westward to command fantastic prices in the markets of Europe.

By the time Columbus set sail in the fifteenth century, the demand in Europe for spices from the East was seemingly unquenchable, and the resentment of the stranglehold the Muslim and Italian middlemen in Venice and Genoa had over the spice markets was high. To bypass the middlemen, an alternative route to the East was needed. Columbus and his men set out to find a shortcut to the East by sailing west. They found a new world and a strange fiery plant that they thought was pepper because it burned the mouth like the pepper they were seeking. It turned out to be the chile, and within a century after its discovery, chiles from the New World were planted in the East Indies and became an important ingredient in a majority of the dishes cooked in Southeast Asia.

The Portuguese were the first to find a direct sea route around Africa to India, the source of the lucrative trade that Arab merchants had concealed from their European customers for centuries. Though the Portuguese never succeeded in completely breaking the Arab hold on the spice route, for the first time Europeans were now actively trading along the whole length of it. But Portuguese dominance in Europe was not to last. Toward the end of the sixteenth century, the Dutch and the English were determined to become involved in direct trade with India and Southeast Asia or, as it was called, the East Indies. The Portuguese were ejected by the Dutch, who established their colonial empire there in 1605 and succeeded in systematically exploiting Indonesian resources for three centuries in order to finance the prosperity of Holland. Dutch rule lasted well into the twentieth century.

Four great external culinary influences have shaped the cuisines of Indonesia and Malaysia—Indian, Chinese, Arabian and Dutch colonial—and all four have been absorbed and adapted to fit into the native style of each region. From Hindu cuisine, natives adopted the practice of cooking in coconut milk, and from the Chinese they learned the technique of stir-frying and the eating of noodles. But they held onto their own traditions of spicing and flavoring, with spice combinations varying from one region to another. Sumatran food has strong Indian and Arab influences. Lamb is often used in currylike dishes, and pilau-style rice dishes cooked together with meat are also common. Dishes that are sweet, sour and fiery-hot may be found in the central area of Java, while in western Java meat and fish are cooked more simply, often in banana leaves. Raw vegetables are preferred. Bali, as the only Hindu state in Indonesia, is not bound by Islamic dietary laws and has its own varied cuisine, which includes pork. As in other countries of Southeast Asia, street vendors ply their delicacies all day, the most popular being the ubiquitous satay—marinated meat on bamboo skewers, which originated in Java but has spread throughout Indonesia, Malaysia, Singapore and Thailand.

As in the rest of Southeast Asia, the main cooking utensil, adopted from the Chinese, is the wok, or *kwali,* as well as the mortar and

pestle. And as in most Asian countries, rice is the main staple and the foundation of every meal. With rice, there could be as few as one and as many as six or twenty-six dishes, if one has a battery of servants as the Dutch colonial rulers did when they served their *rijsstafel*, or rice table. The other staple of the islands is fish, which is commonly eaten with rice. Blessed with thousands of miles of shoreline, Southeast Asia has always looked to the sea as a major food source, and every region has its own way to prepare it. Moreover, there would be no Indonesian cuisine without chiles. These are used in great quantities everywhere; yet every dish with chiles and every fiery-hot sambal is meant to be eaten spread over and mixed in with a large quantity of bland rice to balance and quell the heat.

Indonesian-Malay Pantry

To keep shopping to a minimum, and to speed preparation and cooking time, it is helpful to keep these Indonesian and Malay staples on hand in your kitchen.

Ingredients with a Long Shelf Life

black and white peppercorns, ground

candlenuts, macadamia nuts, Brazil nuts or almonds

cardamon, ground

cinnamon, ground and whole sticks

chiles, whole, dried

cloves, whole and ground

coconut milk, unsweetened, canned

coriander, ground

cumin, ground

dried red pepper flakes

dried shrimp paste (*terasi*) or anchovy paste

Indonesian chili sauce (*sambal ulek*, recipe on page 192)

Indonesian sweet soy sauce (*kecap manis*, recipe on page 192)

nutmeg, ground

onion flakes (bawang goring)

red pepper, ground

salam leaves (Indonesian bay leaves) or dried curry leaves

soy sauce

tamarind water or lime juice

turmeric, ground

Fresh Ingredients

chiles (red and green)

coriander leaves (cilantro)

garlic

ginger

lemongrass

lemons

limes

onions

■ Rice ■

White Rice

Nasi Putih

As in common throughout most of Asia, boiled white rice is central to all Indonesian cooking. Long-grain, highly milled and polished rice is generally preferred. The recipe for cooking Boiled Rice, Chinese Style on page 26 is recommended.

Yellow Rice

Nasi Kuning

Yellow is traditionally a sacred color in Southeast Asia and India. In Indonesia, yellow rice is a ceremonial dish eaten during the *Slametan*, a ritual feast combining elements of pagan, Hindu and Islamic religions. The feast was originally held to ward off evil spirits and to celebrate happy occasions, such as the rice harvest, weddings or the birth of a child. It began with prayers and was followed by a sumptuous feast. Today the Slametan is still a significant occasion, but it can also be held solely as a social gathering for friends and family who

wish to enjoy an extensive selection of Indonesian food. The *nasi tumpeng*, a tall cone of yellow rice, is the centerpiece of the Slametan. It is decorated with morsels of meat, eggs, vegetables and nuts, and capped at the peak with a fresh red chile, decoratively cut to look like a flower. It is surrounded by a variety of fish, poultry and vegetable dishes. The Slametan is believed by some to be the origin of the Dutch *rijsstafel,* or rice table.

1 tablespoon vegetable oil
½ medium onion, finely chopped
1 cup (225 g) long-grain rice
1¾ cups canned unsweetened coconut
    milk (shake can well before measuring),
    or unsalted chicken stock or water,
    or a combination of these ingredients
    (eliminate or reduce amount of coconut
    milk for a lower-fat dish)
1 teaspoon ground turmeric
¼ teaspoon ground coriander
¼ teaspoon ground cumin
2 whole cloves
1 cinnamon stick
Slices of cucumber, fresh red chile or
    red bell pepper and green onions
    (scallions), decoratively cut for garnish

1. Heat a medium saucepan over medium-high heat, and add the oil. Stir-fry the onion until it softens, 1–2 minutes. Add the rice and stir-fry 3–4 minutes. The grains will begin to turn opaque and white.
2. Add the coconut milk, stock and/or water. Stir well, and then add the spices. Bring to a boil, reduce the heat to low cover and cook for 15–20 minutes. Do not take the lid off during cooking. After cooking, remove the lid, taste for doneness, stir with a large fork and discard the cinnamon stick. Transfer to a

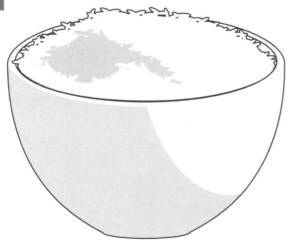

warmed serving dish and garnish as desired.

Makes 2–3 servings

Indonesian Fried Rice
Nasi Goreng

Like Indonesian fried noodles, Indonesian fried rice is a first cousin to its Chinese equivalent. Basically, the recipe is the same as for fried noodles: stir-fry the meat and vegetables, add the seasonings and combine them with the cold rice. Feel free to make any additions or substitutions in the following recipe. It is important to use rice that has been cooked several hours before it is fried, and using day-old rice is even better. The grains of freshly cooked rice are not dry enough and will stick together.

1 tablespoon vegetable oil

1 onion, cut into quarters and thinly sliced

2 large cloves garlic, thinly sliced

6–8 oz (175–200 g) chicken, beef or pork, cut into bite-size cubes

2 green onions (scallions), chopped

3 oz (50 g) fresh or frozen green peas

1 tablespoon Indonesian sweet soy sauce (*kecap manis*, see page 192) or 1 tablespoon reduced-sodium soy sauce mixed with 1 teaspoon brown sugar

1 teaspoon Indonesian chili sauce (*sambal ulek*, see page 192) or fresh or dried chiles or chili sauce or ground red pepper, to taste

4 oz (100 g) small fresh or cooked shrimp, peeled (optional)

3 cups (600 g) cold cooked rice (separate grains as much as possible)

2–3 tablespoons ready-made onion flakes (*bawang goreng*), sold in a jar or packet in many supermarkets, for garnish (optional)

Sliced cucumber, for garnish

1. Heat a nonstick wok (or skillet) over medium-high heat. Add the oil and stir-fry the onion until it softens, about 2 minutes. Add the garlic and stir-fry a few seconds. Add the chicken, beef or pork and stir-fry for about 2 minutes, or until it loses it is no longer pink. Drop in the chopped green onions and green peas and stir-fry a few seconds.
2. Stir in the sweet soy sauce and the chili sauce. Mix well.
3. Add the shrimp and cook briefly until they become opaque, about 1 minute.
4. Add the rice a little at a time, stirring constantly. Continue turning the mixture over until the rice has heated through. Transfer to a warmed platter and garnish with the onion flakes and cucumber slices.

Makes 2–3 servings

■ Satay ■

Grilling foods over a wood or charcoal fire is one of the most ancient cooking methods. Satay, or *sate*, the best known of Southeast Asian grilled dishes—popular in Thai and Singaporean cooking—originated in Indonesia. The word *satay*, probably derived from the English word *steak*, means skewered and grilled over coals. It does not connote a particular flavor. The master chef of satay is the street vendor with his portable kitchen. Each vendor has his own favorite recipe and every island in the Indonesian archipelago also has its own style of preparing satay. The Balinese who are Hindu prefer pork satay. The other islands, being pre-

place a sheet of aluminum foil on the pan under the broiler to catch drips and make cleaning easier.

Satay

Sate

Two basic satay marinades are offered here. One is sweet, the other is hot.

Sweet marinade

> 2 large cloves garlic, finely chopped or crushed
>
> 2 tablespoons tamarind water (see page 245) or fresh lime or lemon juice
>
> 2 teaspoons ground coriander
>
> ½ teaspoon ground cumin
>
> 2 tablespoons Indonesian sweet soy sauce (*kecap manis*, see page 192) or 2 tablespoons reduced-sodium soy sauce sweetened with 1 tablespoon brown or white sugar
>
> 1 tablespoon vegetable oil

Spicy marinade

> 2 large cloves garlic, finely chopped
>
> 2 teaspoons ground coriander
>
> ½ teaspoon ground cumin
>
> 2 tablespoons sambal ulek (see page 192) or ready-made hot chili sauce such as Sriracha brand
>
> 2 tablespoons reduced-sodium soy sauce
>
> 1 tablespoon vegetable oil
>
> 8-12 oz (200–300 g) lean, boneless pork, beef or chicken, cut into ½-in (1½-cm) cubes or strips up to 2 in (5 cm) long
>
> Bamboo skewers

1. Combine the sweet or spicey marinade ingredients in a bowl. Add the meat and toss about until pieces are evenly coated. Marinate for 30 minutes at room temperature. If there is no time to marinate the meat, baste several times while it is cooking.

2. Preheat the oven broiler to high.

dominantly Muslim, eschew pork in favor of beef and chicken.

Quick and economical, this style of cooking has spread all over Southeast Asia. The meat is marinated, grilled, and served with a variety of peanut sauces, which may be made hotter, milder, sweeter or saltier according to your taste. In Java, the sauce is very sweet, while in Sumatra it is flaming hot. The recipes for both the marinade and the peanut sauce are infinitely variable, so feel free to make adjustments to suit your own taste. In Southeast Asia, a satay is always cooked over burning coals, so it makes a good outdoor summer barbecue. On the other hand, it is just as good cooked under an oven broiler or, in a pinch, in a lightly oiled skillet. Be sure to

Note: Kecap manis and sambal ulek are available commercially prepared in Asian food stores and major supermarkets.

3. Thread the meat on the skewers. Broil them about 3 inches (7½ cm) from the heat for about 5 minutes, turning occasionally, until the meat is crisp and brown. Otherwise, forget about using the skewers and simply brown the meat in a hot, lightly oiled skillet for 4–5 minutes, or until done. Serve with Peanut Sauce, Indonesian Style (below) or Sweet-and-Sour Chili Sauce (page 192). In my opinion, the satay is tasty enough as it is and does not need a dipping sauce.

Note: To keep wood skewers from burning, soak them in water before using.

VARIATION: *For a shrimp satay, substitute shrimp for the meat or chicken and add ½ cup unsweetened coconut milk to either marinade.*

Makes 2 servings

■ Sauces ■

The following sauces are used frequently in Indonesian, Malay and Singaporean cuisines, and all are delicious with satay. They are available in jars in Asian food shops and major supermarkets, which saves a lot of time for the hurried cook. But for those who wish to make them from scratch, I offer some simplified recipes. Traditionally, the peanuts are ground by hand in a mortar.

Peanut Sauce, Indonesian Style

Sambal Kacang

1 teaspoon vegetable oil
1 large clove garlic, crushed or minced
1 tablespoon minced shallot or onion
¼ cup (50 ml) canned, unsweetened coconut milk (shake can well before measuring) or water
4 tablespoons smooth or crunchy peanut butter
½–1 teaspoon brown sugar
Ground red pepper, to taste
1 tablespoon fresh lime juice
1 tablespoon Indonesian sweet soy sauce

(*kecap manis*, see page 192) or 1 tablespoon reduced-sodium soy sauce sweetened with 2 teaspoons brown sugar

Heat the oil over low heat. Add the garlic and shallot or onion and cook for about 1 minute. Add the remaining ingredients and cook, stirring constantly, for 2–3 minutes until well blended. If necessary, thin the sauce with additional coconut milk or water.

Makes about ¾ cup

Sweet-and-Sour Chili Sauce

> 5 cloves garlic, crushed and finely chopped
> One 2-in (5-cm) piece fresh ginger, peeled and sliced, or grated
> 5 fresh or dried red chiles, seeded
> 1 teaspoon vegetable oil
> ½ cup (100 g) sugar
> ¼ teaspoon salt
> 1 cup (250 ml) vinegar

Though Nonya-Singaporean in origin, this sauce is a common condiment in Indonesian-Malay cooking. To make, combine the garlic, ginger and chiles in a food processor and blend into a paste. Alternately, you can finely chop these ingredients and cook them in their chopped form. Heat the oil in a small saucepan, add the mixture and stir for a few seconds. Add the remaining ingredients and simmer for a few minutes until they are well blended and the sugar is dissolved. Cool and store in a container with a tight cover.

Makes about 1 cup

Indonesian Sweet Soy Sauce
Kecap Manis

> 1 cup (250 ml) reduced-sodium soy sauce
> ½ cup (150 ml) dark molasses
> 2 tablespoons brown sugar

Combine the ingredients in a saucepan. Cook over low heat until the sugar dissolves. Store in a jar with a tight cover.

Makes about 1 ½ cups

Sambal Ulek

> 10 fresh red chiles, stemmed
> 1 teaspoon salt
> 1 teaspoon white vinegar

Combine the chiles, salt and vinegar in a food processor and grind to a coarse paste. Store in a jar with a tight cover.

Makes about ½ cup

■ Chicken ■

Spicy Chicken Sambal
Sambal Goreng Ayam

Sambal goreng is a general name for a type of sauce made with chiles in which many kinds of meat are cooked. This one is for chicken, but it can also be used for red meat (*sambal goreng daging)* or for shrimp *(sambal goreng udang*). The word *sambal* also refers to a whole range of chile-based condiments, such as *sambal ulek* (used in this recipe), which is a paste of fresh red chiles preserved with salt or vinegar. (A bottled version is available commercially, and a recipe for a homemade version is offered on page 192.) Indonesian chile condiments are fiery hot and are not for those who prefer lightly seasoned food. One solution is to leave out the condiments altogether and substitute milder strains of fresh red or green chile (jalapeño and Anaheim peppers are milder), or use just a touch of dried chile, making up the color difference by adding paprika. The finished dish will have the required pinkish-red color, but not the incendiary taste. A vegetable is added to this recipe to make it a one-dish meal.

> 1–1½ tablespoons vegetable oil
> 1 large or 2 medium onions, coarsely
>   chopped
> 2 large cloves garlic, finely chopped
> 8–12 oz (200–300 g) chicken breast meat,
>   cut into ½-in (1½-cm) cubes
> 1 teaspoon sambal ulek (see page 192),
>   or to taste, or chopped fresh or dried
>   chiles or ground red pepper, to taste,
>   with ½ teaspoon paprika for color
> 1 tablespoon grated fresh ginger
> 3 tablespoons fresh lemon juice
> 10 asparagus spears or 1 handful of
>   snow peas, tips and strings removed
>   (optional)

1. Start rice. Prepare the ingredients and place them within easy reach of the stove.
2. Heat a nonstick wok (or skillet) over medium-high heat. Add the oil and stir-fry the onions for 1–2 minutes, or until they soften. Add the garlic and stir-fry a few seconds.
3. Add the chicken and stir-fry about 2 minutes, or until it begins to brown.
4. Stir in the sambal ulek, ginger, lemon juice and 2–4 tablespoons of water. Reduce the heat to low and simmer for 2–3 minutes to blend the flavors.

5. Add the asparagus or snow peas and simmer for another minute or so, until they are tender but still crisp. Serve with rice.

VARIATION: *Substitute lean tender flank steak for the chicken.*

Makes 2 servings

Coconut Chicken Curry
Opor Ayam

This moderately seasoned dish is very popular all over Java. It is a mild curry using chicken pieces, bones and all. The sauce is white because it does not contain chiles or turmeric, and white pepper is used instead of black. The fastest way to make this dish is to use already-cooked chicken from the supermarket rotisserie.

> 1 tablespoon vegetable oil
> 1 onion, coarsely chopped
> 2 large cloves garlic, chopped
> 1 teaspoon ground coriander
> ½ teaspoon ground cumin
> ½ teaspoon ground white pepper
> 8–12 oz (200–300 g) chicken meat, cut into
>   ½-in (1½-cm) cubes
> 3 candlenuts or macadamia nuts or brazil
>   nuts or 6 blanched almonds, ground or
>   chopped
> 1 cup (250 ml) canned, unsweetened
>   coconut milk (shake can before
>   measuring)
> 1 tablespoon tamarind water (see page
>   245) or fresh lemon or lime juice

1. Start rice. Prepare the ingredients and place them within easy reach of the stove.
2. Heat a nonstick wok (or skillet) over medium-high heat. Add the oil and stir-fry the onions for 1–2 minutes, or until soft and trans-

parent but not brown. Add the garlic and stir-fry 3–4 seconds. Stir in the spices and pepper and mix well.

3. Add the chicken and stir-fry 1–2 minutes until it begins to brown.

4. Add the nuts and coconut milk, stirring constantly until bubbles appear around the edge of the wok. Reduce the heat to low, cover the wok partially and simmer for about 5 minutes. Do not boil or the coconut milk may curdle. Add the tamarind water or lemon or lime juice and more pepper and salt if desired. Serve with rice and a salad or vegetable of your choice.

Makes 2 servings

Green Chicken
Ayam Hijau

Cooking red, yellow, and green meat dishes refers to the color of the sauces—red (*habang*) from red chiles, yellow (*kuning*) from turmeric, and green (*hijau*) from green chiles. It takes a lot of chiles to color a sauce, which means the traditional recipe for this dish may be too fiery for most tastes. In this simplified recipe, green bell peppers are used for color. Add only as many hot green chiles as you can tolerate.

Seasoning paste

1 onion, chopped
2 large cloves garlic, chopped
1-5 fresh green chiles, seeded and chopped
2 slices peeled fresh ginger
½ teaspoon ground coriander

• • •

1 tablespoon vegetable oil
8-12 oz (200–300 g) chicken meat, cut

into ½-in (1¼-cm) cubes, or about 1 lb (450 g) chicken parts
2 salam leaves (Indonesian bay leaves) or dried curry leaves
½ cup of water
2 green bell peppers, seeded and cut into 2-in (5-cm) strips
1 tomato, cut into wedges (optional)
Salt and freshly ground black pepper, to taste

1. Start rice. Prepare the ingredients and place them within easy reach of the stove.

2. Combine the paste ingredients in a small food processor and blend until smooth. If you don't have a food processor, finely chop these ingredients and go on to Step 3.

3. Heat a nonstick wok (or skillet) over medium heat. Add the oil and stir-fry the paste ingredients for about 1 minute. If using hand chopped ingredients, stir-fry them until the onion softens.

4. Add the cubed chicken and stir-fry 1–2 minutes or until it begins to brown. If you're using chicken parts, cook them 5–10 minutes longer, depending on size. Add the *salam* or curry leaves and water. Bring to a boil.

5. Add the bell peppers, tomato, salt and pepper and cook for 3–4 minutes longer, or until the peppers are done but still firm. Serve with rice.

Makes 2–3 servings

Chili-Chicken Stew
Ayam Masak Di Buluh

This simple, stewlike dish is traditionally cooked with a large quantity of hot pepper in a bamboo container (*buluh* means bamboo) over a charcoal fire.

1 lb (450 g) chicken breast or chicken legs or
   any combination of chicken parts, cut into
   small pieces for faster cooking (remove
   skin if a low-fat dish is desired)
Salt and freshly ground black pepper, to taste
4 ripe tomatoes cut into wedges, or one 14-
   oz (450 g) can stewed tomatoes
1 onion, thinly sliced
2 large cloves garlic, thinly sliced
1 green bell pepper, seeded and cut into
   narrow strips (optional)
1 stalk fresh lemongrass (bottom 6 inches
   of the plant only), tough outer leaves
   discarded, sliced, or use grated zest of
   ½ lemon
1-4 fresh chiles, seeded and chopped, or
   dried red pepper flakes or ground red
   pepper, to taste
2-4 tablespoons unsalted chicken stock
   or water
Chopped fresh coriander leaves (cilantro)
   or parsley or sliced green onions
   (scallions), for garnish

1. Start rice.
2. Place the chicken in a heavy
   saucepan. Season with the salt
   and pepper. Add the remaining
   ingredients and bring to a boil.
   Taste for seasoning. Add more hot
   pepper if desired, or more water if
   the mixture seems dry. Reduce the
   heat and cover the pan. Simmer
   for about 15–20 minutes, or until
   the chicken is tender. Garnish with
   the chopped fresh herbs or green
   onions and serve with rice.

Makes 2–3 servings

Simple Broiled Chicken

Ayam Panggang

This is very simple to prepare and
easy to cook. Buy kecap manis ready-
made or use the substitute suggested
in the recipe.

Marinade

2-3 tablespoons Indonesian sweet soy
   sauce (*kecap manis*, see page 192), or
   2 tablespoons soy sauce mixed with 1
   tablespoon brown sugar
1 tablespoon sambal ulek (see page 192) or
   1-3 fresh red chiles or dried red pepper
   flakes or hot chili sauce, to taste
2 large cloves garlic, chopped
2 tablespoons fresh lemon juice or white vinegar
1 tablespoon vegetable oil

• • •

1 lb (450 g) chicken breast or chicken legs
   or any combination of chicken pieces,
   cut into small pieces for faster cooking

1. Start rice.
2. Combine the marinade ingredients
   in a food processor and blend
   them into a coarse paste. If you do
   not have a processor, finely chop
   the ingredients, place in a large
   bowl and coat the chicken pieces
   well on all sides. Let stand 5–10
   minutes. The longer the chicken
   marinates, the stronger the flavor
   will be. If there is not enough time
   to marinate the chicken, baste it
   frequently while cooking.
3. Preheat the broiler to high. Broil
   the chicken until nicely browned
   and tender, turning and basting
   occasionally with the marinade.
   Larger pieces of chicken will take
   longer to cook. While the chicken
   is broiling prepare a cooked vegetable or a salad. Serve with rice.

Makes 2 servings

Spice-Rubbed Chicken Breast

This is a very simple recipe. You will
need a supply of ground spices on
hand. In a pinch, you can substitute
about 1 tablespoon curry powder for
the cumin, coriander and turmeric.

Indonesia & Malaysia

Marinade

1 tablespoon reduced-sodium soy sauce

1 large clove garlic, finely chopped

½ tablespoon ground cumin

½ tablespoon ground coriander

⅛ teaspoon turmeric

½ teaspoon brown sugar

1 tablespoon fresh lemon juice

Ground red pepper, to taste

Freshly ground black peppper, to taste

•   •   •

2 skinless, boneless chicken breast halves
(about 12 oz/300 g)

Fresh coriander leaves (cilantro) or parsley,
for garnish

1½ tablespoons vegetable oil

1. Start rice. Make a salad or vegetable of your choice.
2. Blend the marinade ingredients in a bowl with ½ tablespoon of the vegetable oil. Add the chicken and coat the pieces well. If there is time, let them stand for a few minutes.
3. Heat a nonstick wok (or skillet) over medium-high heat. Add the oil and brown the chicken on both sides until tender, about 15 minutes total. Do not overcook. Garnish with the coriander leaves or parsley and serve with rice.

Makes 2 servings

Chicken Drumsticks with Orange-Soy Glaze

This is an excellent combination of flavors—fruity, sweet-and-sour and hot. You can control the degree of sweetness and heat as you wish.

1 tablespoon vegetable oil

6 chicken drumsticks (about 1 lb/450 g)

1 onion, coarsely chopped

2 large cloves garlic, finely chopped

½ teaspoon sambal ulek (see page 192)

or minced fresh or dried chile and ½
teaspoon paprika for color or ground
red pepper, to taste

5 tablespoons fresh orange juice

2 tablespoons fresh lemon juice

1–2 tablespoons Indonesian sweet soy
sauce (*kecap manis*, see page 192) or
1–2 tablespoons reduced-sodium soy
sauce mixed with ½–1 tablespoon
brown sugar

2 tablespoons unsalted chicken stock or water

Freshly ground black pepper, to taste

Chopped fresh coriander leaves (cilantro)
or parsley, for garnish

1. Start rice. Prepare the ingredients and place them within easy reach of the stove.
2. Heat a nonstick wok (or skillet) over medium-high heat. Add the oil and brown the chicken legs on both sides, about 8–10 minutes. Remove from the wok and keep warm.
3. Add the onion and stir-fry until soft and translucent. Stir in the garlic and sambal ulek. Add remaining ingredients and mix well.
4. Return the chicken to the wok and mix with the sauce. Simmer gently for about 5 minutes, or until the chicken is done and flavors are blended. If the mixture seems dry, add an additional tablespoon or two of water to prevent scorching. Garnish with the chopped coriander leaves or parsley and serve with rice.

Makes 2 servings

Chicken Curry, Java Style

Soto Ayam Jawa

The cooking of Java tends to be more moderately spiced and to use more vegetables. I recommend serving chili sauce at the table. This will allow diners to control the amount of heat to suit their own tolerance.

> 1 tablespoon vegetable oil
> 1 onion, thinly sliced
> 2 large cloves garlic, thinly sliced
> 1 tablespoon curry powder, preferably Javanese curry powder (*bumbu soto*, see page 200)
> 8-12 oz (200-300 g) boneless, skinless chicken meat cut into ½-in (1¼-cm) cubes
> 2 tablespoons unsalted chicken stock or water
> 1 stalk fresh lemongrass (bottom 6 inches of the plant only), tough outer leaves discarded, sliced, or use grated zest of ½ lemon
> Salt and ground red pepper, to taste
> ½ teaspoon sugar
> 1 carrot, scraped and cut into thin strips
> 10 green beans, trimmed and cut lengthwise into thin strips
> ¾ cup (175 ml) canned, unsweetened coconut milk (shake can well before measuring)
> 2 tablespoons roasted peanuts and chopped fresh coriander leaves (cilantro), for garnish

1. Start rice. Prepare the ingredients and place them within easy reach of the stove.
2. Heat a nonstick wok (or skillet) over medium-high heat. Add the oil and stir-fry the onion until it is soft and translucent, about 2 minutes. Add the garlic and stir-fry for 3–4 seconds. Mix in the curry powder and stir well.
3. Add the chicken cubes and stir-fry briskly until they begin to brown, about 2 minutes.
4. Stir in the stock, lemongrass, salt, ground red pepper and sugar and bring to a boil. Add the vegetables and cook until they are tender-crisp, about 2 minutes. Add a little more stock or water, if necessary, to prevent scorching.

5. Reduce the heat and add the coconut milk. Stir frequently until heated through. Do not boil or the coconut milk may curdle. Garnish with the peanuts and coriander leaves. Serve with rice and chili sauce.

Makes 2–3 servings

Chicken and Shrimp, Balinese Style
Sambal Goreng Ayam Udang

This is a spicy combination of chicken, shrimp and coconut milk that is very quick cooking.

Seasoning paste
> 1 onion, coarsely chopped
> 2 large garlic cloves, finely chopped
> 1-in (2½-cm) piece peeled fresh ginger, thinly sliced or grated
> ½ teaspoon ground turmeric
> ½ teaspoon ground coriander
> 1 teaspoon sambal ulek (see page 192) or 1-3 chopped fresh or dried chiles or chili sauce or ground red pepper, to taste

• • •

> 1 tablespoon vegetable oil
> 6 oz (175 g) skinless, boneless chicken breast, cut into thin strips
> 1 cup (250 ml) canned, unsweetened coconut milk (shake can well before measuring)
> 1 tablespoon fresh lime or lemon juice
> 1 teaspoon brown sugar
> 6 oz (275 g) raw or cooked shrimp, peeled
> Snipped chives or chopped parsley, for garnish

1. Start rice. Prepare the ingredients and place them within easy reach of the stove.
2. Combine the paste ingredients in a small food processor, beginning with the wet ingredients, and blend until smooth. You may need to add 1 tablespoon of coconut

milk or water to facilitate the blending. If you don't have a processor, finely chop the ingredients and go on to Step 3.

3. Heat a nonstick wok (or skillet) over medium-high heat. Add the oil and fry the blended ingredients for 1–2 minutes, stirring constantly. If using hand chopped ingredients, stir-fry them until the onions are soft and transparent, but not brown.

4. Add the chicken pieces and stir-fry them until they begin to brown, about 2 minutes.

5. Add the coconut milk and cook, stirring constantly, over medium heat until bubbles appear around the edge of the wok. Do not let the coconut milk boil or it may curdle.

6. Add the lime juice, sugar and shrimp and stir well. If you're using raw shrimp, cook over low heat only long enough for the shrimp to change color. Do not overcook or the shrimp will toughen. If you're using pre-cooked shrimp, cook only long enough to heat through. Remove to a serving dish and garnish with the chives or parsley. Serve with rice.

Makes 2–3 servings

Lamb

Skewered Lamb Kebabs
Sate Kambing (Magbub)

The Arab influence is evident here with the use of lamb. Variations on this dish are found throughout the Muslim world. Substitute beef and you will have a variation on the American hamburger.

8-12 oz (225-350 g) ground lamb or beef
½ small onion, finely chopped
2 large cloves garlic, finely chopped or crushed

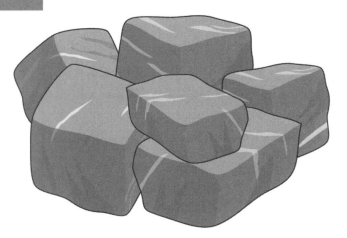

1 tablespoon finely grated fresh ginger (optional)
1 teaspoon ground coriander
½ teaspoon ground cumin
1 tablespoon tamarind water (see page 245) or fresh lime or lemon juice
¼ teaspoon palm or brown sugar
Salt and pepper, to taste
Bamboo skewers, soaked in water

1. Start rice.
2. Heat the broiler to high.
3. Combine all the ingredients and mix thoroughly.
3. The meat may be prepared as skewered kebabs or patties. (To make patties, skip to step 5). To make kebabs, form the mixture into sausage shaped kebabs 2 inches (5 cm) long and 1 inch (2⅓ cm) thick, then mold them around the skewers.
4. Place the skewers on a baking sheet or broiler pan and broil about 3 inches (7½ cm) from the heat until nicely browned and well done, turning occasionally.

5. To make patties, shape the meat mixture into patties and pan-fry them in a hot skillet with a little oil until they are well done.

Makes 2 servings

Serving Suggestion

Serve plain or with Peanut Sauce, (page 191) or Sweet-and-Sour Chili Sauce (page 192) or another chili sauce.

Lamb Curry

Soto Kambing

Lamb in Southeast Asia usually means mutton, which requires a long cooking time. However, if young lamb is used, there is no reason why a curry can't be produced in 30 minutes or less. The curry powder in this recipe is a particular blend of spices, much like the five-spice powder used in Chinese cooking. I have tried to approximate this blend while simplifying the recipe. If your supply of ground spices is low, a commercial curry powder may be substituted.

Seasoning paste

1 onion, chopped

2 large cloves garlic, sliced

1–4 fresh or dried red chiles or dried red pepper flakes, chili sauce or ground red pepper, to taste

1 tablespoon grated fresh ginger (optional)

• • •

1 tablespoon vegetable oil

1 tablespoon Javanese curry powder (*bumbu soto*, see page 200) or commercially-prepared curry powder

1 tablespoon curry powder, preferably Javanese curry powder (*bumbu soto*, see page 200)

1 lb (450 g) lean, tender lamb, preferably from the leg, cut into ½-in (1¼-cm) cubes

2 tablespoons water

2 tablespoons fresh lemon juice

Grated zest of ½ lemon

2 tomatoes, chopped (optional)

½ teaspoon sugar

1 cup (250 ml) canned, unsweetened coconut milk (shake can well before measuring)

1. Start rice. Prepare the ingredients and place them within easy reach of the stove.

2. Combine the seasoning paste ingredients in a small food processor and blend until smooth. If you don't have a food processor, finely chop the ingredients and go on to Step 3.

3. Heat a nonstick wok (or skillet) over medium-high heat. Add the oil and stir-fry the paste ingredients for about 1 minute. If using hand-chopped ingredients, stir-fry them until the onions soften. Add the curry powder and mix well.

4. Add the lamb and stir-fry 3–5 minutes, stirring well to the coat meat with the spice mixture.

5. Mix in the remaining ingredients, except the coconut milk, and cook for another 1–2 minutes, stirring constantly.

6. Stir in the coconut milk and cook over medium heat until bubbles appear around the edge of the wok. Do not let the coconut milk boil or it may curdle. Reduce the heat and simmer for about 10 minutes, or until the meat is tender. Serve with rice.

Makes 2–4 servings

Aromatic Lamb

This simple lamb recipe requires no coconut milk or hot chiles, only a blend of spices and onion, but it is important that the spices be fairly fresh. Toasting them enhances their flavor and aroma, and is a technique common to Indian cooking. Two tablespoons curry powder may be substituted for the spice mixture.

Spice mixture

1 tablespoon ground coriander

1 teaspoon ground cumin

1 teaspoon freshly ground black pepper

¼ teaspoon ground cloves

¼ teaspoon ground nutmeg

¼ teaspoon ground turmeric

One 2-in (5-cm) cinnamon stick or ¼ teaspoon ground cinnamon

• • •

1 tablespoon vegetable oil

1 large onion, cut in half and thinly sliced

1 lb (450 g) lean lamb, cut into ½-in (1¼-cm) cubes

One 1-in (2½-cm) piece of fresh ginger, peeled and sliced

Salt, to taste

½ cup water

Chopped fresh coriander leaves (cilantro) or parsley, for garnish

1. Combine the spices (except the cinnamon stick) and place in a small dry pan. Toast them over very low heat for up to to 1 minute. Or put the spices in a piece of aluminum foil and toast them over low heat in a toaster oven. Be careful not to burn them.

2. Heat a nonstick wok or skillet over medium-high heat. Add the oil and stir-fry the onions until they soften.

3. Add the lamb pieces and stir-fry them until they begin to brown, 2–3 minutes.

4. Add the spices and stir to mix well with the meat. Add the ginger, salt and water and bring to a boil. Reduce the heat and simmer for about 10 minutes, or until lamb is tender. Add more water, if needed, to keep from the lamb scorching. Garnish with the coriander leaves or parsley and serve with rice

VARIATION: *The lamb can be substituted with chicken parts cut into small pieces or, for even faster cooking, boneless chicken cut into bite-size cubes.*

Makes 2–3 servings

■ **Spices** ■

Javanese Curry Powder

Bumbu Soto

This is a nice combination of aromatic spices. Adjust the amount of pepper depending on how much heat you want.

1 tablespoon ground coriander

1 teaspoon ground cumin

¼ teaspon ground turmeric

½ teaspoon ground cinnamon

½ teaspoon grated nutmeg

½–1 teaspoon ground black pepper

¼ teaspoon ground cloves

¼ teaspooon ground cardamom

Mix the spices together and store in a jar with a tight cover.

Makes about 2 tablespoons

■ Beef ■

Beef Randang

Kalio

Kalio is another variation on curry-like dishes cooked in coconut milk. The dish takes on the name *Rendang* (a dry curry), when it is cooked a long time, until all the water in the coconut milk evaporates and the meat becomes dark brown and dry. This cooking method probably developed out of a need to preserve meat in a tropical climate without refrigeration, and also to tenderize buffalo meat. The quick version here is meant to be served with a lot of very peppery sauce, and will be quick-cooking only if very tender beef is used. To make Rendang, continue to cook and stir over low heat until all the sauce disappears and the meat is dry.

Seasoning paste

    1 onion, coarsely chopped
    2 large cloves garlic, finely chopped
    1 slice fresh galangal, chopped or ½
        teaspoon powder (optional)
    One 1-in (2½-cm) piece fresh ginger,
        peeled and thinly sliced
    1-4 fresh red chiles, seeded and chopped,
        or ground red chile or chili sauce or
        ground red pepper, to taste

• • •

    1 tablespoon oil
    1 teaspoon ground coriander
    ½ teaspoon ground cumin
    ½ teaspoon turmeric
    1 stalk fresh lemongrass (bottom 6 inches
        of the plant only), tough outer leaves
        discarded, sliced, or use grated zest of
        ½ lemon
    2 salam leaves or curry leaves
    8-12 oz (225–350 g) flank steak or other
        lean tender beef, cut into ½-in
        (1¼-cm) cubes

    1 cup (250 ml) canned, unsweetened
        coconut milk (shake can well before
        measuring)
    Chopped fresh coriander leaves (cilantro)
        or parsley, for garnish

1. Start rice. Prepare the ingredients and place them within easy reach of the stove.
2. Combine the seasoning paste ingredients in a small food processor and blend until smooth. If you don't have a food processor, finely chop the paste ingredients and go on to Step 3.
3. Heat a nonstick wok (or skillet) over medium heat. Add the oil and stir-fry the paste ingredients for about 1 minute. If using hand-chopped ingredients, stir-fry them until the onion softens. Add the spices, lemongrass and *salam* (or curry leaves) and mix well.
4. Add the beef and stir-fry 1–2 minutes, stirring well to coat the meat with spice mixture.
5. Stir in the coconut milk and cook over medium heat until bubbles appear around the edge of the wok. Stir frequently. Do not let the coconut milk boil or it may curdle. Simmer gently over very

Indonesia & Malaysia

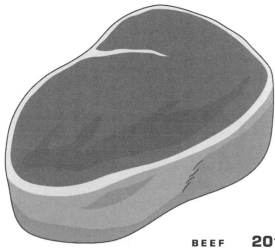

low heat until the meat is tender, 5–10 minutes. Garnish with the coriander leaves or parsley and serve with rice.

VARIATION: *Chicken pieces may be substituted for the beef.*

Makes 2 servings

Balinese Beef

Daging Masak Bali

The Balinese season their food with liberal amounts of soy sauce, both sweetened and dark, and are also fond of hot-sour-sweet mixtures. And of course, as in most of Indonesia, chiles are used in large quantities. Adjust the level of heat to suit your own taste.

Seasoning paste

1 onion, coarsely chopped
2 large cloves garlic, finely chopped
One 1-in (2½-cm) piece fresh ginger, peeled and sliced
1-4 fresh red chiles, seeded and chopped, or chili sauce or ground red pepper, to taste
¼ teaspoon shrimp paste (*terasi*) or anchovy paste

• • •

1 tablespoon vegetable oil
8-12 oz (225-350 g) lean tender beef or pork, cut into thin 2-in (5-cm) strips
1 tablespoon tamarind water (see page 245) or fresh lemon or lime juice or white vinegar
1 tablespoon Indonesian sweet soy sauce (*kecap manis*, see page 192) or 1 tablespoon reduced-sodium soy sauce and 1 teaspoon brown sugar
2-4 tablespoons water
Chopped fresh coriander leaves (cilantro) or parsley, for garnish

1. Start rice. Prepare the ingredients and place them within easy reach of the stove.
2. Combine the seasoning paste ingredients in a small food processor and blend until smooth. If you don't have a food processor, finely chop these ingredients and go on to Step 3.
3. Heat a nonstick wok (or skillet) over medium-high heat. Add the oil and stir-fry the paste ingredients for about 1 minute. If using hand-chopped ingredients, stir-fry them until the onion softens.
4. Add the beef or pork and stir-fry about 2 minutes, or until the meat begins to brown.
5. Add the remaining ingredients, bring to a boil, reduce the heat to low and simmer gently for about 5 minutes, or until the meat is tender and the flavors are blended. Add more sugar if desired. Garnish with the chopped coriander leaves or parsley and serve with rice and a salad.

Makes 2 servings

Spicy Beef Sambal with Leeks

Sambal Goreng Daging

Beef stir-fried with strips of leeks makes an excellent meal. Adjust the quantity of kecap manis and sambal ulek to suit your own taste. You can also substitute the beef with pork or lamb.

1-2 tablespoons vegetable oil
1 large or 2 medium onions, thinly sliced
2 large cloves garlic, chopped
8-12 oz (225-350 g) flank steak or other lean tender beef, cut across the grain into thin, narrow slices about 2 in (5 cm) long

4-6 stalks from a small young leek, cut
   into thin narrow strips about 2 in
   (5 cm) long
1-2 teaspoons sambal ulek (see page 192) or
   chopped fresh or dried chiles, to taste,
   and ½ teaspoon paprika for color
½-2 tablespoons Indonesian sweet soy
   sauce (*kecap manis*, see page 192) or 2
   tablespoons reduced-sodium soy sauce
   mixed with 1 tablespoon brown sugar
3-4 tablespoons unsalted beef stock or
   water
Chopped fresh coriander leaves (cilantro)
   or parsley, for garnish

1. Start rice. Prepare the ingredients and place them within easy reach of the stove.
2. Heat a nonstick wok (or skillet) over medium-high heat. Add the oil and stir-fry the onions until soft and transparent. Add the garlic and stir-fry 3–4 seconds.
3. Add the meat and stir-fry about 2 minutes or until it begins to brown.
4. Add the leek strips, sambal ulek, kecap manis and stock or water. Stir well to combine the ingredients. Bring to a boil, reduce the heat to low and simmer for 3–5 minutes. Garnish with the chopped coriander leaves or parsley and serve with rice.

Makes 2–3 servings

Stir-Fried Beef with Sweet Soy Sauce

Semur Daging

Aromatic spices and sweet Indonesian soy sauce give this simple stir-fry its character. Fresh tomatoes are added, but you may substitute another quick-cooking vegetable of your choice.

1 tablespoon o.
1 onion, thinly slice.
2 large cloves garlic, slic
8-12 oz (225–350 g) flank stea.
   lean, tender beef, cut across the
   into thin narrow strips about 2 in
   (5 cm) long
2 tomatoes, cut into small wedges, or
   other quick-cooking vegetable of your
   choice
½ teaspoon grated nutmeg
6 whole cloves or ½ teaspoon ground
   cloves
1 cinnamon stick
1-2 tablespoons Indonesian sweet soy
   sauce (*kecap manis*, see page 192) or 2
   tablespoons reduced-sodium soy sauce
   mixed with 1 tablespoon brown sugar
2 tablespoons unsalted beef stock or water
Chopped fresh coriander leaves (cilantro),
   parsley or green onions (scallions), for
   garnish

1. Start rice. Prepare the ingredients and place them within easy reach of the stove.
2. Heat a nonstick wok (or skillet) over medium-high heat. Add the oil and stir-fry the onions until they are soft and transparent, 1–2 minutes. Add the garlic and stir-fry a few seconds.
3. Add the beef and stir-fry until it begins to brown, about 2 minutes.
4. Stir in the tomato or other vegetable, and stir-fry another minute or two.
5. Add the remaining ingredients and stir for 2–3 minutes, or until the flavors are blended. If necessary, add the stock or water to keep the mixture from scorching. Garnish with the chopped coriander leaves, parsley or green onions and serve with rice.

Makes 2–3 servings

Indonesia & Malaysia

■ **Seafood** ■

Baked Fish Packets

Ikan Panggang

This is a quick, tidy way to prepare fish, with no pans to clean. Southeast Asian cooks often wrap foods in banana leaves and place the packets directly on a charcoal fire or in a steamer. The word *panggang* means grilled or barbecued. Of course, the banana leaf also imparts some additional flavor and moisture to the dish, but aluminum foil makes a good substitute.

Seasoning paste

1 onion, coarsely chopped

2 large cloves garlic, chopped

One 1-in (2½-cm) piece fresh ginger, peeled and sliced

2 tablespoons tamarind water (see page 245) or fresh lemon or lime juice

1 tablespoon reduced-sodium soy sauce

1 teaspoon sambal ulek (see page 192) or 2-3 fresh or dried red chiles, seeded, or hot chili sauce, to taste

¼ teaspoon shrimp paste (*terasi*) or anchovy paste

2 candlenuts or macadamia nuts or 4 toasted blanched almonds, finely chopped

½ teaspoon ground coriander

½ teaspoon brown sugar

• • •

8-12 oz (225-350 g) firm-fleshed fish fillets of choice or 2 small whole trout, scaled and washed

Heavy aluminum foil

Lime wedges and cucumber slices, for garnish

1. Start rice.

2. Preheat the oven to 450°F (230°C).

3. Combine the seasoning paste ingredients in a small food processor, beginning with the wet ingredients, and blend until smooth. If needed, add a tablespoon of water to facilitate blending. If you don't have a processor, finely chop everything and mix well.

4. Coat the fish fillets with the mixture. If you're using a whole fish, place some inside its cavity.

5. Lay out two large sheets of aluminum foil. (If using thin aluminum foil, use double sheets to prevent leakage.) Place each serving of fish in the center of the foil. Fold the foil around the fish so that it forms a packet, and securely wrap it so it will not leak, keeping the seam side up. Place the packet in the center of the hot oven (or in a baking dish) and bake for about 15–20 minutes. Open the packet to see if the fish is done. Bring the packet to the table on a platter, and serve with rice and a salad.

VARIATION: *Peeled shrimp may be substituted for the fish, or a combination of fish and shrimp may be used.*

Makes 2 servings

Indonesia & Malaysia

Pan-Fried Fish with Spicy Coconut Sauce

Sambal Goreng Ikan

In this recipe the fish is pan-fried and kept warm while the sauce cooks separately. The sauce is a little more work-intensive than most others in this book, but it is very tasty and well worth the effort.

2 tablespoons vegetable oil
8-12 oz (225-350 g) firm fleshed fish
fillets or steaks or two small whole
trout, trimmed, scaled and washed

Seasoning paste

1 large or 2 medium onions, coarsely
chopped
2 large cloves garlic, finely chopped
One 1-in (2½-cm) piece fresh galangal
or ginger, peeled and thinly sliced or
grated
1 teaspoon sambal ulek (see page 192) or
1-3 fresh or dried chiles, chopped, or
chili sauce or ground red pepper, to
taste
¼ teaspoon shrimp paste (*terasi*) or
anchovy paste

• • •

2 tablespoons tamarind water (see page
245) or fresh lemon or lime juice or
mild vinegar
½-1 tablespoon Indonesian salty soy sauce
(*kecap asin*) or Japanese soy sauce
1 teaspoon brown sugar
⅓ cup (75 ml) unsweetened coconut milk
Fresh parsley or coriander leaves
(cilantro), for garnish

1. Start rice. Prepare the ingredients and place them within easy reach of the stove.
2. Heat a nonstick wok (or skillet) over medium-high heat. Add half of the oil and brown the fish 1–2 minutes on each side, depending on thickness, until golden brown.

Do not overcook. Remove and drain on paper towels. Place on a warmed serving plate and keep warm.

3. Combine the seasoning paste ingredients in a small food processor, beginning with wet ingredients, and blend until smooth. You may need to add a tablespoon of coconut milk to facilitate blending. If you don't have a blender, finely chop everything and go on to Step 4.
4. Heat the remaining oil in the same wok in which fish was cooked and add the paste. Cook for 1–2 minutes, stirring constantly. If using hand-chopped ingredients, stir-fry them until the onions soften and the mixture is well blended.
5. Add the remaining ingredients, reduce the heat to low and simmer gently for 3–4 minutes. Do not allow the mixture to boil or the coconut milk may curdle. Pour the sauce over the fish. Garnish with the coriander leaves or parsley and serve with rice.

Makes 2 servings

Pan-Fried Fish with Hot-and-Sour Sauce

Ikan Asam

A fruity-sour mixture, combined with chiles, make up the main flavors of this sauce.

1½ tablespoons vegetable oil
8-12 oz (225-350 g) firm-fleshed fish
fillets or fish steaks of your choice
½ small onion, finely chopped
2 large cloves garlic, finely chopped
1 tablespoon grated fresh ginger
1-3 fresh red chiles, seeded and chopped,
or dried chiles, chili sauce or ground
red pepper, to taste

3 tablespoons fresh orange juice

3 tablespoons tamarind water (see page
   245) or fresh lime or lemon juice

10 fresh basil or mint leaves or a
   combination of both, coarsely chopped

1. Start rice. Prepare the ingredients and place them within easy reach of the stove.
2. Heat a nonstick wok (or skillet) over medium-high heat. Add ½ tablespoon of the oil and lightly brown the fish until done, 1–2 minutes on each side, depending on thickness. Do not overcook. Drain the fish on a paper towel. Remove to a warmed serving plate and keep warm.
3. Add the remaining oil and stir-fry the onions until soft and translucent. Stir in the garlic, ginger and chiles and cook for about 1 minute.
4. Stir in the remaining ingredients, reduce the heat to low and simmer for another 2 minutes until the flavors are well blended. Pour the sauce over the cooked fish. Alternatively, you may place the fish back in the wok to reheat and simmer in the sauce. Serve with rice.

Makes 2 servings

Stir-Fried Shrimp in Coconut Milk

Sambal Goreng Udang

Shrimp cooked this way is popular all over Indonesia and Malaysia, as well as in other places in Southeast Asia. Of course, there are many variations, but it is basically a quick stir-fry (a technique learned from the Chinese), but with Indonesian seasonings. To save preparation time,

you may wish to use shelled and pre-cooked shrimp.

1 tablespoon vegetable oil

1 small onion, thinly sliced

2 large cloves garlic, thinly sliced

1-3 fresh red or green chiles, seeded
   and thinly sliced, or dried red pepper
   flakes, chili sauce or ground red
   pepper, to taste

1 teaspoon ground coriander

1 tomato, cut in half, then into thin wedges

8-12 oz (300-450 g) medium shrimp,
   peeled and deveined, leaving tails
   intact

½ cup (125 ml) canned, unsweetened
   coconut milk (shake can well before
   measuring)

1 tablespoon Indonesian sweet soy sauce
   (*kecap manis*, see page 192) or 1
   tablespoon soy sauce mixed with 1
   teaspoon brown sugar

1 tablespoon tamarind water (see page
   245) or fresh lime or lemon juice

Chopped fresh coriander leaves (cilantro)
   or parsley leaves, for garnish

1. Start rice. Prepare the ingredients and place them within easy reach of the stove.
2. Heat a nonstick wok (or skillet) over medium-high heat. Add the oil and stir-fry the onion until it softens. Add the garlic, chiles, ground coriander and tomato and stir-fry about 2 minutes.
3. Add the shrimp and stir-fry 1–2 minutes, or until they turn pink. If you are using pre-cooked shrimp, stir-fry just to warm through, about 15 seconds.
4. Stir in the coconut milk, sweet soy sauce and tamarind water or lime juice. Simmer while stirring over very low heat, about 2 minutes, to blend flavors. Do not allow the coconut milk to boil or it may curdle. Also, do not overcook the shrimp or it will toughen. If

the mixture seems dry, add more coconut milk or a little water to prevent scorching. Garnish with the coriander leaves or parsley and serve with rice.

Makes 2 servings

Sweet-and-Sour Shrimp

Udang Nenas

This is a sweet-sour-peppery dish. The shrimp is cooked in the shell to keep it from becoming dry and to add more flavor to the sauce. Though this requires less preparation for the cook, it means more work for the diner. You may remove the shells before cooking if you dislike doing it while you eat. Fresh pineapple is best in this dish, but canned may be substituted.

1 tablespoon vegetable oil

8–12 oz (300–450 g) medium shrimp, unpeeled, rinsed and patted dry, or peeled and deveined, leaving tails intact

½ small onion, finely chopped

2 large cloves garlic, finely chopped

1 red or green bell pepper, cut into narrow strips

2–3 slices slightly under-ripe fresh pineapple, peeled and cut into small bite-size cubes (reserve the juice) or canned pineapple, drained and cubed (reserve the juice)

1–2 teaspoons sambal ulek (see page 192) or chopped fresh or dried chiles, chili sauce or ground red pepper, to taste

1 tablespoon reduced-sodium soy sauce

1 tablespoon brown sugar

2 teaspoons tamarind water (see page 245) or fresh lime juice added to 3 tablespoons of the reserved pineapple juice

Chopped fresh parsley or coriander leaves (cilantro), for garnish

1. Start rice. Prepare the ingredients and place them within easy reach of the stove.
2. Heat a nonstick wok (or skillet) over medium-high heat. Add the oil and stir-fry the shrimp for 1–2 minutes, or until they turn pink. Remove from the wok and keep warm.
3. Add the onions and stir-fry until softened. Add the garlic and stir-fry 2–3 seconds. Add the bell pepper, pineapple cubes and sambal ulek and stir-fry about 2 minutes.
4. Stir in the soy sauce, reserved pineapple juice, sugar and tamarind water or lime juice. Bring to a boil, reduce the heat to low and simmer another minute. If necessary, add another table-spoon or two of pineapple juice or water to prevent scorching.
5. Return the shrimp to the wok and cook only long enough to heat through. Do not overcook or the shrimp will toughen. Garnish with the chopped coriander leaves or parsley and serve with rice.

Makes 2–3 servings

Javanese-Style Shrimp

Udang Panggang Jawa

Shrimp—one of nature's fast cooking foods—is plentiful in southeast Asian waters. This is a very quick and tasty way to prepare them. They may be threaded onto skewers and grilled or broiled, or they may be stir-fried.

Marinade

2 large cloves garlic, finely chopped

3 tablespoons reduced-sodium soy sauce

3 tablespoons fresh lime or lemon juice

2 teaspoons brown sugar

½ teaspoon dried red pepper flakes, chili
   sauce or ground red pepper, to taste

• • •

8-12 oz (300–450 g) medium shrimp,
   peeled and deveined, leaving tails
   intact
1 tablespoon vegetable oil (if stir-frying
   shrimp)
Fresh coriander leaves (cilantro) or mint
   leaves, for garnish
Bamboo skewers (if grilling or broiling the
   shrimp), pre-soaked in water

1. Start rice.
2. Combine the marinade ingredients and add the shrimp, coating
   them well. Marinate for 10 minutes or more. If there is no time
   to marinate the shrimp, baste
   them frequently during cooking.
   They will be just as delicious.
3. Thread shrimp onto skewers for
   grilling over coals or for broiling
   under an oven broiler. Cook for
   1–2 minutes on each side, depending on size, until they change color.
4. For stir-frying, heat a nonstick wok
   (or skillet) over medium-high heat
   and add a tablespoon of the oil.
   Lightly stir-fry the shrimp for 1–2
   minutes on each side, or until they
   turn pink. Do not overcook or the
   shrimp will toughen. Garnish with
   the coriander leaves or mint leaves
   and serve with rice.

Makes 2 servings

Corn and Shrimp Fritters

Perkedel Jagung

Corn is a North American grain
that originated in the Valley of
Mexico. It was brought to Europe by
Columbus, and again by the Spanish
after the conquest of Mexico and
Guatemala in the sixteenth century.
During the Portuguese, Spanish,
English and Dutch colonial incursions into Asia, corn was carried
to the new European colonies (as
were hot chiles). It was introduced
to Indonesia in about 1625 by
the Spanish and planted in areas
not conducive to rice cultivation.
Indonesians embraced corn (and
chiles) as well as the Dutch technique of making fritters.

2 eggs, lightly beaten
½ small onion, finely chopped
1 clove garlic, crushed
2 oz (75 g) cooked shrimp, cut into small
   pieces
¼ cup (25 g) rice flour or all-purpose flour
¼ teaspoon baking powder
½ teaspoon ground coriander
⅛ teaspoon ground cumin
⅛ teaspoon ground turmeric
Freshly ground black pepper or ground red
   chile, to taste
2 green onions (scallions), very finely sliced
One 15-oz (400 g) can whole kernel corn or 2
   cups (350 g) fresh or frozen corn kernels
Vegetable oil, for frying

1. Beat the eggs well in a large
   bowl. Stir in the onion, garlic and
   shrimp. Sift or mix together all of
   the dry ingredients and stir them
   into the egg mixture. Add the
   green onions and corn. Mix well.
2. Heat a nonstick skillet over
   medium heat and add a little the
   oil. Drop large tablespoons of the
   egg mixture into the pan. Brown
   one side, then turn over and
   brown the other. Remove the fritters and drain on paper towels.
   Serve plain or with a little chili
   sauce, soy sauce or applesauce.

*Makes about 12 fritters, or about
2–3 servings*

Indonesia & Malaysia

■ Salads ■

Gado-Gado

Gado-Gado is a well-known and much-loved Indonesian salad that combines vegetables from Europe, Asia and North America. There are many versions of this salad, which usually include cooked vegetables such as potatoes, green beans, carrots and cabbage, as well as raw ones such as cucumbers. It becomes a full meal when fried tofu and hard-boiled eggs are added. Make a selection of vegetables that would fill a serving bowl enough for two servings. The combination that follows is flexible. Add or subtract, depending on what you prefer and what is available. The easiest version uses only raw vegetables and is described in the variation at the end of this recipe.

    3 whole eggs
    3 small new potatoes
    8 oz (175 g) green beans, cut in half
        lengthwise into 2-in (5-cm) lengths
    2 carrots, cut into thin 2-in (5-cm) strips
    1 handful fresh bean sprouts, trimmed
    6 broccoli or cauliflower florets (optional)
    ¼ small head Chinese (napa) cabbage,
        coarsely shredded
    1 small bunch watercress, cut into sprigs,
        discarding tough stems
    Cucumber and tomato slices, for garnish
    Ready-made onion flakes (*bawang
        goring*), sold in jars or packets in many
        supermarkets, for garnish (optional)
    Peanut Sauce, Indonesian-style (see page 191)

1. Boil the eggs over medium heat until hard, about 10 minutes Cool and peel.
2. Boil (unpeeled) the potatoes until tender. Peel and slice.
3. Steam or blanch the beans, carrots, bean sprouts and broccoli sepa-

rately in boiling water, rinsing them in cold water to stop cooking as soon as they reach desired degree of tenderness. Cabbage and bean sprouts require only a few seconds to cook. Do not overcook. The vegetables should remain crunchy.

4. Place the watercress on a large platter and arrange the vegetables in separate sections. Garnish with the cucumbers, tomatoes and hard-boiled egg slices. Sprinkle the onion flakes over all. Serve with peanut sauce.

VARIATION: *Gado-Gado with raw vegetables. If you have very limited time, make a selection of your favorite uncooked vegetables. Choose from watercress, lettuce, cucumbers, bean sprouts, carrots, tomatoes, green and red bell peppers, as well as broccoli and cauliflower florets and spinach. Slice and arrange them attractively on a platter, and decorate the circumference of the salad with alternating slices of hard-boiled eggs and tomato. Cubes of pasteurized, firm tofu,*

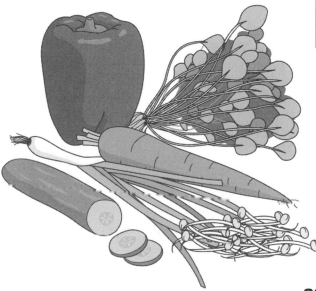

which needs no cooking, may also be included. Just dip the tofu cubes in a little soy sauce for flavor and add them to the salad. To really save time, use commercially-prepared peanut sauce from a jar.

Makes 2–3 servings

Vegetable and Fruit Salad

Asinan

Asinan combinations vary from region to region. They are sour, salty and usually spicy to a greater or lesser degree, and some combinations include tofu. Feel free to leave out or substitute vegetables and fruits. The dressing is a sweet-sour-hot sauce that you can adjust to your own taste.

    1 small cucumber, cut into 2-in (5-cm)
        matchsticks
    2 carrots, scraped and cut into 2-in (5-cm)
        sticks
    1 handful fresh bean sprouts, trimmed
    1 apple or 1 pear or ¼ pineapple, cut into
        pieces
    3 oz (75 g) jícama, peeled and cut into thin
        2-in (5-cm) strips
    ½ bunch watercress, trimmed and cut into
    2-in (5-cm) pieces, or a few green lettuce
        leaves, cut into small pieces
    6 fresh mint or basil leaves, chopped, and
        a few roasted peanuts, for garnish

Dressing
    4 tablespoons fresh lime or lemon juice or
        mild vinegar
    1-2 tablespoons brown or white sugar
    1 teaspoon sambal ulek (see page 192)
        or minced fresh chile, or dried red
        pepper flakes, chili sauce or ground red
        pepper, to taste
    2 tablespoons boiling water
    Salt, to taste

1. Prepare the salad ingredients.
2. Combine the dressing ingredients in a salad bowl. Add the boiling water and mix to dissolve the sugar. Add the salad ingredients and toss well.

Makes 2–3 servings

Vegetable Salad with Sweet Vinegar Dressing

Acar Kuning

Acar refers to mixed vegetable dishes, spiced and lightly pickled with vinegar. *Kuning* means yellow, and refers to the color of the turmeric in the dressing. These dishes keep well and are usually served at room temperature. Vary the vegetable depending on availability and preference.

Sweet vinegar dressing
    1 teaspoon vegetable oil
    2 thin slices peeled fresh ginger
    3 large cloves garlic, thinly sliced
    2 candlenuts or 4 blanched almonds,
        chopped (optional)
    ½ teaspoon ground turmeric
    ½ cup (125 ml) water

Serving Suggestion

To make this a main-course meal, cut 1 block (14 oz/400 g) firm tofu into bite-size cubes and serve it with the salad. Flavor the cubes by dipping them into a light soy sauce. If you buy pasteurized tofu, it needs no cooking. Otherwise, poach the cubes in simmering water for 2–3 minutes.

½ cup (125 ml) white or cider vinegar

2 tablespoons, or more, sugar

Salt and freshly ground black pepper, to
    taste

Vegetables

8 oz (175 g) Chinese long beans or green
    beans cut into 2-in (5-cm) pieces

6 oz (250 g) cauliflower florets

2 carrots, peeled and cut into thin 2-in
    (5-cm) sticks

2–4 fresh red and green chiles, stemmed
    (optional)

1 small cucumber, peeled, seeded and cut
    into 2-in (5-cm) strips

1. To make the sweet vinegar dressing, heat the oil in a large saucepan over medium heat. Stir-fry the ginger and garlic for about 10 seconds, or until the garlic begins to brown. Add the nuts and turmeric and stir a few seconds longer. Add the water, vinegar, sugar, salt and pepper. Turn the heat to medium-high and bring to a boil.

2. Stir in the beans, cauliflower, carrots and chiles. Return to a boil, cover the pan and cook for about 2 minutes. Add the cucumber and boil about 10 seconds more. Stir well. The vegetables should be crunchy and only partially cooked. Remove from the heat and place in a glass bowl. Serve hot or cold, as you wish. The salad will keep several days in the refrigerator.

Makes 3–4 servings

Sweet-and-Sour Cabbage Salad
Acar

I think of this *acar* recipe as a kind of piquant coleslaw without the calories of mayonnaise.

Dressing

¼ cup (50 ml) white or cider vinegar

2 tablespoons boiling water

2 tablespoons sugar

1 large clove garlic, sliced

2 thin slices peeled fresh ginger

Salt and ground red chile or ground red
    pepper, to taste

• • •

½ small head white cabbage, finely
    shredded

1 small carrot, scraped and shredded

1 small cucumber, sliced lengthwise,
    seeded and very thinly sliced

½ small red onion, very thinly sliced

Combine the dressing ingredients in a salad bowl. Stir until the sugar dissolves. (You may need to heat the dressing to be sure the sugar dissolves.) Add the vegetables and toss well. The flavor is stronger if the salad is refrigerated or set aside for a while before serving.

Makes 2–4 servings

Cucumber Salad

This cool and tangy salad is especially good on a hot day.

Dressing

3 tablespoons fresh lime or lemon juice or
    mild vinegar

½ teaspoon sugar

1 teaspoon sambal ulek (see page 192),
    or chopped fresh red chile, dried red
    pepper flakes, chili sauce or ground red
    pepper, to taste

Salt and freshly ground black pepper, to taste

• • •

1 cucumber, peeled (leaving some green
    for color), seeded and sliced

½ small red onion, thinly sliced

1 tomato, quartered and sliced

Chopped fresh mint leaves, for garnish

Combine the dressing ingredients in a salad bowl and stir until the sugar dissolves. Mix in the cucumber, onion and tomato slices. Garnish with chopped mint leaves.

Makes 2 servings

VARIATION: *For spinach salad, bring water to a boil in a saucepan and blanch 1 bunch of fresh spinach (stemmed and washed) for about 10 seconds. Remove immediately and drain. Toss the spinach with the dressing used for* Cucumber Salad.

Spicy Fruit Salad
Rujak

This is a delicious, tangy, spicy-sweet salad that may be served with any dish. Substitute fruits of your choice and adjust the seasonings as you wish.

1 navel orange, peeled, sectioned, tough membranes removed

1 tart green apple, peeled and cored
¼ small fresh pineapple, peeled
1 firm mango, peeled and pitted
1 firm pear
1 small cucumber, peeled, halved length-wise, seeded and sliced
Fresh mint leaves and lime wedges, for garnish

Dressing
1 tablespoon rice vinegar
3-4 tablespoons fresh lime or lemon juice
¼ teaspoon shrimp paste (*terasi*) or chopped fresh red chile, or chili sauce, dried red pepper flakes or ground red pepper, to taste
2-3 tablespoons brown sugar

Cut the fruit and cucumber into bite-size pieces and place in a salad bowl. Combine the dressing ingredients, add to the fruit and mix well. Garnish with mint leaves and lime wedges. Alternately, you may serve the dressing separately as a dipping sauce.

Makes 2–3 servings

Eggs

Crab Omelet
Telur Dadar Kepiting

This distinctively-shaped omelet is quick to make and guaranteed to be delicious. Typically, after it is cooked, the omelet is rolled up and sliced into strips.

4 whole eggs or 2 whole eggs and 4 egg whites
4 oz (75 g) fresh or canned crabmeat, shredded
1 green onion (scallion), thinly sliced
½ teaspoon grated fresh ginger
½ teaspoon sambal ulek (see page 192) or

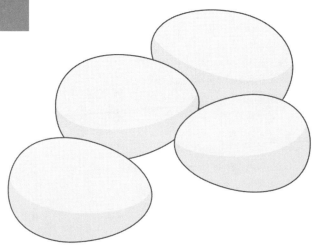

1 small fresh red chile, minced, or chili
   sauce, dried red pepper flakes or ground
   red pepper, to taste
Salt and freshly ground black pepper, to
   taste
1½ tablespoons vegetable oil for cooking
   the omelet
Finely chopped fresh coriander leaves
   (cilantro), for garnish

1. Lightly beat the eggs. Mix in the remaining ingredients, except the oil and garnish.
2. Heat a nonstick skillet over medium heat and add half of the oil. Add half of the egg mixture and cook until just set. Do not overcook. Turn the omelet over carefully. Remove the skillet from the heat and let it stand a few moments to continue to firm. Roll the omelet into a sausage-shaped log. Put the skillet back on the heat. Cook until firm. Remove to a warmed platter. Make the second rolled omelet in the same way.
3. Cut the omelets with a sharp knife into diagonal 1-inch (2½-cm) strips. Sprinkle with the chopped coriander leaves.

Makes 2 servings

Tofu Omelet
Tahu Telur

Perfect for a quick meal, this very simple omelet is a good source of protein for vegetarian diners.

4 whole eggs or 2 whole eggs and 4 egg
   whites
4 oz (125 g) firm tofu, cut into ¼-in
   (6-mm) cubes
1 small fresh chile, seeded and minced, or, for
   a milder flavor, substitute Anaheim or a

red or green bell pepper
Salt and freshly ground black pepper, to taste
1 tablespoon vegetable oil
Snipped fresh chives, for garnish

1. Beat the eggs in a bowl and add the tofu, chopped red or green bell peppers, salt and pepper.
2. Heat a nonstick skillet over medium heat. Add half of the oil. Pour half of the egg mixture into the skillet, tilting it in all directions to make a thin omelet. Cook until set and lightly browned. Fold the omelet in half and lightly brown both sides. Remove to a heated plate and keep warm. Add the remaining oil and make the second omelet in the same way. Sprinkle with the snipped chives.

Makes 2 servings

Omelet, Balinese Style
Dadar Bali

This highly seasoned omelet is sweetened with minced meat filling. Only one skillet is necessary to make both the filling and omelets.

1½ tablespoons vegetable oil
1 small onion, finely chopped
6 oz ground chicken breast meat
1 tablespoon curry powder
¼–½ teaspoon sambal ulek (see page
   192) or chopped fresh or dried red
   chiles, or chili sauce or ground red
   pepper, to taste
½–1 teaspoon Indonesian sweet soy
   sauce (*kecap manis*, see page 192) or
   reduced-sodium soy sauce mixed with
   ¼–½ teaspoon brown sugar
1 small tomato, coarsely chopped
1 tablespoon fresh parsley or coriander
   leaves (cilantro), finely chopped

4 whole eggs or 2 whole eggs and 4
   egg whites, lightly beaten with 2
   tablespoons water
½ teaspoon brown sugar (optional)
Salt and freshly ground black pepper, to
   taste

1. To prepare the filling, heat a nonstick skillet over medium heat and add ½ tablespoon of the oil. Stir-fry the onion until softened. Add the chicken and curry powder, stir-frying and separating the minced chicken bits when they stick together. Cook until the chicken begins to brown, about 3 minutes.

2. Add the sambal ulek and kecap manis and stir well. Add the tomato and the parsley or coriander leaves. Cook for 1–2 minutes, or until the chicken is done and the mixture is well blended. Remove from the skillet and keep warm. Wipe the skillet clean with paper towels.

3. Beat the eggs and add the sugar, salt and pepper. Heat the nonstick skillet over medium heat and add ½ tablespoon of the oil. Pour half of the eggs into the skillet and cook until they set. Turn the omelet over to cook the other side. Add half of the filling to the omelet and fold the sides over. Remove from the skillet to a warmed plate and keep warm. Add the remaining oil to the pan and make a second omelet in the same way. Serve immediately.

Makes 2 servings

The Philippines

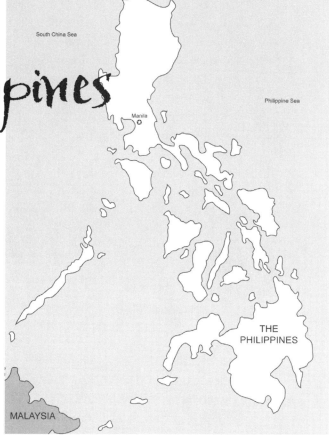

The Philippines, a nation made up of more than 7000 islands off the southeast coast of mainland Asia, is situated between Indonesia and Taiwan. A Christian country—the only one in Asia—it is the most Westernized of the Asian countries, both in customs and taste. Nearly 400 years of Spanish rule popularized the Roman Catholic Church, and today the majority of its 68 million people are Roman Catholic. Most Christians live on Luzon Island in the north where the capital city of Manila is located. Muslims form a sizeable minority in the south.

The earliest migrants were the Malays, who pushed northward out of the Indies to conquer the aboriginal inhabitants, but in subsequent centuries, Chinese traders and Muslim Arabs made their mark on the islands. Western culture arrived in 1521, in the form of the Portuguese navigator, Ferdinand Magellan. The Spanish came twenty-one years later and named the islands in honor of Prince Philip of Spain. For the next 350 years, Spain ruled the islands, only to cede them to the United States in 1899 after the Spanish-American war. Fifty years of American occupation brought more of the West to the Philippines, and it was not until 1946 that the Philippines became completely independent.

Today, their Spanish heritage is apparent in a number of ways aside from religion. Most Filipinos bear Spanish names, not because they have Spanish ancestors, but because late in the nineteenth century the Spanish governor ordered them to adopt names from an official list. There are three official languages—Spanish, English and Tagalog—as well as many regional dialects. No Filipino is considered educated unless he or she knows Spanish as well as English. In Manila, the Basque game of jai-alai is one of the principal gambling sports, and all over the country Spanish dances have been incorporated into the Philippine repertory of folk dances. In every small city and town, community life focuses on a broad central plaza, a Mediterranean custom otherwise alien to Asia.

Naturally, this multicultural heritage is reflected in the food. While rice and fish, simply cooked, are the mainstay of the Filipino diet for the majority of people, the cuisines of their traders and invaders have been borrowed and adapted. From the Chinese they have learned various ways to prepare noodles, and every region has a *pancit* (noodle dish) of its own. There are also many Filipino versions of Chinese dumplings and spring rolls (*lumpia*). From the Spanish, upper class Filipinos learned to prepare elegant fiestas, and many of the less elaborate dishes and cooking methods introduced by the Spanish spread throughout all classes of Philippine society. All these dishes, whether of Spanish or Chinese origin, have Spanish names.

The basic cooking methods of Spain—sautéing and stewing—have also been adopted. Most typical of this style are the dishes known as

Today the Spanish colonial heritage is apparent in a number of ways, but it's especially reflected in the food of the Philippines.

guisado (sauté). It begins with olive oil, in which onions and garlic, and sometimes tomatoes, are sautéed before meat is added. The Spanish also bequeathed to Filipinos a taste for rich desserts, which is not found anywhere else in Asia.

Many other Filipino dishes use the seasonings of the Malays, which are related to those of other countries in Southeast Asia. There is the salty fish sauce called *patis* that is similar to the Thai *nam pla* and the Vietnamese *nuoc mam*. There is also an equivalent to *kapi*, the fermented shrimp paste of Thailand, and the *terasi* of Indonesia, which the Filipinos call *bagoong*. Not surprisingly, the use of these condiments, and of chiles, is restrained, so thoroughly have the centuries of colonial rule toned down the native Malay foods.

Still, Filipino food does have a unique personality that is marked by several traits: a fondness for sour tastes, a predilection for frying with garlic and onions, and a tendency to cook several seemingly unrelated foods together. The dish that embodies all these characteristics is the *adobo,* the most popular and well known of the sour dishes. There are many variations of adobo, but chicken and pork cooked together is the most common. Like the Sumatran *rendang,* to which it may be related, adobo originated as a means of preserving food during long journeys without refrigeration. Vinegar, tamarind and calamansi, a sour lime, are used. Another example of the Filipino inclination to cook many seemingly unrelated foods together is a savory stew called the *puchero*. In it, one may find pork, beef, sausage, sweet potatoes, tomatoes, cabbage, chickpeas and a cooking-variety banana, as well as other vegetables. It is eaten mixed with rice and relishes.

In these health-conscious times, the high fat and cholesterol content of Filipino food is important to consider. This defect is blamed on the Spanish, who taught Filipinos to sauté in lard as well as in olive oil. While Filipinos use the Chinese wok, they did not pick up the Chinese technique of quick stir-frying. Instead, they sauté in the Spanish style, with large quantities of lard or oil and tend to leave food in the fat much longer than their Asian neighbors.

Not only did the Spanish alter Filipino food, but they also influenced their eating habits. Though rice and fish comprise the typical native breakfast, spicy pork sausage and fried eggs are also popular. Filipinos drink coffee, not tea, and hot chocolate and a sweet cake are a

common mid-morning snack. Lunch and dinner are both big meals, and in the afternoon, before dinner, there is the *merienda,* which can be compared to an English high tea. This can be anything from a simple snack to an elaborate spread, including egg rolls (lumpia), a noodle dish, and various cakes and rich desserts made with coconut milk. No rice appears at a merienda since it is intended to be a snack, not a meal. However, rice always makes an appearance at dinnertime, proving that Filipinos are essentially an Asian people despite the Western influences.

The Filipino Pantry

*To keep shopping to a minimum, and to speed preparation and
cooking time, it is helpful to keep these Filipino staples
on hand on your kitchen.*

Ingredients with a Long Shelf Life

black peppercorns

chili sauce or ground red chiles

dried chiles or red
   pepper flakes

fish sauce (*patis*) or Thai *nam
   pla* or Vietnamese *nuoc
   mam*

red pepper, ground

soy sauce

tomatoes, canned

turmeric

Fresh Ingredients

chiles

coriander leaves (cilantro)

ginger

green onions (scallions)

limes or lemons

onions

tomatoes

■ Rice ■

Plain Rice

As is common throughout most of Asia, boiled white rice is central to Filipino cooking. Long-grain, highly milled and polished rice is preferred. The recipe for Boiled Rice, Chinese Style on page 26 is recommended.

■ Noodles ■

Savory Noodles
Pancit Guisado

This is a cousin to Chinese noodle dishes with a Filipino spin. It is an excellent one-dish meal. The meats may be raw or cooked leftovers, and the amount and quantity of each is flexible, as it is with the vegetables.

6 oz (175 g) dried Chinese egg noodles, or
    other flat or round egg noodle
1–2 tablespoons vegetable oil
1 onion, halved and thinly sliced
3 large cloves garlic, chopped
All, or a selection, of the following:
    4 oz (100 g) raw or cooked
      chicken, cut into thin strips
    4 oz (125 g) raw or cooked pork or
      beef, cut into thin strips
    2 oz (75 g) cooked ham, cut into
      thin strips
    4 oz (100 g) white or Chinese (napa)
      cabbage, shredded
1 tomato, cut into quarters

6 small cooked or raw shrimp (optional)
1–2 tablespoons reduced-sodium soy
    sauce
Freshly ground black pepper and
    ground red chile or ground red
    pepper, to taste
Chopped fresh coriander leaves
    (cilantro) and lemon wedges, for
    garnish

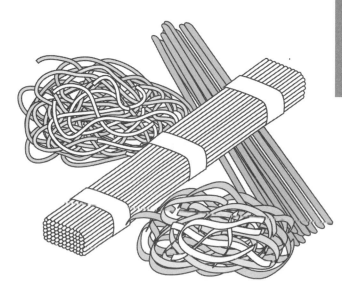

The Philippines

1. Boil a large quantity of water and cook the noodles until just tender, or according to the instructions on the package. Do not overcook. Rinse the noodles with cold water to stop the cooking process. Drain immediately and set aside.
2. Heat a nonstick wok or skillet over medium-high heat and add half of the oil. Add the onions and stir-fry for about 1 minute. Then add the garlic and continue to stir-fry until the onions are soft and translucent.
3. Add your selection of chicken and/or meat and stir-fry briskly until browned, 2–3 minutes.
4. Stir in the cabbage and tomato.

Cook for 2 minutes, tossing the mixture briskly, until the cabbage wilts and the tomato softens. Add the shrimp, if using, soy sauce and black pepper. Mix well. If you're using uncooked shrimp, cook only as long as it takes for the shrimp to turn pink.
5. Add the noodles a little at a time, stirring well with each addition, and cook until heated through. Transfer to warmed serving platter and garnish with the chopped coriander leaves and lemon wedges. Serve with soy sauce, if desired.

Makes 2–3 servings

■ Soups ■

Shrimp and Vegetable Soup

This tasty soup—suitable for lunch or a light dinner—is simple to prepare and delicious.

1 tablespoon vegetable oil
1 onion, coarsely chopped
1 large clove garlic, finely chopped

6 oz (175 g) Chinese (napa) cabbage, finely shredded
2 cups (475 ml) unsalted chicken stock or water
3 tablespoons fresh lemon or lime juice
2 large tomatoes, quartered and cut into thin slices
1 large green bell pepper, seeded and cut lengthwise into thin slices
1-2 fresh red chiles, seeded and thinly sliced, or dried red pepper flakes or ground red pepper, to taste
8 oz (300 g) shrimp, peeled and deveined, leaving tails intact
Salt and freshly ground black pepper, to taste
1 teaspoon reduced-sodium soy sauce, or to taste
1 green onion (scallion), sliced, for garnish

1. Start rice. Prepare the ingredients and place them within easy reach of the stove.
2. Heat a soup pot over medium heat. Add the oil and stir-fry the onions for about 2 minutes, or until they soften. Add the garlic and stir-fry 3–4 seconds.

3. Add the cabbage and stir-fry 2 minutes, or until it begins to wilt. Stir in the stock or water and the lemon or lime juice and bring to a boil. Turn the heat down and simmer about 2 minutes.
4. Add the tomatoes, bell pepper and chiles, and cook for 3–4 minutes.
5. Add the shrimp, salt and pepper.

Simmer until the shrimp turn pink, 1–2 minutes, depending on their size. Do not overcook or they will toughen. Season with a little soy sauce, and garnish with sliced green onion.

Makes 2 servings

■ Chicken ■

Sweet-and-Sour Grilled Chicken

A pineapple sweet-and-sour marinade makes for an easily prepared, enticing chicken dish. To make more than 2 servings, simply double the marinade ingredients. Leftovers will be good the next day. The chicken may be baked in the oven, grilled over coals or stir-fried.

Marinade

1 large clove garlic, crushed
1 tablespoon grated fresh ginger
¼ cup (50 g) brown sugar
¼ cup (50 ml) pineapple juice
2 tablespoons reduced-sodium soy sauce
2 tablespoons white vinegar
1 tablespoon honey (optional)
Freshly ground black pepper, to taste

• • •

1 lb (450 g) chicken parts cut into small pieces for faster cooking. If desired, remove skin to reduce fat.

1. Start rice.
2. Combine the marinade ingredients in a large bowl and stir until the sugar dissolves. Add the chicken and coat well with the mixture. The chicken may marinate a few minutes or several hours, or overnight in the refrigerator. The longer the marination, the stronger the flavor. If there is no time to

marinate the chicken pieces, then baste them frequently.
3. To cook the chicken, you may grill it over hot coals, broil it in the oven, or stir-fry it in 1 tablespoon oil. Brown both sides of the chicken and baste it while it cooks.

Makes 2–3 servings

Chicken Adobo

If the Philippines can be said to have a national dish, *adobo* would be it. A method of cooking using vinegar, soy sauce and garlic, adobo, in its many variations, turns up everywhere. Pork, seafood and vegetables are also cooked in adobo style, and some versions contain coconut milk as well as fish sauce.

All of the recipes I surveyed use a lot more soy sauce than my version, and an incredible amount of garlic—in one case an entire head. This recipe will take a little longer than most in this book, but the distinct and complex flavor of adobo is worth it.

1 cup (250 ml) coconut palm vinegar or
    other mild vinegar
1 cup (250 ml) water
4 large cloves garlic
1 teaspoon freshly ground black pepper
4 bay leaves
1 whole chicken breast and 2 chicken legs,
    cut into small serving pieces, fat and
    skin removed
2 teaspoons reduced-sodium soy sauce
Chopped fresh parley, for garnish

1. Start rice.
2. In a large saucepan, combine the vinegar, water, garlic, pepper and bay leaves. Add the chicken and bring to a boil. Turn the chicken pieces to coat with the sauce. Cover and simmer over low heat for 15–20 minutes. Stir in the soy sauce.
3. Remove the chicken pieces to a serving platter and keep warm in a heated oven.
4. Boil the sauce, uncovered, until it is reduced to about half its original volume. Pour over the chicken.
5. Garnish with the parsley and serve with rice.

Makes 4 servings

Chicken Braised with Tomatoes and Potatoes
Chicken Fritada

The Spanish influence is obvious here. Though this one-pot meal contains potatoes, it is usually served with rice.

1 tablespoon vegetable oil
1 large onion, thinly sliced
3 large cloves garlic, crushed
1 lb (450 g) chicken parts, cut into small
    pieces for faster cooking (if desired,
    remove skin to reduce fat)
2 large tomatoes, chopped, or one 14-
    oz (400 g) can low-sodium stewed
    tomatoes, drained
Salt and freshly ground black pepper, to
    taste
¼ cup (50 ml) unsalted chicken stock or
    water
2 fresh green chiles, seeded and thinly
    sliced, or 1 small green bell pepper,
    thinly sliced, and chile or ground red
    pepper, to taste
2 new potatoes, peeled and cut into small
    cubes
Chopped fresh parsley, for garnish

1. Start rice. Prepare the ingredients and place them within easy reach of the stove.
2. Heat a nonstick wok or skillet over medium-high heat. Add the oil and stir-fry the onions until softened, about 2 minutes. Add the garlic and stir-fry a few seconds.
3. Add the chicken pieces and brown on both sides. Mix in the tomatoes, salt, black pepper, stock or water, and green peppers. Stir well, and bring to a boil.
4. Add the potatoes and more stock or water if the mixture seems dry. Reduce the heat and cook until the potatoes and chicken are tender, about 10–15 minutes. Garnish with the chopped parsley and serve with rice.

Makes 2–3 servings

The Philippines

■ **Seafood** ■

Shrimp in Coconut Milk

Having few ingredients, this tasty shrimp dish is simple and quick to make. For a complete meal, serve with Green Bean Salad (page 226).

> 1 cup (250 ml) canned, unsweetened coconut milk
> 2 large cloves garlic , finely chopped
> 1–2 teaspoons grated fresh ginger
> Salt and freshly ground black pepper, to taste
> 8–12 oz (300–450 g) medium shrimp, peeled and deveined, leaving tails intact

1. Start rice.
2. Combine the coconut milk, garlic, ginger, salt and pepper in a medium saucepan and bring to a slow simmer. Do not boil. Simmer over low heat for 5 minutes.
3. Add the shrimp and cook for 2–4 minutes, depending on their size, until they become opaque. Do not overcook or they will toughen. Serve with rice and a salad.

Makes 2–3 serving

Fish Adobo

This recipe is one of several possible variations on *adobo*, the national dish of the Philippines. The amount of vinegar and soy sauce in this recipe are modest. Add more if you like a stronger taste.

> 1 tablespoon reduced-sodium soy sauce
> 2–4 tablespoons rice vinegar or fresh lemon or lime juice
> 8–12 oz (225–350 g) firm fish fillets, cut into 2–3 serving pieces
> 1 tablespoon vegetable oil

> 1 large onion, thinly sliced
> 4 large cloves garlic, finely chopped
> 6 oz (100 g) fresh or frozen green peas
> 1 large tomato, quartered and cut into thin sections
> ¼ cup (50 ml) unsalted seafood stock or water
> Salt and freshly ground black pepper, to taste

1. Start rice. Prepare the ingredients and place them within easy reach of the stove.
2. Combine the soy sauce and vinegar in a large bowl. Place the fish pieces in the mixture and coat on all sides.
3. Heat a nonstick wok or skillet over medium-high heat. Stir-fry the onion until softened, about 2 minutes. Add the garlic and stir-fry a few seconds.
4. Add the peas, tomato and stock or water. Bring to a boil and simmer for 1–2 minutes.
5. Add the fish with its marinade, the salt and pepper, and simmer until the fish is done, 2–4 minutes, depending on the thickness of the fish fillets. Do not overcook. Garnish with the parsley and serve with rice.

The Philippines

VARIATION: *Shrimp may be substituted for the fish. Be sure to cook the shrimps only long enough for them to turn pink, or they will toughen.*

Makes 2–3 servings

Fish Poached with Fresh Ginger

Pesa

You may cook a small whole fish this way, or fish steaks or fillets. The whole fish looks very elegant and appetizing when sliced tomatoes and green onions (scallions) are artfully placed on top of it.

> 1 tablespoon vegetable oil
> 3 tablespoons grated fresh ginger
> 1 whole fish, about 1 lb (450 g), cleaned and scaled, or 8-12 oz (225-350 g) fish fillets or fish steaks
> 2 green onions (scallions), cut into 2-in (5-cm) lengths
> 2 tomatoes, quartered
> Salt, and a generous grinding of black pepper
> 2 bay leaves

> Reduced-sodium soy sauce or fish sauce (*patis*, *nam pla* or *nuoc mam*), to taste
> Fresh coriander leaves (cilantro) and lemon wedges, for garnish

1. Start rice.
2. Heat a nonstick skillet over medium heat. Add the oil and gently stir-fry the ginger until lightly browned.
3. Put the fish in the skillet on top of the ginger. Place the green onions and tomatoes on the fish and sprinkle with salt and pepper. Add enough water to almost cover the fish, and place the bay leaves in the water. Bring to a boil and immediately reduce the heat to low. Cover and simmer until the fish is done, about 5 minutes, depending on thickness. (Cook 8–10 minutes to the inch, measuring the fish at its thickest part.) Test for doneness with a fork. The meat will flake easily when done.
4. Transfer to a platter and garnish with the coriander leaves and lemon wedges. Serve with rice and a little soy or fish sauce.

Makes 2–3 servings

■ Beef ■

Picadillo

This is yet another easy one-pot meal. Cooked with potatoes and eaten with rice, *Picadillo*, meaning "minced meat," is South American in origin. It is sometimes made with a sweet-and-sour sauce. For the sake of speed, this recipe uses ground instead of minced meat.

> 1 tablespoon vegetable oil
> 1 large onion, thinly sliced
> 3 large cloves garlic, crushed
> 8-12 oz (225-350 g) lean ground beef

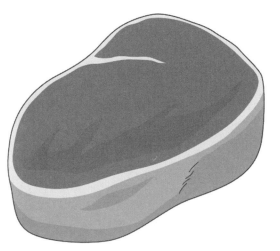

2 large tomatoes, chopped, or one 14-oz
  (400-g) can low-sodium stewed tomatoes,
  drained and cut into small pieces
Freshly ground black pepper, to taste
¼ cup (50 ml) unsalted chicken stock or
  water
2 new potatoes, peeled and diced
Chopped fresh parsley, for garnish

1. Start rice.
2. Heat a nonstick wok or skillet over medium-high heat. Add the oil and stir-fry the onions about 2 minutes, or until softened. Add the garlic and stir-fry a few seconds.
3. Add the beef and stir-fry until it begins to brown, separating the pieces if they stick together.
4. Mix in the tomatoes, pepper and stock or water. Stir well and bring to a boil.
5. Add the potatoes and more stock or water if the mixture seems dry. Reduce the heat and cook until the potatoes are tender, 10–15 minutes. Garnish with the chopped parsley and serve with rice.

Makes 2–3 servings

Meatballs, Filipino Style
Almondigas

Most cuisines have their own style of meatballs. This delicious recipe—with the flavors of garlic, onions, tomatoes and soy sauce—is typically Filipino.

8-12 oz (225-350 g) ground lean meat (half
  beef and half pork) or use a combination
  of ground meats including lamb, chicken
  or turkey, or even a mixture of lamb
  and shrimp
Salt and freshly ground black pepper, to
  taste
1 egg, lightly beaten
1 tablespoon oil
1 onion, finely chopped

2 large cloves garlic, finely chopped
2 large tomatoes, chopped, or one 14-oz
  (400 g) can low-sodium stewed tomatoes,
  drained and cut into small pieces
1 cup (250 ml) unsalted beef stock or water
1 tablespoon reduced-sodium soy sauce
2 green onions (scallions), thinly sliced

1. Start rice. Prepare the ingredients and place them within easy reach of the stove.
2. Combine the ground meat, pepper and egg. Mix well. Form the mixture into balls about the size of a walnut.
3. Heat a nonstick wok (or skillet) over medium-high heat and add the oil. Add the onions and stir-fry 1 minute, then add the garlic and continue to stir-fry until the onions soften. Add the tomatoes and stir-fry until softened, then combine with the onions.
4. Stir in the stock and soy sauce and bring to a boil. Add the meatballs and simmer slowly until they are cooked through. Test for doneness with a fork. Garnish with the green onions and serve with rice.

Makes 2 servings

Filipino-Style Steak
Bistek Filipino

A good steak is always good. But the Filipino way is to make it tangy and to add a lot of fried onions on the side. An irresistible combination.

Marinade
  4 tablespoons fresh lime juice
  1-2 tablespoons reduced-sodium soy sauce
  1 teaspoon sugar
  Salt and freshly ground black pepper, to taste
  • • •
  2 beef tenderloin steaks, about 6–8 oz
    (175-225 g) each

1 tablespoon vegetable oil
4 onions, thinly sliced into rings
2 large cloves garlic, chopped
Fresh chopped parsley or coriander leaves
(cilantro), for garnish

1. Start rice, unless you prefer to serve the steak with some crusty bread.
2. Combine the marinade ingredients in a bowl. Stir until the sugar dissolves. Place the steaks in the marinade and let stand up to 20 minutes. While the steaks are marinating, prepare a salad or vegetable of your choice. The Green Bean Salad (below) works well this this steak.
3. Heat a nonstick skillet over medium-high heat and add the oil.

Remove the steaks from the marinade and drain well, reserving the sauce. Sear on both sides. Cook to your preference—rare, medium or well done. Remove from the skillet to individual plates and keep warm.

4. If necessary, add a little more oil to the skillet. Sauté the onion rings until they soften. Add the garlic and continue to sauté until the onions are lightly browned. Add the remaining marinade to the onions and simmer up to 1 minute. Place the onions on top of the steaks and garnish with the parsley or coriander leaves. Serve with rice.

Makes 2 servings

■ Salads ■

Green Bean Salad

In this simple-to-make Filipino salad, blanched fresh green beans are tossed with a versatile and delicious dressing that can be used on any vegetable or salad.

The Philippines

12 oz (350 g) green beans, trimmed and cut
on the diagonal into bite-size lengths
1 tablespoon chopped fresh mint leaves or 1
teaspoon dried mint

Dressing
3 tablespoons fresh lemon or lime juice or
a mild vinegar
2–3 tablespoons olive oil or other
vegetable oil
Salt and freshly ground black pepper

1. Boil 4 cups (1 liter) of water in a saucepan, add the beans, cover, reduce the heat and simmer until tender, no longer than 10 minutes. Test after 5 minutes. The beans should be tender-crisp. Drain, rinse with cold water, and place in a serving bowl.
2. Combine the dressing ingredients and mix with the cooked beans. Mix in some of the mint, retaining some to sprinkle on top before serving.

Makes 2–3 servings

Singapore

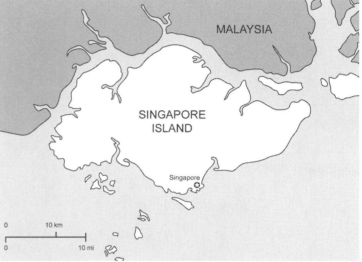

The republic of Singapore, an island located off the tip of the Malay Peninsula and connected to Malaysia by a causeway, is the only nation, outside mainland China and Taiwan, where the majority of the population is Chinese. Formerly a Malaysian fishing village, Singapore, literally "Lion City," takes its name from the Malaysian *singa pura,* which has it's roots in the Sanskrit *simha pura.* Although little is known about Singapore's early history, from the sixteenth to the early nineteenth centuries it was a part of the Sultanate of Johore, Malaysia. In 1819 Sir Thomas Stamford Raffles of the British East India Company arrived, saw the strategic advantages of its location, and urged Britain to sign a treaty with the Sultan of Johore establishing Singapore as a major British trading post in Southeast Asia. It was later made a crown colony by Britain in 1867. Singapore saw instant growth and immigration from various ethnic groups. Chinese and Indian traders, Indian laborers, and Malays began arriving in

large numbers, and the population increased rapidly, with the Chinese outnumbering all other groups.

Because of its strategic position and excellent natural harbor, Singapore has become a major industrial and financial center. Also, as one of Asia's so-called "Little Tigers" (along with Hong Kong, Taiwan, and South Korea), it has one of the world's most rapidly growing economies. It is a densely populated and prosperous nation whose people enjoy one of the highest standards of living. Singapore is also one of the cleanest and most orderly cosmopolitan centers in Asia.

Like southern Malaysia, Singapore's culinary heritage is the result of a melting pot of Chinese, Malay and Indian cultures. But it is also a cosmopolitan city of enormous diversity, with people from Japan, Taiwan, Indonesia, Vietnam and Thailand living side by side.

While Chinese cuisine is the most popular food in Singapore, Malay food is also abundant. Indonesians and Indians remain dominant minorities there, and their cuisines are all richly represented. This city-state, often called a gourmet's paradise, teems with first-class restaurants offering the widest variety of Asian and Western food in all of Asia. Street food is also plentiful and is one of Singapore's great attractions. Hawkers' stalls turn out a huge array of tasty local dishes in various styles. You can walk into street markets and find outdoor eating areas side-by-side, serving specialties from each cuisine. Even Mexican and Italian dishes are represented, as well as American fast food. Satay, a delicious Indo-Malay style of barbeque popular throughout Southeast Asia (pages 189–191), is the most common street food in Singapore.

Perhaps the most interesting of all the culinary styles is Straits Chinese *Nonya* cooking, which originated in the time of British rule. This came about when Chinese laborers were recruited in the nineteenth century to work in the docks and ports of Singapore. Only men were permit-

Singapore is a cosmopolitan city-state of enormous diversity, and its culinary heritage is the result of a melting pot of Chinese, Malay and Indian cultures.

ted to leave China, and when they came to the Straits settlements they married Malay women. The women are *"Nonyas,"* the men *"Babas"* and together they are known as *"Peranakan."* Nonya cooks use a mixture of Chinese and Malay ingredients and Malay methods of preparation. Nonya cooks prefer thinner coconut milk and less turmeric, chile and pepper than the Malays use, but more than would be used by a Chinese cook. They also add Malay spices, especially the sweeter Indian spices, to produce dishes that look like those of Malaysia and Indonesia but have a distinctive character of their own.

What sets Nonya apart from Chinese cooking is the use of the *rempah,* or seasoning paste. Where a Chinese cook would slice or mince each ingredient separately—for example, garlic, ginger, onion, chiles and spices—then stir-fry them in a wok, a Nonya cook begins by pounding them together in a mortar and pestle and cooking the resulting paste in the wok, before adding meat and vegetables. In this high-tech kitchen age, appliances, food processors, blenders and grinders have largely replaced the *batu lesong* (mortar and pestle) and the *batu giling* (grinding stone). Nonya cooking also uses some Chinese ingredients, such as pork, which the Malays, being Muslim, are forbidden to eat.

Singaporean Pantry

To keep shopping to a minimum, and to speed preparation and cooking time, it is helpful to keep these Singaporean staples on hand in your kitchen.

Ingredients with a Long Shelf Life

bean sauce, yellow or brown

black pepper, ground

chili sauce (Sriracha brand, made in Thailand, is recommended)

coconut milk, unsweetened, canned

coriander, ground

curry powder

egg noodles

Indonesian chili sauce (*sambal ulek*, recipe on page 192)

Indonesian sweet soy sauce (*kecap manis*, recipe on page 192)

shrimp paste (*terasi*) or anchovy paste

soy sauce

tamarind water or lime juice

turmeric, ground

Fresh Ingredients

chiles

coriander leaves (cilantro)

garlic

ginger

green onions (scallions)

lemongrass or lemon zest

onions

■ Rice ■

Plain Rice
Nasi Putih

As is common throughout most of Asia, boiled white rice is central to all Singaporean cooking. Long-grain, highly milled and polished rice is preferred. The recipe for Boiled Rice, Chinese Style on page 26 is recommended.

■ Noodles ■

Fried Egg Noodles
Bami Goreng

This is one of many Indonesian-Malay versions of Chinese *laomien*, "tossed and mixed noodles," a very popular one-dish meal. Almost any meat, fish or vegetable, whether leftover or fresh, can be stir-fried, seasoned with sambal ulek (Indonesian chili sauce) and kecap manis (sweet soy sauce), and mixed with the noodles. It can also become a vegetarian meal by substituting tofu. (See variation at the end of the recipe.)

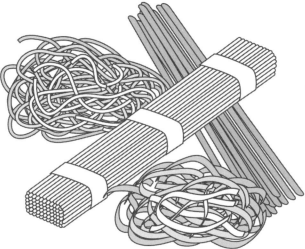

12 oz (350 g) fresh egg noodles or 8 oz (175 g) dried egg noodles
1 tablespoon vegetable oil
2 large cloves garlic, chopped
6-8 oz (175-250 g) cooked or raw chicken, cut into small thin pieces
4 oz (100 g) Chinese cabbage, shredded
4 fresh mushrooms, sliced
½-1 teaspoon sambal ulek (Indonesian chili sauce, see page 192) or fresh or dried chiles, chili sauce or ground red pepper, to taste
1-2 tablespoons kecap manis (sweet soy sauce, see page 192) or 1-2 tablespoons reduced-sodium soy sauce and 1-2 teaspoons brown sugar
10 small peeled raw or cooked shrimp
1 or 2 handfuls fresh bean sprouts, trimmed
Sliced green onions (scallions) and red bell pepper or chiles (depending on whether you like spicy heat or not), and lemon wedges, for garnish

1. Bring a large pot of water to boil and prepare the noodles according to the instructions on the package. Otherwise, drop the noodles in the boiling water, allow to return to a boil and continue boiling 1–3 minutes, depending on the type of noodles. Usually it takes about 1½ minutes for fresh noodles

Singapore

and about 3 minutes for dried to cook. Keep testing one strand after another. They should remain firm to the bite. Drain in a colander, rinse with cold water and set aside.

2. Heat a nonstick wok (or skillet) over medium-high heat. Add the oil and stir-fry the garlic for 3–4 seconds. Add the chicken and stir-fry about 2 minutes.

3. Add the cabbage and mushrooms and stir-fry 1–2 minutes.

4. Stir in the chili sauce and sweet soy sauce, followed by the shrimp. Cook until the shrimp become opaque, about 1 minute. Do not overcook or the shrimp will toughen. Mix well. If the mixture seems dry, add a tablespoon or two of stock or water to prevent scorching. If you're using pre-cooked shrimp, add them in Step 5 after the noodles have been added.

5. Add the noodles a few at a time and stir-fry them gently until they are heated through. Add the bean sprouts and toss until wilted. Serve garnished with the green onions, red pepper and lemon wedges.

Makes 2–3 servings

VARIATION: *For a vegetarian dish, eliminate chicken and shrimp and substitute one block (about 14 oz/400 g) firm tofu. Cut the tofu into 2-inch (5-cm) squares, and lightly brown them in a little oil. Add them in Step 4, in place of the shrimp. Stir into the sauce.*

■ Soups ■

Chicken Cucumber Soup
Huang Quar Gai Tong

This simple and elegant soup can be a main course for a light meal or a delicious accompaniment to another dish.

> 12 oz (300 g) chicken breast meat, sliced into thin strips
> 2 egg whites, whipped
> 3-4 cups (700 ml-1 liter) unsalted chicken broth
> ¼ teaspoon sugar
> 1 tablespoon reduced-sodium soy sauce
> 1 cucumber, peeled and seeded, cut into thin strips
> 1 teaspoon sesame oil
> Salt and freshly ground black pepper, to taste

1. Coat the chicken strips with the egg whites.

2. Bring the broth, sugar, and soy sauce to a boil.

3. Stir in the chicken and cucumber. Cook until the chicken is done, not a moment more.

4. Add the sesame oil, salt and pepper. Serve hot.

Makes 2–4 servings

Singapore

■ **Seafood** ■

Pan-Fried Fish Nonya Style

Ikan Goreng Taucheo

Nonya cooking, also known as Straits Chinese, is a combination of Chinese and Malay styles. A seasoning paste called *rempah*—a mixture of spices, onion and garlic that is similar to the curry pastes of Thailand—give Chinese ingredients a distinctive Nonya flavor. The seasoning paste ingredients are pounded together in a mortar. In this recipe, yellow bean sauce is used. It is a light tan color and is the Malay variety of bean sauce, as opposed to brown bean sauce, which is the Chinese variety.

> 1½ tablespoons vegetable oil
> 8-12 oz (225–350 g) fish fillets or steaks or a 1-lb (450-g) whole fish, cleaned and scaled

Seasoning mixture

> 1 onion, finely chopped
> 2 large cloves garlic, crushed
> 1-3 fresh chiles, seeded and chopped, or

> ½ teaspoon sambal ulek (Indonesian chili sauce, see page 192) or other chili sauce or ground red pepper, to taste
> 1 tablespoon grated fresh ginger
>
> • • •
>
> 1 teaspoon yellow bean sauce (*taucheo*) or Chinese bean sauce
> ¼ cup tamarind water (see page 245) or fresh lime or lemon juice
> ½ teaspoon sugar
> Fresh coriander leaves (cilantro) or mint leaves, for garnish

1. Start rice. Prepare the ingredients and place them within easy reach of the stove.
2. Heat a nonstick wok (or skillet) over medium heat. Add half of the oil and lightly brown the fish on both sides, about 2 minutes. Do not overcook. Cooking time will depend on the thickness of fish. Pierce with a fork to determine doneness. Remove to a heated platter and keep warm.
3. Combine the seasoning ingredients in a small food processor and blend to a coarse paste. If you do not have a processor, finely chop the ingredients and go on to Step 4.
4. Heat the wok over medium heat. Add the remaining oil and stir-fry the paste for 1–2 minutes. If you're using hand-chopped ingredients, stir-fry them until the onion becomes soft and transparent, about 2 minutes.
5. Stir in the bean sauce, tamarind water or lime juice, and sugar and cook over low heat until the mixture thickens slightly. Pour over the fish, garnish with the coriander or mint leaves and serve with rice.

Makes 2 servings

Singapore

Squid Cooked in Coconut Milk

Opor Sotong

With its rich and delicious sauce, this quick and easy recipe rewards you with an incredible amount of flavor for only a short time spent in preparing it.

   2 tablespoons vegetable oil
   2–3 cloves garlic, chopped
   1 onion, chopped
   ½ teaspoon turmeric
   2 tablespoons ground coriander
   1 teaspoon ground cumin
   12 oz (350 g) squid, cleaned and cut into
      small pieces
   ¾ cup (175 ml) coconut milk
   1–2 tablespoons grated fresh or
      unsweetened dried coconut
   Salt and freshly ground black pepper, to taste

1. Heat the oil in wok (or skillet) and stir-fry the garlic and onion.
2. Stir in the spices.
3. Add the squid and stir-fry about 3 minutes.
4. Add the coconut milk, grated coconut, salt and pepper. Cook until heated through.

Makes 2–3 servings

Chili Crab

This is a very spicy, full-bodied dish made with fresh red chiles and garlic. The recipe is usually made with unshelled crab or lobster pieces. To speed preparation time, cooked crabmeat is used here.

Sauce
   ½ cup (125 ml) water
   1 tablespoon sugar
   1 teaspoon soy sauce
   1 teaspoon cornstarch
   2 tablespoons tomato ketchup

   1 tablespoon fresh lime juice or white vinegar

   • • •

   2 tablespoons vegetable oil
   2 cloves garlic, chopped
   2 or more fresh red chiles, stemmed,
      seeded and chopped
   12 oz (175 g) cooked crabmeat, picked over
   2 green onions (scallions), sliced
   Fresh coriander leaves (cilantro), chopped

1. Start rice. Prepare the ingredients and place them within easy reach of the stove.
2. Combine the sauce ingredients in a small bowl.
3. Heat the oil in a hot wok (or skillet). Stir-fry the garlic for 30 seconds. Add the chiles and stir-fry 30 seconds to 1 minute. Add the crabmeat and stir-fry until heated through. Add the sauce and stir well. Stir in the sliced green onions.
4. Garnish with the coriander leaves and serve with rice.

Makes 2–3 servings

Shrimp Curry, Nonya Style

Sambal Udang

Shrimp and pineapple, an usual combination, is enhanced in this recipe by the distinct flavor of lemongrass. Be careful not to overcook the shrimp.

Seasoning mixture
   1 small onion, chopped
   2 stalks lemongrass (use bottom 6 inches
      only), chopped, or grated zest from ½
      lemon
   2 large cloves garlic, chopped
   1–2 fresh red chiles or ½ teaspoon sambal
      ulek (Indonesian chili sauce, see page
      192) or other chili sauce, or ground red
      pepper, to taste
   ½ teaspoon shrimp paste (*terasi*) or
      anchovy paste

Singapore

3 tablespoons ground coriander

1 teaspoon turmeric

• • •

1 tablespoon vegetable oil

8-12 oz (300–400 g) medium shrimp, peeled and deveined, leaving tails intact

1-2 slices fresh or canned pineapple, cut into small pieces

1 cup (250 ml) canned, unsweetened coconut milk (shake can before measuring)

2 green onions (scallions), sliced, for garnish

1. Start rice. Prepare the ingredients and place them within easy reach of the stove.

2. Combine the seasoning ingredients in a small food processor and blend to a coarse paste. If you do not have a processor, finely chop the ingredients and go on to Step 3.

3. Heat a nonstick wok (or skillet) over medium-high heat and add the oil. Add the paste mixture and cook for 1–2 minutes. If using hand chopped ingredients, stir-fry them until the onion becomes soft and transparent, about 2 minutes.

4. Add the shrimp and quickly stir-fry them until they turn pink, 1–3 minutes depending, on their size. Add the pineapple and coconut milk and bring slowly to a gentle simmer, stirring constantly. Do not boil. Cook for about 1 minute or until heated through. Garnish with the green onions and serve with rice.

Makes 2 servings

■ **Chicken** ■

Chicken in Spicy Tomato Sauce

Ayam Goreng

Singapore, often called a gourmet's paradise, teems with restaurants offering Chinese, Malay, Indonesian, Indian and Pakistani food, as well as the popular Nonya cooking style. This spicy dish—a kind of hybrid coconut-curry with a tangy tomato sauce—reflects Singapore's culinary melting pot.

1-1½ tablespoons vegetable oil

About 1 lb (450 g) boneless, skinless chicken breasts or parts, cut into small pieces, for faster cooking

Seasoning mixture

1 small onion, chopped

2 stalks lemongrass (use bottom 6 ines only), chopped, or grated zest from ½ lemon

2 large cloves garlic, chopped

1-3 fresh red chiles or 1 teaspoon sambal ulek (Indonesian chili sauce, see page 192) or other chili sauce, or ground red pepper, to taste

• • •

1 tablespoon curry powder

2 tablespoons canned tomato sauce or tomato ketchup

2 tomatoes, quartered

1 teaspoon sugar

1 tablespoon fresh lime juice or vinegar

½ cup (125 ml) canned, unsweetened
  coconut milk (shake can before
  measuring)
6 fresh mint leaves

1. Start rice. Prepare the ingredients
   and place them within easy reach of
   the stove.
2. Heat a nonstick wok (or skillet)
   over medium-high heat. Add half
   of the oil and cook the chicken on
   both sides until brown, 7–10 minutes, depending on their thickness.
   (Boneless chicken will take about 2
   minutes more to stir-fry.) Remove
   from the wok and keep warm.
3. Combine the seasoning ingredients
   in a small food processor and blend
   to a coarse paste. If you do not
   have a processor, finely chop the
   ingredients and go on to Step 3.
4. Heat the wok over medium heat.
   Add the remaining oil and stir-fry
   the paste 1–2 minutes. If using
   hand-chopped ingredients, stir-fry
   them until the onion becomes soft
   and transparent, about 2 minutes.
   Stir in the remaining ingredients,
   except coconut milk and mint
   leaves, and cook for another minute or two, stirring constantly.
5. Stir in the coconut milk and
   reserved chicken pieces. Cook over
   moderate heat until bubbles appear
   around the edge of the wok. Do
   not boil or the coconut milk may
   curdle. Simmer about 5 minutes or
   until the chicken is done. Fold in
   the mint leaves and serve with rice.

Yield 2 servings

Chicken Braised with Onions

There is a large quantity of onions in
this recipe, so it will probably need to
be cooked in two batches.

1 tablespoon ground coriander
½ teaspoon ground turmeric
Salt and freshly ground black pepper, to
  taste
8–12 oz (200–300 g) boneless chicken
  meat, cut into bite-size pieces, or 1 lb
  (450 g) chicken parts, cut into small
  pieces, for faster cooking
2–3 tablespoons vegetable oil
2 large cloves garlic, finely chopped
1–3 fresh or dried red chiles, seeded and
  chopped, or ground red pepper, to
  taste
4 large onions, thinly sliced
¼–½ cup (50–125 ml) water
Fresh parsley or coriander leaves
  (cilantro), for garnish

1. Start rice. Prepare the ingredients
   and place them within easy reach
   of the stove.
2. Combine the ground coriander,
   turmeric, salt and pepper, and rub
   into the chicken. Set aside.
3. Heat a nonstick wok (or skillet)
   over high heat. Add 2 teaspoons
   of the oil. Stir-fry the garlic,
   chiles and half of the onions
   until they soften and begin to
   brown. Remove from the wok
   and place on paper towels. Add
   a little more oil, if needed, and
   cook the remaining onions.
   Remove from the wok and place
   on paper towels.
4. Heat a little more oil and stir-fry
   the chicken pieces until they begin
   to brown, about 2 minutes.
5. Return the onions to the wok, add
   the water and stir well. Cover and
   simmer gently until the chicken is
   tender. Larger pieces of chicken
   will take longer to cook. Transfer
   to a serving dish and garnish with
   the coriander or parsley leaves.

Makes 2–3 servings

Singapore

ACKNOWLEDGMENTS

I wish to acknowledge the help and inspiration of those who made this book possible. First, I am indebted to all the writers and cooks whose works brought me closer to the culture and cooking of Asia. This endeavor would not have been possible without the knowledge and understanding that I gained from reading their writings.

I would also like to give special thanks to those individuals who generously gave of their time to help me with some of the chapters. Their opinions and knowledge were invaluable: Zhang Yaqi, formerly an exchange teacher from Hunan Teachers University, for the chapter on China; Prasad Vasireddi, for India and Pakistan, who generously shared with me his lively interest and study of the culture of his country India and its neighbor; Jan Vanlent, who lived and worked in Indonesia for more than thirty years; Grace Kobayashi, for her expert help and enthusiasm regarding Japan; and Clare You, who besides being a wonderful Korean cook, teaches Korean at the University of California, Berkeley, and writes about Korean language and linguistics. Thanks also to Helen Black, R.D., for her professional opinions on diet and cooking technique, and to Lynda Robinson for her help in making some difficult decisions. Last but not least, my debt to Sara Sclarenco, for her encouragement when my energies flagged. I am deeply grateful to all.

Thanks also to The Centre—a meeting place for families from all over the world who are visiting the United States as students and scholars—at the University of California, Berkeley. They have enriched our lives by generously sharing their foods and customs.

To make shopping easier, and to cut preparation and cooking time, unfamiliar ingredients have been kept to a minimum. Substitutes are given when possible.

BAGOONG: *See* shrimp paste.

BAI MAKRUT: *See* kaffir lime leaves.

BAMBOO SHOOTS: Readily available canned. Once opened, may be stored in the refrigerator in water, changed daily, for up to a week. To rid them of a tinny taste, blanch briefly in hot water.

BASIL: Several native varieties of this herb are used in Indian and Southeast Asian cooking. Holy basil (*horapa*), is the one most commonly used in Thai cooking. Substitute the large-leaf sweet basil leaves used in Western cooking. If that is not available, substitute fresh mint, though it is not the same. Dried basil is not a good substitute.

BEAN SAUCE, YELLOW: A salty, pungent soybean sauce, used as a flavoring in some Chinese and Singaporean dishes. The Malaysian variety (*taucheo*) is light tan in color; the Chinese variety (brown bean sauce) is dark caramel. Substitute brown bean sauce or Japanese *miso*.

BEAN SAUCES OR PASTES: Throughout Asia, soybeans are fermented and processed into sauces for use in cooking or as table condiments. They have a pungent, salty flavor and are used sparingly to add color and flavor, and to help thicken sauces. There is also a hot bean sauce called *koch'ujang* that is used in Korean cooking. All these sauces are sold in jars in Asian food shops and major supermarkets.

BEAN SPROUTS: Usually sprouted from mung beans, the tender new shoots add a pleasing crunch to many dishes. They should be scrupulously fresh, crisp and white. Canned bean sprouts are not recommended. Although you may substitute matchstick slices of celery for texture, it is not quite the same.

BEANS, CHINESE YARD-LONG: Sold in Asian groceries and some supermarkets, yard-longs are slender, dark green and, despite their name, grow from 12 to 18 inches long. They are often used in ceremonial dishes because they symbolize long life. Though yard-long beans have a stronger flavor and more crunch, ordinary green beans may be substituted.

BENI SHOGA: *See* pickled ginger.

BLACK BEANS, FERMENTED: These small black soybeans, fermented with salt, have a wonderful flavor when combined with garlic. Sold in cans, jars and plastic bags. Rinse well before using to prevent over salting. Unused beans may be stored in a sealed container in the refrigerator for up to 3 months.

BOK CHOY: The most popular Chinese green vegetable, this is a leafy green vegetable with a white stem that tastes a little like Swiss chard. The center stem, known as the heart, is topped with yellow flowers. It is very tender and delicate, and is often sold separately. Baby bok choy is increasingly available.

CANDLENUTS (*KEMIRI*): A hard, oily nut used for flavoring and thickening in Indonesian and Malaysian cooking. Macadamia nuts are the best substitute, but Brazil nuts or blanched almonds may also be used.

CARDAMOM: After saffron, the most expensive spice used in many Indian dishes. The pods and seeds of a bush native to South India and Sri Lanka are used in sweet and savory dishes, especially curries. When ground cardamom is called for, the seed pods are opened and discarded, and only the black or brown seeds are ground. Look for cardamom seed pods that are tinged green; white pods have been bleached and are less flavorful.

CHILES: Introduced by the Portuguese in the sixteenth century, these fiery peppers are rich in vitamins A and C, and are an indispensable ingredient in Asian cooking. There are many varieties, varying considerably in degrees of heat. Usually, the smaller they are, the hotter they taste. The pointed red or green, 2-inch-long serrano chiles are preferred by many cooks, but I like the longer Anaheim chile best because it is milder. Thai bird chiles are used extensively in Thai cooking: the small pointed chiles are very, very hot. But even with chiles of the same variety, the degree of heat can be unpredictable. Experiment to ascertain which you prefer. In Southeast Asia, the seeds and ribs, which produce most of the heat, are not usually removed. For the recipes in this book, they are removed, and the number of chiles in each recipe has been reduced dramatically. It should be kept in mind that every fiery-hot dish that Asian cooks prepare is meant to be consumed with a large quantity of rice. Handle all chiles with caution, and wash hands very well afterwards to avoid burning eyes and skin. You may wish to wear disposable rubber gloves when handling them. Dried whole chiles, ground red chile or chile sauce may be substituted.

CHILES, DRIED RED: These have a nice flavor and are convenient to use because they store well. Dried chiles also have a less irritating effect on the hands. Dried red pepper flakes may be substituted. Both are widely available in supermarkets. Ground red pepper may also be substituted.

CHILI SAUCE: There are many bottled varieties of this sauce. A popular one is the Thai *Sriracha* sauce, which is made with chiles, vinegar, garlic and sugar. It comes in mild, medium and hot versions. Indonesian chili sauce is called *sambal uleck*, which may also be bought ready-made.

CHINESE CABBAGE: Also called napa cabbage or celery cabbage, the long, thick heads of Chinese cabbage have crinkly, green-tinged leaves with thick veins. Unlike round cabbages, the leaves of Chinese cabbage are crisp, not chewy, thin and delicately flavored. Look for Chinese cabbage in the produce aisle of large supermarkets.

CHINESE PARSLEY: *See* coriander leaves.

CILANTRO: *See* coriander leaves.

CINNAMON: Cinnamon sticks are rolls of thinly shaved bark from the cinnamon tree. Cassia is the bark of a similar tree. It has a stronger flavor and is cheaper, but it lacks the more delicate taste of cinnamon. The two are usually interchangeable.

CLOVES: The dried flower buds of a tropical evergreen tree that grows in Southeast Asia. The oil contains phenol, which is an antiseptic. Cloves are an ingredient in the Indian spice mix *garam masala* and in Chinese five-spice powder.

COCONUT MILK: A creamy white liquid expressed from the oil-rich flesh of coconuts, not the liquid found inside the nut, conveniently available in cans. It is quite delicious and is one of the most important ingredients of Southeast Asian and South Indian cuisines. I think the best brand comes from Thailand, called Chaokoh. Coconut milk can be refrigerated in a plastic container for a few days or frozen for several weeks after opening. The thick coconut cream rises to the top of the can, as it does in freshly extracted coconut milk. If the recipe calls for coconut cream, skim the top off the milk.

For thick coconut milk, shake the can before opening and use as is. For medium coconut milk, dilute thick coconut milk with half as much water. For thin coconut milk, dilute thick coconut milk with an equal amount of water. There is no substitute for coconut milk that will taste the same. To make a dish different, but still delicious, use yogurt.

CORIANDER: Both a spice and an herb, coriander looks like flat-leafed parsley. The spice has a more subtle and very different flavor from the herb, and cannot be used as a substitute. Dried coriander seeds are an essential ingredient in curry powder and other spice mixtures. They have a slight citrus flavor and impart a subtle perfume. The seeds are more flavorful and aromatic if toasted in a dry pan before using. See Coriander Leaves for description of the herb form.

CORIANDER LEAVES: The pungent fresh leaf, also called Chinese parsley or cilantro, is an indispensable ingredient in Indian, Southeast Asian and southern Chinese cuisines (as well as in Mexican and some Latin American cuisines). It has a brash, musky flavor. Even those who love it (and you either love it or hate it) sometimes cannot tolerate its bitterness. It should always be added to a dish just before serving, although there are some dishes that use a lot of it during the entire cooking process. There is no substitute for flavor, but parsley may be used instead for its color.

CUMIN: Along with coriander, cumin is the most important ingredient in curry powders and spice mixes. It resembles the caraway seed in appearance, and is sometimes confused with it, but the flavors are different. The seeds are more fragrant if they are toasted in a dry pan before grinding.

CURRY POWDER AND PASTES, INDIAN AND THAI: The word *curry* comes from the Tamil *Kari*, which means "sauce." Preparing curry powders and pastes at home is a time-consuming task. Fortunately, there are several canned or jarred mixtures available in Asian shops and most supermarkets that are good tasting and handy. Newcomers to Indian food might do well to sample these mixtures before buying a full-selection of individual spices. These commercially prepared spice mixes and spice pastes are wonderful time-savers for busy cooks. You will have a better choice if you buy the mixes in an Asian or Indian specialty store.

DAIKON: *See* giant white radish.

DASHI: A clear soup made from dried bonito flakes and seaweed. It is an essential ingredient in Japanese cooking, both in soup and as a cooking stock. It is also an ingredient in some dipping sauces. An instant, powdered form of dashi is available in Japanese shops and well-stocked supermarkets.

FENNEL: A spice, sometimes known as sweet cumin, is available in seed or ground form, and is used in spice mixes in India and Southeast Asia. It is similar to cumin, but has a strong anise flavor.

FENUGREEK: The seed is ground and used in spice mixes. Aromatic yet bitter, fenugreek should be used in measured quantities.

FISH SAUCE: A thin, salty brown liquid made from salted, fresh shrimp or fish, fish sauce is an essential flavoring in Southeast Asian cooking. It is called *nam pla* in Thai, *nuoc mam* in Vietnamese and *patis* in Tagalog (the Philippines).

FIVE-SPICE POWDER: An important ingredient in Chinese cooking, this reddish brown powder is a combination of ground star anise, fennel, cinnamon, cloves and Sichuan pepper. Sometimes it contains more than five spices. It is available ready-mixed in jars.

GALANGAL: Known as *kha* in Thailand, *laos* in Indonesia, and *lengkuas* in Malaysia. A rhizome, member of the ginger family, it is more aromatic and less pungent than ginger. Not easy to find in its fresh form, it is available in Asian food shops bottled in brine, frozen, dried in pieces or ground. Fresh ginger can be substituted, though the taste is not the same.

GARAM MASALA: An aromatic, mellow mixture of dry-roasted and ground spices used in Indian cooking. Though there is no standard mixture, it often contains black pepper, cardamom, cinnamon, cumin, cloves and nutmeg. It is generally added at the end of the cooking process or as a garnish just before serving. Ready-ground garam masala is widely available in jars and can be very good.

GARLIC: Garlic is a most vital ingredient in Asian cooking, and almost every recipe in this book has some in it. It is not only used as a flavoring, but is also prized for its medicinal properties. Garlic has been shown to inhibit the tendency to form blood clots, and thus lowers heart attack risk. It is believed to lower blood pressure and cholesterol. Garlic has a long history. Mentioned over 5,000 years ago in Sanskrit writings, it was also a staple in the Sumerian diet. The ancient Egyptians, Romans and Greeks revered it for its curative powers, and there are even claims made for its value in treating infections. Fortunately, it is available everywhere in its fresh form. The amount of garlic called for in this book's recipes is on the mild side. Asian cooks generally use a lot more.

GHEE: The Indian name for clarified butter. Pure butterfat, from which all the milk solids have been removed, it is used liberally in Indian cooking. Because ghee is very high in cholesterol, I have suggested that a light vegetable oil, such as canola or safflower oil, be used in the Indian recipes.

GIANT WHITE RADISH: Daikon, in Japanese, is a white radish that grows large and very long, with a juicy, crispy white flesh. It is widely available in supermarkets. Substitute icicle radish or white turnip.

GINGER: A rhizome with a pungent flavor, ginger is vital in most Asian dishes. Only fresh ginger should be used. Powdered ginger has an entirely different flavor and the two are not interchangeable. Fresh ginger will keep frozen, unpeeled. Cut off what you need and slice or grate it without thawing. Always buy ginger with a smooth, unwrinkled skin. Wrinkles mean the ginger is old and has begun to dry out inside. Some cooks store slices in jars in the refrigerator, completely covering the ginger with dry sherry or vodka. For ginger juice, press ginger slices through a garlic press and catch the juice in a small bowl.

GINGER, PICKLED: Called *beni shoga* in Japanese. Whole fresh ginger is colored red, pickled, sliced paperthin and sold bottled, in packets (and also in bulk) in Asian food stores and major supermarkets. Used as a flavoring, side dish or garnish in Japanese cooking.

GREEN ONIONS: A staple throughout Asia, they are also called scallions or spring onions. The green tops as well as the white bulbs are used.

HOISIN SAUCE: A dark, red-brown sauce made from fermented soybeans, garlic, vinegar, sugar and spices. It is used in Chinese cooking and also at the table as a dipping sauce. An opened jar will keep in the refrigerator for several months.

JAGGERY: *See* palm sugar.

KAFFIR LIME LEAVES: Called *makrut* in Thailand, these leaves from the kaffir lime tree add a lemon-lime flavor and a special fragrance to curries and soups. The leaves have a unique shape and look like they're joined end-to-end. Sold at Asian groceries and some supermarkets. Buy fresh leaves when you see them. Dried leaves will keep a few months. Or substitute citrus leaves or lime and lemon zest.

KALONJI: Small black seeds with a mild flavor, used in India when making breads, vegetables and pickles. Also called "onion seeds." *Kalonji* is one of the ingredients in the Bengali five-spice mixture (*see* panch phoran).

KECAP ASIN: Indonesian salty soy sauce. Substitute Japanese soy sauce.

KECAP MANIS: Indonesian sweet soy sauce. A thick sauce with a molasses base, it is available bottled in Asian grocery stores and major supermarkets. It can be made at home, or substitute ordinary soy sauce and brown sugar.

KELP, DRIED: *See* kombu.

KEMIRI: *See* candlenuts.

KHA: *See* galangal.

KIM: *See* nori.

KOCH'UJANG: A delicious and very hot Korean bean sauce made with fermented soybeans, hot red pepper and sometimes garlic. There is a Chinese equivalent that can be substituted. *See also* bean sauces and pastes.

KOMBU: Kelp seaweed. It is available dried, and is used to flavor stocks and sauces in Japanese cooking.

LAOS: *See* galangal.

LEMONGRASS: Known as *takrai* in Thailand and *sereh* in Indonesia, it is a tall plant, with a strong citrus flavor, used in Southeast Asian cooking. It is available almost all year round in many markets. To use fresh lemongrass, trim the end and peel off or trim the tough outer leaves. Discard the upper part of the leaf, which is fibrous, and use the lower part of the stalk, which is soft and juicy. Use only the lower 4–6 inches (10–15 cm) of the plant. Look for fresh lemongrass at Asian shops and large supermarkets: dried lemongrass is available in many markets, but it has very little flavor. Substitute the grated zest of ½ lemon for each stalk of lemongrass.

LENGKUAS: *See* galangal.

LIMES: Lime juice is used as a souring agent in Southeast Asian cooking; lemon juice is used in Indian cooking. Though Persian limes are not quite the same, they make a good substitute.

LYCHEES: Also spelled "litchis," this small fruit has a red, prickly shell and a juicy, sweetly perfumed white flesh surrounding a single seed. Fresh lychees are available in large supermarkets in June and July. Canned lychees are available all year.

MASUR DAL: A fast-cooking legume, these hulled, salmon-colored split peas, called red lentils, are used in Indian cooking. Masur dal loses the salmon color when cooked and turns yellowish. Look for the lentils in large supermarkets, Indian groceries and health food stores.

MINT: There are several varieties, the most common being spearmint and peppermint. The leaves are used fresh in Indian and Southeast Asian cuisines. Fresh basil may be substituted.

MIRIN: Japanese rice wine. It is sweeter than sake and is used only for cooking. Sake or dry sherry, sweetened with a little sugar, may be substituted.

MISO: A paste made from cooked fermented soybeans used in Japanese soups, stews, sauces and marinades. There are several varieties—white, red, brown and tan. Each has a different taste and a different proportion of salt to sugar.

MUSHROOMS, DRIED CHINESE AND JAPANESE: Used in Chinese, Japanese and Korean cooking. Sold dried in cellophane packs, dried mushrooms are very fragrant with intense flavor and incomparable texture. Soak 25–30 minutes in hot water before using. The dried mushrooms preferred for the recipes in this book are a Japanese variety known as shiitake mushrooms. Stems are seldom used because they are very tough. Standard, cultivated fresh mushrooms may be substituted, but their taste is bland compared to the smoky flavor of dried mushrooms.

MUSHROOMS, STRAW: Small, cultivated mushroom, with a delicate flavor and texture. Available canned, bottled or dried.

MUSTARD SEEDS: Black and brown, these are used whole in Indian dishes. Best if they are lightly toasted in a dry pan to bring out their maximum flavor.

NAM PLA: *See* fish sauce.

NOODLES: The noodle recipes in this book use Chinese wheat, rice and egg noodles, as well as Japanese buckwheat (soba) and wheat (udon) noodles. Instructions and substitutions will be found in the text of the recipes.

NORI: A dried seaweed used in Japanese and Korean cuisine. It is sold in paper-thin sheets and must be toasted before using. Known as *kim* in Korean.

NUOC MAM: *See* fish sauce.

NUTMEG: Ground nutmeg is one of the spices used in garam masala. The outer fiber of the nutmeg kernel, known as mace, is used in powdered form in some Mogul and Kashmiri dishes. Both mace and nutmeg are used in some Thai curry pastes.

ONION SEEDS: *See* kalonji.

ONIONS: In Asia, these come in many varieties. The onion most commonly used in Southeast Asian cooking is similar to a shallot. The recipes in this book substitute the common yellow (Spanish) onion for cooking. The mild red onion is best to eat raw.

OYSTER SAUCE: A thick brown sauce made from oysters, cooked in soy sauce and salt, and used in Chinese cooking. It is available in jars in most supermarkets.

PALM SUGAR: Dark, strongly flavored sugar made from the sap of coconut and palmyrah palms. It is also known as jaggery. Dark brown sugar may be substituted.

PANCH PHORAN: *Panch* means "five" in Hindi. *Panch phoran* is a Bengali combination of five aromatic seeds: whole black mustard seeds, whole cumin seeds, whole fenugreek seeds, whole fennel seeds and whole *kalonji* seeds. (Do not confuse this with the Chinese five-spice powder.) They are added to dishes whole, not ground. Buy panch phoran already mixed from an Indian shop or put the mixture together yourself.

PAPRIKA: A mild, brilliant red spice of European origin. It is useful in making Asian curries for those who have a low tolerance for hot chiles. Paprika will impart the red color without the hot taste that, in authentic Asian cooking, would come from using a dozen or two chiles. Most of the recipes in this book call for a timid amount of one, two or three chiles.

PATIS/PETIS: *See* fish sauce.

PEPPER, BLACK: A vital spice in Asian cooking. Buy the peppercorns and grind them fresh in your pepper grinder.

PEPPER, SICHUAN: These are dried berries that are not related to black peppercorns. Substitute black pepper and a little anise.

RICE WINE, CHINESE: Known also as Shaoxing wine, it is brewed from fermented rice. Pale dry sherry may be substituted.

SAFFRON: The world's most expensive spice is the dried stigma of the saffron crocus. It is used in Indian dishes, especially in the north. The thread-like strands are a dark orange color and have a strong fragrance. It is not to be confused with turmeric, which is often called "cheap" saffron. Soak the threads in warm water and add both the threads and the water to the dish.

SAKE: Japanese rice wine, usually served warm by immersing the wine's container in very hot water for a short time. It is also used in cooking. Pale dry sherry may be substituted.

SALAM LEAVES: These aromatic, young leaves, sometimes referred to as Indonesian bay leaves, contain oils that impart a unique flavor to Indonesian curries. They are sold dried outside the region. If not available, substitute dried curry leaves, which are somewhat similar in flavor.

SAMBAL ULEK: A combination of chiles and salt preserved in vinegar. It is used in Indonesian, Malay and Singaporean sauces, and can also be used as a substitute for fresh chiles. Available ready-made in jars.

SANSHO POWDER: The ground seeds of the sansho tree, it is used as a seasoning in Japanese cooking.

SCALLIONS: *See* green onions.

SESAME OIL: Extracted from toasted sesame seeds, it is used in small quantities as a flavoring in Chinese and Korean cooking, not as a cooking medium. Buy from the Asian shelf of your supermarket, not the health food store. They are very different.

SESAME SEEDS, BLACK AND WHITE: Nutty in flavor, these are used in Chinese, Korean and Japanese cuisine.

SHICHIMI TOGARASHI (SEVEN-SPICE POWDER): Powdered blend of dried chiles, hot mustard seed, sesame seed, pepper leaf, rapeseed, hemp seed and dried tangerine peel, used in Japanese food. Available in small bottles on Asian shelves of many supermarkets.

SHIITAKE MUSHROOMS: *See* mushrooms.

SHRIMP PASTE OR SHRIMP SAUCE: It has a powerful odor and an intense flavor, and is one of the essential ingredients in the cooking of Southeast Asia. Called *kapi* in Thailand, *blacan* or *blachan* in Malaysia, *trasi* or *terasi* in Indonesia, *mam tom* in Vietnam and *bagoong* in the Philippines, it is available in Asian shops and some grocery stores. Though not at all the same in taste, anchovy paste may be substituted.

SOYBEAN CURD: *See* tofu.

SOY SAUCE: An indispensable ingredient in Asian cooking. There are light and dark soy sauces, sweetened soy sauce in Indonesian cooking (*kecap manis*), as well as reduced-sodium varieties.

SRIRACHA SAUCE: *See* chili sauce.

SUL: Korean rice wine. Chinese rice wine or pale dry sherry may be substituted.

SWEET SOY SAUCE: *See* kecap manis.

TAMARIND WATER: Tamarind, the pod-shaped fruit of the tamarind tree, adds a sour note to many Indian and Southeast Asian dishes. At the grocery store, you will find tamarind in different forms: densely pressed blocks of pulp and seeds; fresh, whole pods; or liquid tamarind concentrate.

To make tamarind water, soak the pulp or tamarind block in hot water at a ratio of 1 tablespoon pulp or block (approximately 2 pods) per ½ cup (125 ml) hot water. After 5 to 10 minutes the pulp/block will soften. Pour the tamarind and water through a fine sieve and firmly knead the pulp/block in the strainer to extract the tamarind juice. Discard the pulp and seeds.

Lemon or lime juice, or frozen orange-juice concentrate, may be substituted, but the taste is not the same.

TERASI/TRASI: *See* shrimp paste.

TOFU: A fresh bean curd made from soybeans, tofu is low in calories and high in protein. It has a custardy consistency and, though quite bland on its own, it readily absorbs the flavors of other foods, making it a useful extender. It comes in blocks measuring about 2½–3 inches (6–8 cm) packed in water in plastic tubs, and can be found in the refrigerated or produce section of most major supermarkets. It will keep 4–5 days in the refrigerator in cold water, which should be changed daily. It is called *doufu* in Chinese.

TURMERIC: A rhizome related to ginger, turmeric is available fresh at health food stores and Southeast Asian groceries; ground turmeric is widely available in supermarkets. In its ground form, it contributes the yellow-orange color and pungent flavor to many Indian, Indonesian, Malaysian and Thai dishes. It is also an ingredient in many spice-mixtures. Turmeric is being studied for its anti-cancer properties.

VINEGAR, RICE: Milder than Western vinegars and slightly sweet. Cider vinegar may be substituted. Add a pinch of sugar to cider vinegar and dilute with a little water.

WASABI: A pungent green horseradish used as an accompaniment to raw fish dishes and other Japanese food. Available in cans, powdered like dry mustard, and may be reconstituted quickly with cold water. Also sold pre-mixed in tubes.

YELLOW BEAN SAUCE: *See* bean sauce, yellow.

RECIPES BY COUNTRY

CHINA